Endless

Fortune

Hope you enjoy it x

Ify Adenuga

Ify Adenuga

First published in Paperback in the United Kingdom by:

OWN IT! Entertainment Ltd & Boy Better Know

Company Registration Number: 09154978

Cover design: Jason Adenuga

Paperbck ISBN: 978-1-9160523-6-9

www.ifyadenuga.com

Dedication

This is who I am today. The mother of Joseph Junior, Jamie, Julie and Jason, and married of course to the love of my life Joseph Adenuga Senior, all of whom I dedicate this book to: my family with whom I am well pleased.

Contents

IFY ADENUGA'S FAMILY TREE
From Great Grandparents to Grandchildren.

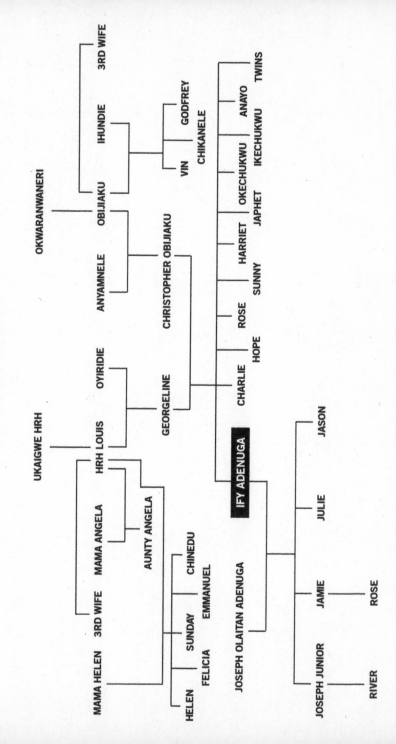

Introduction

'I'm just so thankful. I've been trying to do this music stuff and work it out for so long, but it was the moment when I was like, "Yo, let's do this for ourselves, for the family," [that] all these songs travelled the world, no record label or nothing, we just travelled the world. We just did this for us, but the love is very appreciated. Love you bro, love you Matt, Kane, for life bro, we did it. And lastly, my mum and dad [and] all my friends' mums and dads because they made us, they gave us that voice in our head... to keep us in line, to keep us in check. Thank you very much. More blessings, more love, more greatness, more support. Konnichiwa!'

– Joseph Junior 'Skepta' Adenuga,
Mercury Prize speech, 2016

Junior's *Konnichiwa* album won the Mercury Prize Album of The Year in September 2016. The room was in a frenzy following the announcement; people jumped to their feet, chairs were thrown to the floor, champagne was sprayed. It's possible that even I got carried away – grabbing a bottle of what I thought was champagne, I accidentally ended up covering Kano's mother in red wine – I'm very sorry Ms Richards! We were all so thrilled because while there are many awards – the BRITs, the MOBOs – this is the one that meant the most to my son Junior, AKA Skepta. We all joined him on stage, and as Junior accepted the award, I couldn't help but do a little celebratory dance. It quickly went viral on social media, with several outlets reporting on my impromptu moves. *The Fader* ran a story called 'The Internet Couldn't Get Enough of Skepta's Mum' and the *NME* reported on 'All the people who fell in love with Skepta's Mum'. After the awards we went to the afterparty near the venue where I was interviewed by a number of media journalists, including the BBC. Junior's friend Lasha stood by me for support as I spoke. Reporters were hanging on every word I said about how I had raised my children and not trained them. As well as my dance moves, social media also went crazy about my choice of words around how I had brought up my children.

After a very late night going to various parties, I jumped in my car the next morning to head for my physio session at Chase Farm Hospital, and my phone was ringing off the hook; friends and well-wishers rang constantly to congratulate me and the kids. I answered call after call, and as I drove to the hospital a BBC journalist rang to interview me. He wanted to know more on the story he must have heard Jamie rap about. It was the time he and Junior nearly set fire to our old house when they were little. I told the reporter that I'd heard Jamie coming up the stairs crying, running into my bedroom to tell me, 'Mummy, fire, fire'. I quickly jumped up and rushed downstairs and, glancing into the living room and seeing the burning teddy bear by the foot of the wall-unit, I dashed into the kitchen, headed for the sink where I grabbed a handful of dirty plates with water in them and threw them mindlessly onto the fire to put it out. The BBC reported my story like no other, claiming that it was because of the kids setting fire to our old house that we moved to north London! In fact, we moved into our own two-bedroom flat which we bought for £41,000 on Mount Pleasant Road in Tottenham because we had finally gotten the money together.

It was then it dawned on me that my family was becoming public property and it made me aware how much the press can blow up a story. I didn't know whether to laugh or cry for that brief moment. I was so smitten by the attention that it didn't bother me what readers might think of the report – plus I knew how much Junior deserved the prize, which the story mentioned.

The Mercury Prize was a huge milestone for both Junior and the family, a family that began over three decades ago when I met and married Joseph Adenuga (Junior) who became Joseph Adenuga (Senior) after the birth of our first child. Our four children are Joseph Junior (aka Skepta); Jamie (aka Jme), also an artist in the Grime scene, who together with Junior founded Boy Better Know (BBK). Following them is the only girl in the mix, Julie, a cultural figure in the UK who was the voice of Apple Music's radio station Beats 1 in London when it launched in 2015 and Jason, the producer and graphic designer behind some of his siblings' and family's artwork and music, he produced tracks on *Konnichiwa*.

Joe explained to me during our courtship that it was a family tradition for the eldest son to have the same name as his father. The names of the firstborn – Joseph and Olaitan – go back for as far as he can remember, with his great granddad bearing the names prior to travelling to the UK. He in turn inherited it from his father, who passed away barely a year into our relationship. Joe became the Senior and passed Junior down to his first-born son. As for the rest of the family's JA initials, all of my family members have the initial J – that was Joe's idea – except me. I liked it but I turned down the suggestion to change my name from Ify to Jiffy! That wasn't happening, I said. First off, Ify is short for my name Ifeomagwu, which coincidentally means the same thing as Olaitan in Joe's language – endless fortune. And I wasn't going to bare the same name as a cleaning product, no way!

I'm writing this book to document my life journey. I have been keeping a journal since a child, and so I've been writing this book most of my life, really. With the interest in our family and how Joe and I have raised our children in a way that is perhaps at odds with traditional African or British ideologies, it now feels like a great opportunity to explore my transitional moments and the coping mechanisms I applied to pass through both good and bad times. *Endless Fortune* is also my way of expressing my unconditional love for my family: my children firstly and the love of my life, my dearest husband, Dad. Most of all, it's to tell them that I would go through it all again to relate to every single one of them that constitutes my family – the ADENUGA FAMILEE – as we like to say to ourselves! This book, if you like, is giving my children the opportunities that I missed in my own life growing up. I want them to know my backstory, something that I could only imagine of my parents, who never really spoke about their own lives. I'm hoping my kids will come to understand how and why I raised my family differently to the way my parents raised me and my siblings, while still sharing the same goals with them as economic migrants in pursuit of greener pastures.

My own parents left Eastern Nigeria for Lagos, the then-capital of Nigeria where they birthed and raised us. Following in their footsteps, I journeyed to the United Kingdom at the start of the 80s where I had and raised my own family.

My life started in Lagos where I lived in my young years until civil war broke out in Nigeria. I grew up fast as a result of the Biafran war in the mid-60s which raged through the country until January 1970. It was an agonising journey into the unknown for me from 1966 when my parents had to escape with six of us siblings back to the eastern region of Nigeria where I spent a decade – including my secondary education – before I returned to Lagos in 1976 in search of employment. I worked for four years in the city before I left for the UK in 1980 with the hope of accessing a better life. Like my father, my goal remained the same. I too was seeking something else. But I wanted more. Where my father had travelled to Lagos, I looked to London for my future. It was here I wanted to make my life – and it was here that I did.

It wasn't until my early thirties that I realised I could be happy for me, and I mean just for me. I needed to re-evaluate my predefined concept of happiness taught to me by my parents that simply meant pleasing everyone else but me. My life journey to date has been the struggle to assert my own definition of happiness while seeing life through my cultural and traditional lens, as well as being a black Christian woman migrant from Africa. I had to find happiness in a foreign environment that doubled the amount of learning and growing up I needed to do to achieve my true happiness. So you may ask the question: who am I today? My cultural tradition by definition is fluid and, most of all, I am none other than a chip off the existing old humanity block who feels and remains forever hungry to learn, in order that I recognise, respect and understand OUR WORLD, both as it is and as it ought to be in the interest of all of us Citizens of the World. That's who I have become! This book explores my literal and emotional journey but also in many ways my philosophical one. When you take away all that identifies us – our race, the colour of our skin, our gender – I am merely a human trying to figure it all out. I hope this book provides an insight into my life for my kids and grandkids, but also helps them to think about who they are and their place in this world of ours.

This is *Endless Fortune*; it's my story, it's the story of my family. It's the story of both struggle and survival, of joy and pain. It is the story of Ify Adenuga. I hope you enjoy it.

Chapter 1

Papa had already had six children before my Uncle Vincent, his younger stepbrother, followed his footsteps. Papa sponsored his move to Lagos to live and work. He had passed through Modile Way and found himself a job and accommodation like others before him and moved on. He lived in a 'face-me-I-face-you' accommodation common in townships. It comprised two rows of single rooms with a corridor in the middle. The tenants could be single, married or with children. Uncle Vin played a huge part in my early years learning development when he lived with us. He taught me how to spell my name despite his stammering. 'P-p-p-p-aa-t-t-tieeenccce, s-s-ssaay it!' he would command, cane in his raised hand above me. I used to cry myself silly trying to spell my name without copying his stammering. Each time I stumbled with the spelling he slammed the cane on my shoulder. My parents could be sitting in the next room or in the parlour minding their own business while we practised at the front of the house. They would not even bat an eye, let alone get involved. I learned to spell my name 'cause I knew

..e wouldn't leave me alone until I got it right. I did eventually, months down the line.

My uncle and his wife, Julianna, lived in Bariga and had two daughters. He would drop by once or twice during the week to catch up with Papa. He and his family often dined with us at weekends. It was during this period, on the evening of 24th September 1966, it was a Saturday, that my uncle, his daughters, Stella and Lucy, and pregnant wife visited for dinner. I sensed there must be more to their visit than met the eye this time as I observed them locked in nonstop discussion with my parents. While they chatted seriously, the maid, Vicky, ordered Charlie and me to clear the plates from the parlour back into the kitchen. I tried as hard as I could to catch a hint of what they were talking about as I returned to collect more plates. If only I'd understood Igbo at that time it would have helped me to guess the drama unfolding before me. Papa fiddled with his portable transistor radio knob as he talked. He was trying to tune into a favourite station, but I was still wondering what might be so amiss that my uncle and family weren't in a haste to return to their home in Bariga.

And no matter how hard I strained my ears I was still none the wiser. Then I heard Papa mention 'travel' and 'Ala Igbo' (Igboland) from the little I could make out. It was getting very late by now and Vicky told us to retire to our rooms. My cousins Stella and Lucy came along to share the room with us girls. I fell asleep with those two words playing on my mind. Maybe they were planning for all of us to visit Ala Igbo, the east. Not that such travel wasn't possible but it was weird that they were whispering about it. We woke up in the morning and the contents of every room had been packed and boxed up apart from the beds we'd been sleeping in. Even the kitchen was ordered into boxes. It was really weird!

It was now Sunday morning and my parents had Mr. Iwu and Mr. Igwe join them. There was no courtesy entertainment of food and drink like we used to – usually the rare occasions the house china came out of the closet. Today, however, I woke early to see them in the parlour on a lockdown in deep discussion. I said good morning sir but got no reply from them as I made my way to the kitchen where my siblings and cousins were already assembled. Vicky had made them brush their teeth and get ready for breakfast. She looked up at me as I wandered into the kitchen and before she could remind me I completed my U-turn and went to the bathroom to brush my teeth. Minutes later I joined everyone for a breakfast of tea and bread. We all dipped our bread pieces in a bowl of tea to eat till we were full. The maid asked us to return to our rooms where we waited till we could hear our neighbours return from church. Soon enough we could all go out and play.

Our friends didn't show, instead their parents came to join the other six adults in our house where their discussions intensified in Igbo. Not knowing what to make of our playmates' no show, I was bored stiff. I decided to ask Vicky's permission to go out and play as my parents were in a meeting with neighbours. As soon as she nodded for me to leave the house, I dashed into our room for my book of songs; my escapism whenever I found myself confused and alone in my thoughts. I would sing aloud from the book sitting or lying down. It was now early evening and the adults' meeting had been going on all day except for when they stopped to have Sunday lunch which I helped Vicky serve. We had ours in the kitchen. Soon it was bedtime and our neighbours left to return to their homes. My uncle and family spent a second night with us which was so unusual that my anxiety increased, even though as a young child I didn't have a clue what I was supposed to be worried about. We were sent to our rooms and asked to sleep on rafter mats with everything packed up around us.

I lay there as Vicky told me all about what I had been dying to know. She began by telling me what she'd heard on the street.

'They're killing the Igbos. They want to kill all the Igbos in Lagos. That's why we are going back home to the east,' she concluded almost in a whisper as we lay on the mat.

'Why are they killing just the Igbos?' I asked.

She kissed her teeth. 'Sshh. Come on, go to sleep.'

I wasn't a stranger to her telling me off but it was the dismissive way she said it that ran through me, like my mother's stern chastising voice. My curiosity turned into confusion as I lay still but wide awake with thoughts fearfully running riot in my head. While the Igbos on the street ran around, it was business as usual for Mama Erine, Mama Lanre and Mama Bosa's families and the other non-Igbos. They didn't join in the ad-hoc meetings that went on among the Igbos on our street. The anger in me welled up as I began to think perhaps

Papa meant for us to travel that weekend or the next, as this was a Sunday night. I couldn't get to sleep. If we were not Igbo, my family would have been exempt from this madness that was threatening to bring my life in Lagos to an abrupt end. Why was I created Igbo I pondered as I finally dozed off.

The next morning, Papa didn't get ready for work, Mama hadn't prepped anything for the kiosk on Akerele Road kerb at the top of Modile Way. Vicky informed us that we would not be selling anything at the kiosk. I began to wonder what might happen next when my uncle and his wife upped and left to return home briefly, leaving my cousins with us. Suddenly, Modile Way, where I played with my mates and watched people go by – especially 'fine girls' walking by on high heels – was falling apart before my very eyes and there was nothing I could do about it. Us children barely stepped outside again. Mama asked us to capture and tie up all of our chickens in the kitchen as opposed to putting them in their wooden basket from where we would release them into the backyard in the mornings. We caught all ten of them. Papa slaughtered them for my mother to prepare a pot of red tomato stew and a pot of ogbono (Irvingia gabonesis, or African wild mango nuts) soup. Vicky and I boiled white rice to go with the red stew and made garri for the ogbono soup. We were going to eat the food en route to the east. That was it. Nothing more was explained to us even though I'd no idea how much the maid knew that I didn't. All we knew so far was we were leaving at some point with what we had hastily put together to journey into the unknown.

Later that evening before we readied for bed, I saw a gwongworo (a wooden frame pickup lorry) parked at the front of our house and Mr. Iwu, Mr. Igwe, Uncle Vin and Papa spent the rest of the night loading the lorry with the belongings of all four families. There was just enough room for us all to sit on four long benches cutting across the width of the vehicle behind the driver. They loaded everything up in the lorry and on the roof, securing it with a heavy tarpaulin draped over the whole vehicle.

Very early the next day, 27th September, we left Modile Way, all squashed up in the lorry, bound for the east. Charlie and I were the only ones of our siblings who had visited the village with Mama before. I was nonetheless looking forward to exploring those thatched roofs and jungles I'd seen on TV. Plus a chance to see my grandparents in the flesh again. My parents would refer to them a lot when talking to us. Even though I was young, I could still remember the faces of my grandmother, Anyamnele and step-grandmother, Ihundie, mother to Uncle Vin and his siblings.

Our vehicle left 10 Modile Way and as we drove out of our street I knew we weren't on holiday; not the type I was used to the couple times I had ever been home with Mama. In Lagos Iddo Motor Park, the driver slowly drove into a space and parked the vehicle with us seated quietly in it.

Charlie glanced sideways at me and asked, 'Are we getting down?'

Before I could respond Mama warned, 'Don't you dare! Sit where you are and we will soon be leaving.' I looked at the faces of the other children and back at Charlie as if to say 'it's tough luck, bro' to him and I meant it. I was beginning to feel the heat of the humid atmosphere.

The park was jam-packed with people. Igbo chatter filled the air as many of the adults haggled with vehicle operators who seemed to be enjoying the chaotic atmosphere! It was a sea of mostly Igbos – men, women, babies and even pregnant mothers – moving about the packed gwongworos, full of people and their properties. I gasped at the sight of so many Igbos leaving Lagos to head home like we were.

'Mama, please can we raise the tarpaulin a little? I'm hot.'

The driver who was sat behind his wheel came to our rescue. We sat and watched the madness playing out in front of us while waiting on our fathers who were in negotiations with the vehicle operators. The noise increased by the minute as crowds of people filled not just the motor park but the roads in the surrounding areas. So many vehicles all with their horns blazing as if they were about to start a race in the traffic.

'Mama, what are we waiting for?' I asked without glancing at her. Somehow I felt that sense of responsibility as the oldest to ask what the rest of the children would probably also like to know as many became restless just sitting there in the heat. A couple of younger ones were starting to bicker with their siblings.

Mama said to me, 'We don't leave till your father, Nnayi (Mr.) Iwu and Igwe are back. Then we go.' She said it with this straight face that said to me that the mothers had long resigned to letting our fathers take control. It felt grave to think that my mother was powerless to fulfil my needs. 'The two men walking back with them are coming with us,' Mama said aloud. I looked and could see both Mrs. Iwu and Igwe nod in agreement. There's something more to our unusual group holiday trip to the region than meets the eye – the adults know it but are not telling us, I thought.

I did not question why these men were to come with us in our already cramped gwongworo. And with precision, the two strangers sat in front; one of them swapping position with our initial driver that brought us to the park. The tarpaulin was draped down in place and we left the park around 10am onto the main road heading east.

As our vehicle was leaving Shagamu behind, Mama lowered her head to whisper to me, 'We need those two drivers for our safe drive-through home.' I was now really confused. I only got to find out after we were safely home and I overheard my parents telling the story to homeland people that they had three drivers in all for us to go through the checkpoints. The northern driver drove us out of Lagos to Ore where the western driver took over to take us to the Niger Bridge and our eastern and initial driver drove us across the bridge into Onitsha and took us on the last leg to our villages. This was the arrangement that took place while we sat waiting at the Iddo Park – this way, they made crossing those checkpoints a little easier when the respective driver had to deal with their tribal officers at the stops.

A tremendous amount of fear and confusion were going

through my mind as our gwongworo galloped along the almost pitch-black motorway except for other car headlights. Lagos to my village federal road junction is around 458km or thereabout, a few hours journey by road today, but it took us nearly the whole day to complete the journey with the route changes and stopovers we encountered along the way, both to stay safe and avoid the back roads rumoured to be deathtraps for fleeing Igbos and dealing with the checkpoint officers accordingly.

It suddenly dawned on me that I was leaving the city for the village for the very last time. There's no way of coming back from this one – not if we'd packed up all we could of our belongings… my thoughts were racing. No more hang outs with my friends on our street and in school. Cramped up with our luggage, there wasn't much room to move about so we just ate, drank, ate more and dozed off to sleep. We had rest stops along the way to ease ourselves and for the parents to see to the children who saw the stopovers as opportunity to run amok, particularly the little ones of all the families who, after peeing, stood on the road shoulder and mimicked the sound of vehicles passing while our mothers tried to clean them up and haul them back into their seats.

There were fourteen of us children and ten adults in total on that trip, so each rest stop would take a good half an hour. The adults were the Iwus, Igwes, Uncle Vin and wife Julianna, Vicky, and Auntie Angela who had joined us at the house very early that morning. There were six of us siblings: myself, Charlie, Hope, Rose, Sunny also known as Nelson, and Harriet plus my two cousins. Three Iwu boys and three Igwe children: two boys and a girl. The Igwe's eldest daughter, Angelina, who was about to start university in the new year, did not come with us. She was presumably over eighteen because her parents allowed her to stay behind under some adult's supervision I supposed, otherwise the parents who were as strict as mine would have forced her to come along.

We remained seated in the vehicle for however long we spent at each checkpoint. I kept imagining what was going on each time I heard Papa's raised voice outside the vehicle at checkpoints. He would be talking back to the military officers at the post.

'Look here, officer, I am an upright citizen and a civil servant like yourself. Make you let us go. We have all our family members here and are going home.'

'Mr. Civil Servant, make you keep quiet there. Shut up or I'll shoot you,' we would hear an officer's voice say to him.

'God! Papa Patie doesn't know when to keep quiet. Until he kills me would he shut up.' I was beginning to understand Mama's phrase now – that her life is at stake is usually when she cannot deal with a problem. She saw the problem as going to kill her.

Mrs. Igwe came up with the suggestion that 'Papa Patie should remain seated at checkpoints 'cause he argues too much and these people are not joking when they say they will kill!'

Mrs. Iwu seconded the opinion. 'It's true. He should not go down at checkpoint again; let the drivers do the talking. Isn't that why they joined us? Mama Patie, we really need to stop him.'

Mama didn't say a word, rather she kept shifting on her seat and tending to our littlest but I knew she was angry. I'd seen her quite a number of times in that mood.

But my father ignored them every time.

'I'm leaving all my life savings behind and I have to have your permission to return to my father's compound!' This was his response to an officer at a stop past Ore and heading to Niger Bridge.

'Hey Mr. Man, I can let your people go and detain you here...'

'And why might you do that?'

'Keep you for as long as I want to punish you for not keeping your mouth shut. I could even shoot you dead!'

And unbelievably, Papa couldn't wait to respond. 'I don't care what you do to me. You kill me, and I die. Just let my family go! I don't care...'

If I didn't know my father, I would have thought he was possessed. Papa is fearless, I kept thinking while at the same time I was fearful that he might not survive the trip if he kept talking at each stop. The whole scenario was scaring the hell out of me this time. I'd been awake all along while the children had fallen asleep at some point on our journey.

Our sitting arrangement in the vehicle wasn't helping matters either. I sat close to Mama with Harriet between us whom we checked from time to time including to feed her. The Iwu and Igwe children sat close to their parents on each of the bench rows behind the front seat dividing panel. My family sat on the last bench row close to the suitcases and our boxed-up belongings. Several hours into our journey, while most of the children were fast asleep, we approached River Niger Bridge. I was wide awake still as we rode through the steel bridge alongside a convoy of other vehicles returning to the eastern regions. It was getting dark and we still had to get to the motorway junction, the Iwu and Igwe temporary stop to join separate transport to their villages in Mbano and Umuahia.

Upon crossing the bridge, we emerged into a totally changed atmosphere. Men, women and young people were celebrating that evening of the 27th, bellowing war songs with the broadest smiles on their faces as our gwongworo and other motorcades came off the bridge and drove through Onitsha. People lined the highways and war songs filled the air, one of which I still remember.

E jirim ukwu ala ga Enugu ga nara Ojukwu egbe
Ga nara Ojukwu mma
Ga nara ya dagger
E jirim ukwu ala ga Enugu ga nara Ojukwu egbe
Ogaghi ewutem o Gowon ga nwu echi o

Translated:

I trekked to Enugu to ask Ojukwu for a gun
machete and dagger

I am not worried about my trekking drill
because Gowon will die tomorrow.

People from all the surrounding communities filled
everywhere, hailing the returning convoys – the Igbo travellers
from the north and west of Nigeria escaping the threat of
war. Our gwongworo went through many local communities
to get to Owerri township before we headed for Anara, the
main motorway junction. We were driving past more jubilant
crowds of people along the way. An hour later, our gwongworo
parked up as we finally got to Anara Junction. The Iwu and
Igwe families joined the rest of the adults in helping to bring
down their belongings.

'How long have we got to go to get home?' I muttered to
my mother as she and my father climbed back into the vehicle.

'Not long now,' she replied. Although I desired more
clarity than that, I was hopeful. After their belongings had
been loaded up and the Iwu and Igwe men said their bye-byes
to my parents and boarded another shuttle to take them to
their respective towns, we continued our own journey to my
village. While my two youngest siblings slept, we drove past
Umunachi before we got to Okwelle. I now know these places
that I was ignorant of then. Everywhere looked the same to
me as we drove through the hugely popular Okwelle market
and a couple Okwelle villages before we finally reached the
junction to my village.

Our gwongworo turned off at the junction and eased
along the ungraded footpath, rocking from side to side as it

rolled from one small hill to another, the bushes slapping the tarpaulin until we got to the small hilly slope that gave way to a wooden bridge over Aku stream. We could see blocks of thatched houses spread in what looked like a valley in front of us from the bridge. There were flickers of lights dotted around these huts too, though it was pitch black and quiet. As we crossed the bridge, two women and a teenage boy walked out slowly from the bank of the Aku stream. The women were carrying clay pots of water on their heads while the boy carried fishing tackle equipment and the fish he had caught. The women were so excited to see us! My mother stepped out of the vehicle as the women, who now recognised her, did a little native dance and sang '*lekwe nu ndina puru anyi ola beke unu alolo*' (here they come the white goldsmiths of our village. You are welcome) as they touched Mama's arms, moving their hips to the sway of the folk song they were bellowing happily. What an irony I thought, my parents were returning home empty-handed with six little mouths to feed.

My mother got back in the lorry while the women and their teenage companion kept pace with the lorry which slowly rolled on, taking a left turn at what looked like a central clearing, where you could continue on the road ahead to cross another stream – the Ikwe – to Alaocha village and onto Okwe town centre. My father's compound was and still is the seventh compound on the left-hand side of the village road. In the middle of our compound stood an unfinished house flanked by two very low thatched houses on either side. You would have to bow your head to step into these nearly identical houses on either side of the dominating unfinished structure. Both had a wide passage between them and the central building running right through from the compound entrance to the backyard gardens.

By the time we parked up, there was a stream of villagers pouring into our compound as we climbed down from the vehicle. Villagers were trooping in, young and old, men and women. Many had followed the crowd behind our vehicle to come to the house to welcome us. You would think we had returned for an August meeting – a yearly event with dining, dancing, networking and organising progressive meetings to better their socio-political lives. It's a magnet for the majority of Igbo communities to this day. People spend their last pennies to prepare for this. It was during such an event when I was very little that Mama took Charlie and I on our first break to the village.

I was now really feeling the transition happening in my life as I thought about the two very different environments I had encountered within the last thirty-six hours. I had left my comfort zone in Lagos to come to the unknown where I was overwhelmed by the village reception. It felt daunting to see so many people, hundreds of them, talk Igbo around us and to us whether or not we understood. They were in a merry mood and looked happy to see us. The largest I'd seen of my community members gathered at one time was at their monthly meetings of no more than fifty or sixty of them at Modile Way except for parties when they swelled to a hundred or so. The reception was truly overwhelming!

I looked around to see if I could spot where to retire within the compound. I needed to catch my breath as the welcoming ceremony was becoming too much for me, especially as I could neither understand the language nor strike up a conversation with anyone. That said, there was joy everywhere as scores of women sang and twirled round in jubilation while the men trooped into the parlour of the unfinished house with Papa. Nearly everyone carried local candles, in the absence of electricity, to make their way to our compound. The candles were made of processed palm oil residue that retains a bit of palm oil to help it burn, then wrapped around long wooden sticks and left to dry under the sun or hung over the fireplace. The compound was alight with yellow flickers, the people's voices filling the air. Several children were shoved in front of Charlie and me by their significant adults and they rambled on in Igbo in front of us. We had no idea what they were saying.

So eager was I to find a resting place that I decided to explore the thatched houses. I dashed into the nearest one to my right and was surprised to find it empty except for a wooden bed and a big clay pot filled with water in one corner of the room. The house must have been about 10 ft by 6 ft at most, and it had no chairs, only a mat on the floor. On the hard mud walls were what seemed like black markers of drawings of little creatures: there was a crab, a snake, a cricket among them. On the other wall were lines crisscrossing each other; up to four to five horizontal lines with a line cutting across them diagonally. These were my old folks' record keeping strategy I later found out. I looked out of the door and caught a glimpse of Charlie's long face looking at me from outside the thatched house. It seemed like everyone had disappeared and he was alone. Some people must have gone home but you could still hear the chatter of many in the unfinished house. Charlie turned round and ran towards the middle house. As I bent over to step out of the house I had wandered into, I was met by an old woman at the door. She immediately hugged me and began to ramble on. Judging by the smile on her face I could only deduce she was happy to see me. I realised as I began to walk away from her that nearly all the old women in our compound had no tops on. They had wraparounds, some with matching headscarves but others had nothing on their hair. A lot of the adult males also had a wraparound, some of them with a string vest or no top on. Some had their traditional woolly hats on and were carrying walking sticks for aid. I remembered a few occasions seeing members of our eastern community club with similar woolly hats and walking sticks at Modile Way.

Here in Umuofeke village, this was it for six siblings and our parents; they didn't have to explain anything to us. The way Mama and Papa acted told us all we needed to know about our exodus to the east. They had left everything in Lagos to return home without any job prospects. Yet the village was happy to see us nonetheless. One old woman stopped and started saying something to me as people dashed back and forth to greet my parents. No sooner had she opened her mouth than I let out the biggest scream for my mother! The sight of her toothless gums scared the hell out of me. I felt spooked like I had just seen one of the cartoon characters I watched on television at No. 4 Modile Way. I had seen old people in Lagos but not so many at once and this close. My mother brought me back to the old woman to apologise where I stood holding tight to my mother's wrapper. The old woman smiled her toothless smile and walked away.

It was a few hours since we'd arrived and villagers were still streaming in and out of our compound as the news spread of our return. We weren't the only family; many others had come back, with more making their way east. The whole environment was completely different to what we were used to in Lagos. Other than the flickers of the locally made candles we were all moving around in semi darkness as people lined up to meet and greet my parents as well as Uncle Vin and his family. I was growing tired of the traffic of visitors into the compound and getting hungry, so I set off to the backyard again this time to look for my siblings. Across at the other thatched house, a few women were chatting with my step-grandma, Ihundie. I remembered her slim face and smiley eyes from my last home visit, albeit I was very young at the time.

The women were still talking when a young girl who looked a little older than me rushed past me and into the hut. I watched her exchange pleasantries with the women in Igbo before she turned round to look at me. Her face beamed with a smile. 'Hello Patie,' she said to me.

'Oh hello. What's your name?' I was happy at last, I met

someone who could communicate with me in English that night.

'My name is Nkechinyere.' It means, whatever the gender of the newborn baby from God is fine by me/us. 'And our house is past Uncle David's,' she told me, pointing away to the opposite side of the village road. We sat on the mat away from the adults who continued chatting and laughing out loud.

'Nkechi,' (as I began to call her by the short form of her name) 'what are they talking about?' I repeatedly asked her. She became my interpreter and friend from that night on as she filled me in on what the adults were saying about me and my family. My step Iye, Ihundie, had said, 'Our daughter already feels at home and has grown into a big girl.' Iye means grandmother Another woman said, 'The eldest boy is shy and very big for his age.' The conversation went back and forth in the hut until Nkechi and I grew tired of listening and left.

'Come let's go into the house,' I said to her as I got up from the mat and expected her to follow.

'OK,' she replied.

We went into the parlour of the unfinished house. 'Many people have gone.' I observed.

'There's still those ones.' Nkechi chuckled, secretly pointing out the last couple of elderly men still talking with Papa in the other corner.

'Let's go.' This time I wanted us to head to our room; the girls' room. 'Nkechi, how did you learn to speak Igbo?' I asked her as we settled on my bed.

'Where we live in Port Harcourt, my two brothers and I

go to an after school club to learn Igbo. My parents insisted we must learn to speak Igbo so that we can speak it when we visit home.'

'Wow, I only understand a little; little words that I picked up from listening to our eastern community club members at our house in Lagos,' I said to her, as if that should suffice.

But it was a fact that, unlike them, we were never made to learn the language. Her father worked with the post office and her mother owned and managed a restaurant in the township, Papa was also a civil servant and Mama a petty trader. I guess my parents got too busy with earning enough of a living to raise us to bother about us speaking the language. And as we weren't encouraged to ask questions, I didn't immediately plan to confront my parents about my lack of Igbo language, not then and not ever. It was the last thing on my mind at that moment. Rather, I settled for listening to Nkechi talk all night about her life in Port Harcourt. It turned out she was a year younger than me, and her two brothers were a lot older than both of us.

We walked out of the room again and back to where my mother was still standing welcoming yet a couple more visiting villagers outside my gran's hut and walked past her.

'Come into Iye Anyamnele to see what she's preparing for dinner for us.' I led the way into my granny's hut. Funny how I was beginning to feel at home and warming to everyone around me, especially my Iyes and Auntie Chikanele and brother Goddy – all of my Uncle Vin's branch of the Obijiaku family. I could see my resemblance to Iye Anyamnele 'cause I look like Papa, who was a carbon copy of his mother and her only child and so, no surprise there, somehow.

Iye had just finished preparing fufu and oha (Pterocarpus mildraedii) soup. 'Egbeocha, my in-law, go get your siblings. Tell them dinner is ready to come now.' She never bothers with my christening name, and instead either called me by my renowned pet name *Egbeocha* (which translates as 'white gun' to mean everything white was desired above anything else, or in my case, that I was a white gun personified in my past life), or *Ogom nwanyi* (still related to my past life as Mama's reincarnated grandmother and so in-law to my grandmother) if all that makes sense.

Mama had called me the name often enough in Lagos. She had explained that her grandmother had earned the nickname following a fight between two prospective suitors that came to ask for her hand in marriage. The two men had coincidentally turned up on the same day, each traditionally bringing with them a keg of palm wine. It didn't matter what the outcome was going to be for the suitors, successful or not in securing marriage with the would-be bride, both kegs were going to be drunk by the prospective in-laws and their villagers, as was and continues to be tradition. Once that ceremony was over, the suitors were dismissed until they received the news about who between them got lucky to marry the said woman, which meant days or even months to wait before the lucky groom is invited along for the formal introduction. This is when the likes of a bar of soap exchanges hands to mean a deal is struck. The man will offer a soap bar to the would-be wife; if she accepts it, the marriage can go ahead, if not then it cannot.

In my grandmother's case, the two potential suitors didn't wait a day let alone seven for the decision! They picked up their empty kegs and left my great-grandparents' compound. They started arguing on their way home to the point that they downed their empty kegs in the middle of Nkwo Okwe market square and engaged in physical combat – despite neither knowing who was being picked by the bride-to-be. The two men nearly killed each other for want of this beautiful woman's hand in marriage, this 'white gun' (i.e a dashing lady) from Alaocha. This, they said, earned me the nickname *Egbeocha*, describing how beautiful I was in my past life. So beautiful that I drove two men to fight in public for my honour! *Egbeocha doro ogu na Nkwo Okwe o* – the white gun that caused a fight at Nkwo Okwe market. And yep, I believed all of that at the time!

Like the toothless old woman I saw earlier that evening, Iye Anyamnele smiled at me with one tooth sticking out like a sore thumb as she asked me to fetch my siblings for dinner. And despite her toothless grin, something in me loved her in an instant. As I got up to go call my siblings Nkechi announced she was going home.

'Ain't you going to eat with us?' I asked as she quickly followed me out of the hut.

'No thanks, I'd eaten before coming to see you.'

'Good to see you, Nkechi. I'll come look for you tomorrow. It's nearly morning now.' We both laughed and waved each other bye. Nkechi headed home while I went in search of my siblings around the compound.

We all assembled for dinner inside the hut. I couldn't believe it was the same meal we were used to at Modile Way. Iye had piled the fufu on two plates, one on each side of the bowl of oha soup that she scooped from her clay pot. It tasted delicious, better than I was used to in Lagos. Instead of kneading the fufu with one hand, I watched my parents join Iye in kneading the fufu with both their hands. I joined them without asking and they looked at me and laughed. Charlie was having none of it; he just fed himself the way he knew how, with one hand, while helping me to feed Sunny and Harriet. Hope and Rose helped themselves also with one hand. Perhaps we didn't eat with both hands in Lagos to avoid being laughed at by friends and neighbours. I found that my family wasn't alone in eating fufu, out of all the swallow foods, with both hands. There are varieties of them which we refer to as such, for instance garri, fufu, pounded yam, etc. The majority of Nigerians swallow these while others, including some Africans, chew them along with the soup condiments. The 'swallow' name is a recent term as far as I understand it used frequently at food joints or eateries. They come as the main part of the dish eaten with meat or fish and vegetable soup. Just like you would have potatoes, rice or spaghetti with sauce of choice.

The soup too, in comparison to what we had in Lagos, was richer in fresh vegetables, dry prawns and fresh fish. Most of these ingredients were locally obtained; the fish and prawns were frequently caught from the scattered rivers and streams around the village. The meat was game or locally reared and the majority of vegetables were locally cultivated. You planted these in your back garden and on your farmland, something we could also do in Lagos but on a very small scale in the backyard, hence these commodities were, and remain, costly in Lagos markets, especially if buying them fresh.

Iye looked happy to see us and didn't stop chatting as we ate. Eventually, after what felt like the longest day ever, we retired to our rooms and my parents went back to the living room to spend time with the few villagers who were still about. I could hear their chatter but their voices trailed away as I thought about what I could be doing now in Lagos – standing by the windowsill at No. 4 watching TV and sneaking back into our house – that is if Papa or Mama didn't find out, which would earn me some seriously painful punishment. Here in the village, in the pitch black lit only by the flicker of local candle lights, I had nothing to do or think about. I simply sat and watched my parents and their friends conversing about running back to the homeland to escape an outbreak of some phantom war. We had no electricity, there would be no going to play with my mates, no going to watch TV or to a friend's house to admire their new toys, which my parents never could afford for us: plastic guitars or pianos or baby dolls and a host of other children's play things that I enjoyed playing with at Nancy's. All of these I had given up just to escape an unconfirmed war. 'What an adult charade,' I suddenly said to myself, my thoughts racing. And then I remembered Angelina

Igwe, who didn't return to the east with her family. She was poised for Christmas to come and go, so that she could start pursuing her career. It was a chance she did not want to miss and I'm sure her parents were supportive too. And so she remained behind to continue her education while the rest of us left good ol' Lagos.

Eventually, after Mama had sprayed mosquito killer fluid in and around our rooms, she asked us to turn in for the night. The smell of the chemical lingered for another half hour before we could sleep. My sisters and I shared a front room with Charlie and Nelson in the room behind ours. My parents' room was opposite ours and their back room was where we kept our foodstuffs, a bit like a utility room. We had a large clay water-pot in one corner and cleaning brushes and brooms in the other with the cooking utensils and a food cupboard arranged by the walls.

I struggled to go to sleep for what seemed like over an hour, my mind still racing. I lay in the dark thinking, my heart pounding so much that I could hear it in my ears! I bet Angelina is comfortably sleeping at No. 8 Modile Way by now, I thought. She never hung around on the street much with us when we played except to come and get her siblings. She also lived away from home much of the time so we hardly saw her, but her younger brother, who was my age group, was one of us and a little boisterous. My mind returned to the present and I started thinking of the mosquitoes that might be lurking in the room with us regardless of the killer fluid. Perhaps the Iwu and Igwe families had also sprayed their bedrooms before going to sleep like Mama had done, to establish who owned the rooms – us or the mosquitoes. I was finding it difficult to shut down, thinking about the events of the last few days in my life and feeling confused and angry. How was I meant to carry on dreaming about happiness and an abundance of friends if I was tucked away in one of the remotest valleys in a little known spot in Igboland called Umuofeke? Where do I go from here? I must have dozed off at some point.

While we kids slept, my parents and their adult companions remained in the living room including Uncle Vin, Auntie Julianna and Goddy, my uncle's brother who had never left the homeland to go anywhere and was happy to see us. They spent what must have been a very late night as two empty palm wine kegs on the living room floor showed the next morning.

'Good morning.' I greeted Mama as she walked into the room with a broom in her hand. She smiled at me and walked through the adjoining door to Charlie's room and out to the backyard and I could hear her broomstick swiping the ground. Auntie Julie came out of her hut and stood by the front door looking flustered as if she hadn't slept in days. Auntie Julie never liked the idea of this homecoming; she'd arrived to live with her husband in Lagos and raise her family barely five years ago. Like my mother she too was having babies like a rabbit.

'Good morning, Auntie,' I said as she stood there.

'Where are your younger ones?' she asked. 'Ask Charlie to

go and bring down some of those ripe pawpaws at the back for me.'

I wasn't going to get my brother, instead I volunteered to climb the pawpaw tree and pluck them myself. Up the tree I went and threw down three ripe pawpaws one at a time. Auntie Julie peeled them and we all had two or more pieces each. Our morning breakfast was done. We didn't need to be told of the looming austerity. We just ate as we came by food, any food. And then came the big eye opener for me. My mother took Harriet with her along the back garden pathway that stretched far back into the bush. They disappeared for a while into bushes that lay beyond. A few minutes later and I saw her walking back with Harriet in hand. I asked her where they had been as they approached the house.

'I took your sister to the latrine,' she replied, unfazed by my reaction as I realised what she said to me.

I was cringing at the thought of going into the bush to do my own business before I quickly asked, 'Could I have tissue for when I want to go?'

'*Nne nnam*, all you need do is strip this bush leaves like this and use them to wipe your bottom after you are done,' she said, casually dropping the bombshell while demonstrating how it was done. It felt like a thunderbolt to my brain. I screamed in disgust. The last time we visited the village, we carried our potties with us and poor Mama saw to all our sanitary needs, so it never registered with me that I would one day be stooping down in an open bush for my convenience! I wonder if my parents had strategically timed our final stopover to ease ourselves on the journey the night before so that we wouldn't need to go again that night, knowing that this would be a culture shock to us.

Brushing our teeth was out of the question so we did the alternative. We chewed icheku, wild sticks that grew in the village. We did nothing all day as the Lagos & Abroad Comeback Kids, except wandering around the village and getting to see more thatched houses as young people hung around us. Everyday saw more Igbos fleeing their townships and retreating into their eastern villages. We saw villagers busy with chores in their respective houses; one might be preparing roof mats, another processing cassava for fufu dinner. Many villagers had also left their homes for the forest and bushes to toil for the day. We passed along, stopping for a few minutes to study our surroundings while listening to the young people trying so hard to communicate with us. Even though they knew we didn't understand or speak Igbo they persisted in communicating with us, switching to broken English for clarity every now and then, explaining they wished we could understand the native language.

My mother called out for us differently here in the village from how she used to in Lagos where she would ask the maid to come get us. Here in the village she practically bellowed our names in the direction she had seen us go off into the village. If by any chance she could not reach us anyone close that heard her calling would raise the alert. It was like every significant adult, including the older youths, had the responsibility to care for you. One big happy village family.

She had called out to us one day. It was lunch time and she wanted us all back to the hut. We came home to boiled white rice, dry fish stew and vegetables, and had coconut and grilled corn for dinner that evening.

I saw a man one early hour, talking and walking past our compound to get round to the other side of the village to our left. He was sounding a twin gong in his hands as he went along. Four to six strikes at intervals to announce the reason for his village crier procession that morning. 'Listen o. There will be a meeting at our chairman Mazi Ike's starting noon this afternoon. If you are owing any levy up to the beginning of this month, remember to bring it with you, else you risk paying it later with interest. Come one come all.'

'Mama, why is he this early?' I asked, woken by the noise even though I was due to get up to begin sweeping the compound but not till much later in the morning.

'Alerting villagers about the meeting before they wake up forgetting and leave home,' she replied and carried on walking to her kitchen as she stepped down the back veranda where we stood, still chatting. Mama was actually holding discussion with me as opposed to telling me to 'shut up' like she would do in Lagos when I 'poked my nose' as she calls it into adults' matters.

'What do you talk about at the meeting?' I asked her.

'It depends on the type of gong. The twin one this morning means both men and women are called to the meeting specially to discuss important matters like organising a rota for cleaning the village church on Saturdays in readiness for

Sunday service. You know it's the duty of the mothers once a week—'

'What will the men be doing?'

A quick surprised glance at me and she replied, 'The men do repair work like patching up the stream bridges when they develop problems; you know, could be as a result of a heavy rainfall and the bridge pillars needing stronger support. But a single gong beat calls for only men to gather.'

The women have their own village crier and a single gong dealing with mainly women's affairs as I later found out, while the men who are perceived as head of the family reserved the right of letting their wife or wives in on matters arising from their meetings at their own risk, if you will.

I was feeling all grown up listening to her. The women don't attend these meetings by default unless indicated by the gong – the different sounds of which are very notable to guide the women's and men's responses to the calls.

Later that morning my parents left for the chair's house for the village meeting. And us children were alone. We also had a number of the village children at our house; quite a number of them, boys and girls, also included some returnee youths and we were getting to know each other. Already good friends with Nkechi and a handful of us that could speak pidgin English at least, we set about force teaching them pidgin.

'How do you say "let's go to the stream together"?' one of the bigger boys asked and Nkechi replied telling him exactly that.

I then asked, 'Where is your school and how far is it?'

Again Nkechi was the go-between, pointing towards the central clearing area, the village square, and telling me, 'The school is at the county. We also have field there to play.'

The feeling of disappointment was going to overwhelm me when I quickly asked, 'What's your name?' The girl I had my gaze fixated on as I asked the question looked on at me, not having a clue what I just said to her. Nkechi stepped right back into her interpreter mode and told her what I just asked and how she should respond.

'My name is Favour.'

I could see her face light up as she said that before asking me to ask her again. Without hesitating to reason why, I looked at her and repeated myself.

'My name is Favour,' came her reply. She went on to repeat it a few times before reverting to Igbo. 'Let's all go into the woods for ugba seeds.'

Looking for oil bean seeds sounded exciting to me seeing as there was nothing else to do. I was beginning to like Favour indeed. Following the majority applause of 'yeah', everyone knew to quickly run home to fetch their machete and basket. I too dashed back to my mother's kitchen for my own gadgets for the woods.

We all set off and had to pass the villagers gathering at the front of the chair's compound close to the the village square to head to the bushes towards Umumgbada. I went round looking for Mama in the gathered crowd to inform her of our planned bush hiking.

'Mama, we are going into the woods. I am going to get you some ugba seeds,' I concluded, feeling good about myself.

'Oh dear, would you recognise ugba if you saw one?' Mama giggled in response looking at the rest of the children who were waiting for me a few feet away.

'Yes I would, Favour will show me,' I replied excitedly.

'OK just be careful and do not stay too long. Where are your siblings?' she asked.

'Charlie is looking after them and Harriet is sleeping,' I replied.

'Alright you go ahead. I will be excusing myself in a minute to return home and look after them myself,' she said with a wave for me to run along and join the others. I rushed off, and off we headed through the long narrow footpath that led into the forest.

As we searched the forest for these seeds, I could see freshly cultivated farm ridges, with cocoyam, corn and hot chilli peppers growing on them and these were located on the several sections of cultivated lands. I observed the number of stems on the ridges carefully guided to wrap themselves round the provided poles. They must be important crop, I reasoned and asked, 'What are these stems on the sticks on top of the ridges?'

'Oh they are yam stems shooting out from the ground so that they grow upwards and not entangle on the ridges or the ground.' Nkechi the translator satisfied everyone. And even though Favour provided the majority of the answers she gave us, I had a feeling Nkechi already knew how yam was grown, for example.

'I will always come home with my mum during yam festival to take some back for her restaurant,' she told us. Port Harcourt was far closer to home than Lagos – besides Mama wasn't in the hotel business anyways. Not sure why jealousy had to keep popping up in my brain each time I compared myself to Nkechi. Not even sure why the comparison.

There was also dry wood scattered here and there in the bushes. You looked up at the trees and you could see rays of sunshine piercing through the huge forest branches downwards to the forest grounds. The wind was also blowing to sway the leaves side to side and you could hear the different types of animal sounds, especially birds. Some were faint but others you could hear and see flying. We could also hear ugba boomerang casings cracking open under that sun and the ugba seeds escaping into the air. They remained wherever they landed however far from the tree until they got picked up by us or anyone else; the fallen seeds germinated and eventually grew into other oil bean trees, unless the land was cleared for farming in which case they were bound to be moved or displaced.

We must have spent about a couple of hours foraging the forest for anything we could find. Many of us had already filled our baskets with forest goodies such as the ugba seeds we were after as well as wild cocoyam, snails and numerous berries that grew in the wild. We reunited again on the main footpath and decided to go down to Ikwe stream to swim before returning home. There was no question of boys swimming separately from the girls neither was anyone going to swim with a suit or trunks on, apart from a handful of us girls; about four of us who came from the city had knickers on. The boys in their group swam and chatted like us girls were doing too. I noticed the absence of the sound of traffic or street traders in and around my village. The nearest tarred road was two kilometres away. It turned out to be a fun village outing that stuck in my mind, because Favour and I grew very close that day and had made the pact to call each other *Nwokem* as in my 'buddy' or 'best friend' and we've never looked back since.

Subsequent days, weeks and months saw more people returning home from Lagos and other Nigerian cities like Ibadan, Abeokuta, Kaduna, Kano, Ife, Maiduguri, Jos, Ilorin, etc. People came home with war-filled stories of those killed while they slept in their houses in townships and many who were killed on their way to work or opening their places of business. Some Igbo civil servants too were rumoured to have been killed, their limbs severed and given to them to feed on their train journey back from the north to the east. Many of these rumours were not only frightening but numbed you into hopelessness. Worse still, you had no way of verifying these stories. Those that could afford transistor radios relied on radio Biafra to inform them while the rest of us in the villages relied solely on the usual oral tradition of 'they said this' and 'they said that' and so on.

And so began the rest of my childhood. I was caught

between adjusting to village life and fostering my dream for the dazzling multicoloured disco lights of the TV shows I'd been dreaming of in Lagos. I was going nowhere till... who knows? I would learn not only to adjust to my new lifestyle, but also to survive with no electricity, no tap water, no bathroom and toilet, you name it. Everything that made life worth living in Lagos was absent – we had to make do for all the amenities. We had no school or any other ordered system of growing up. We had no nearby cinema to go and watch films for free using a handheld mirror like we used to in Modile Way after dinner some Saturday or Sunday evenings.

As our lives transformed in our journey into the unknown, the news broadcast peppered our minds with hourly sad stories that kept coming thick and fast. The radio station played music and more music when they had no news to report. From then on, things were not the same. We had no school to attend. Neither did we look forward to treats like ice cream or shortcakes like we used to. Nothing except the cassava stuff, yam, cocoyam and vegetables which were common in all the village gardens. We could only rely on home grown products for survival. No rice, salt or any other imported stuff into the east. In fact, unless you had premium stuff to sell, you might as well eat what you produced instead of making a wasted journey to the market and not raise enough money to buy what you really needed in return. Suffice to mention the scarcity extended to every other aspects of our lives for business or pleasure. This was the war; it began for me big time just before my 10th birthday!

Chapter 2

'Nne baby,' my father called out to our mother one evening. 'They've just given me the village chairman appointment, and now I also have to elect villagers to join the army.'

'And that's bad news,' Mama replied. Her expressionless face was staring at Papa who stood by the utility room doorway. I felt she knew Papa was as bothered as she was by the worried look on his face. She knew the village men would give him a tough time, particularly those likely to say he had little or no knowledge of the village politics as an 'abroadian' who has just returned from the city.

I went and joined Mama to prep the cocoyam and vegetables for our family dinner. I couldn't help thinking that village politics was about to transform my father from the happy go lucky bicycle riding civil servant I knew to the scared cat he was gradually becoming before my very eyes. First, his antics at the military checkpoints on our way home and now he was up to be killed by his own people where he called home. Us children were learning Igbo as fast as we could through mimicking friends; repeating phrases after them like, *bia ngaa Amadioha amagbu gi* loosely meaning, 'Come here you else you risk being struck down by Amadioha.' I remember wondering who Amadioha was. The curse was bandied about at every little whim between two or more people in the village. Amadioha, as far as I understand it, is a mythical deity and one of many that my people subscribe to that are both revered and feared to date.

Mama asked Papa to turn the chairmanship offer down. Papa was quiet for a few seconds.

'It would be difficult 'cause no one else would take the position. Since Mazi Ike passed, the caretakers called for election last month and no one showed interest to contest. It was the secret ballot result that got me picked unanimously.'

'Tell me about it. Soon you're going to tell me they all chose you out of love, yeah? It's like you don't know your people.'

I couldn't agree more, considering Papa's checkpoint scenarios. From then on, the village gatherings took place at our compound and they would raise their voices arguing now and then on village matters till decisions were made. None of my villagers had joined the army at this time. As well as the village chair, Papa was also the village community link person to Okwe community. He attended meetings with members of his cabinet to represent our village interests. The main discourse at this time was around the war efforts to ensure people's safety and wellbeing. I could imagine like Papa, other Okwe community leaders must also nominate their ready young men to join the Biafran army and the villages were responsible for managing their own security. Our communities were also vulnerable to raids by military conscripts who forcefully removed men to join the army.

Even with all of this going on, Papa had still managed to replace our palm rafter mat roofing with corrugated iron sheets. Other than palm oil trees that were harvested monthly by the villagers and processed into red oil, my parents had no other means of income. His work never ended. Papa was always holding meetings with both the villagers and guests from other villages at the house. Our village now had two young men, Paul and Jacob, who had voluntarily joined the army just before Papa assumed office. We regarded our two soldiers as heroes each time they visited home. They told us both frightening and encouraging stories of the war that we listened to eagerly. Our lifestyle was at a bare minimum, but people managed to stay happy, singing and dancing the Biafran signatory songs as we ushered in 1967, the first year since our return from Lagos. Mama was pregnant. Again. I didn't know whether to love or hate her this time to have allowed herself to fall pregnant when we were barely scraping by. Once a week we had relief agency workers from the Red Cross come to the villages to give us some non-perishable food stuffs like dry cornmeal, dry egg yolk, salted stockfish and semolina, powdered milk, etc. We relied on these handouts to supplement everything else we could farm and gather from the wild. We even hunted crickets, collected snails and slugs at nights to prepare our meals. We had no maid as

Vicky had come back with us and returned to her family who were also from my village. So my younger sisters didn't wait around to be told what to do anymore. This was it. This was life henceforth and no one knew when the war was going to end!

'Mr. Obi, open the door,' a man in military uniform shouted one middle of the night. He was banging at my parents' door opposite ours with the boot of his gun. And my mother was in early pregnancy. I heard the banging from our bedroom so I got up and left our door ajar enough to see the man before Papa could open the door. With a gun pointing at him, Papa was clutching his wraparound to his chest with both hands as the man continued to shout at him.

'Come on, Papa Obi. Let's go,' he said, shoving Papa along the veranda as I watched in fear. Three more uniformed men joined them as they disappeared out of our compound.

We all could hear the command voice, 'Come on, all of you can step outside the house, come on before…'

Cowardly, we all came out of our rooms to face two uniformed men in front of our veranda where we stood, and our mother was slumped at the foot of the living room door, with her head in her hands.

'You and that one.' One of the men pointed at me and then at Charlie. Fear enveloped me. I put my arm round Charlie's neck to keep him close to me. 'We need to eat. Let's go. Come on.' The man waved his rifle at us and we headed the way he indicated and still no clue where we were going with him for this food. I quickly glanced behind us at Mama and she was sobbing still sat on the floor. The man marched us on through the back in silence only to be broken a minute later. 'What's your name?' he asked.

'Patience,' I replied, still on the move before we stopped at the first village barns.

'Go on, get that basket,' he commanded. I brought the basket to him where he was removing yam tubers. He put three in the basket and lifted it onto my head. 'Come on let's go.'

I held onto the basket on my head with one hand and my brother's hand with the other. The man led the way and we followed. We repeatedly went into village backyards only this time it wasn't for yams but chickens. We walked through half a dozen backyards and got nine chickens in total. I carried five with the yam and Charlie carried the remaining – two in each hand – and we made our way back to our house in silence.

'How are you, madam?' the man said to Mama who was now sat in the backyard with Auntie Julianna. Suffice to mention my Uncle Vin must have gone into hiding with the military men about the house. 'A beg, madam here and make us yam pepper soup with the chicken; all of it! Have you any drinks in the house; any palm wine?'

Weirdly I was thoroughly enjoying the whole scenario. 'Come on, you madam,' protruding his lips to indicate my auntie, 'put hot water on fire to clean the chicken.'

The two women got on with preparing the food and an hour or so later Papa returned with the four military men.

And with them were some men and two women handcuffed to one another. The two women had been taken in place of their husbands. We could hear one of the returning soldiers from the parlour where us children were.

'Their men ran away when they saw us. They just took off!'

The women were crying and shouting at my father. 'Christopher, we welcomed you and your family with good heart, why are you doing this to us?'

'Papa Patie, you won't kill me! I told you!' my sobbing mother kept saying to Papa.

The military men left with six village men after their meal which we enjoyed with them. They released the two women. 'Tell your husbands to be ready next time,' one soldier said to them as he undid their cuffs. 'It's all our duty to fight for our fatherland, Biafra!' He spoke loudly followed by two gunshots into the air as they left our compound in the early hours of the morning.

'Patie, run along to Mazi Okwuchi's, the village crier, and ask him to sound the gong first thing this morning,' Papa said to me.

This meant a village emergency gathering at our house that day.

'How on earth they knew to find my house and even knew my name!' Papa was thinking aloud with our mother and Auntie Julianna listening. 'One of our villagers must have told them. One of those living close to Aku no doubt where they must have first gone to…'

'Of course they told them his name and where he lives. What do you know, they also told them he is the chairman,' Mama was saying to Auntie Julianna.

'Nne baby, what is it? Come go and lie down,' Papa shouted before helping her up and they both walked through the living room to go to their room. Auntie Julianna walked back to her hut while us children stayed up and finished what was left of the yam and chicken casserole and ended up spending the night in the parlour; all of us.

The village assembled and the argument raged like fire. They all chatted in Igbo throughout that evening and a number of them asked for drinking water which my siblings and I fetched for them. Unless we were bringing water, Mama warned us to stay away from the meeting area, unlike Papa who was in the thick of it as members jostled to ask him questions. Papa told of how he had deliberately tried to mislead the conscripts by taking them to mostly old people's and widows' homes. But the conscripts got frustrated and decided to ignore his directions and instead they began to search every house they came across. This was how they cornered the number of men and women they arrested. While welcoming Papa's strategic move some argued that he should have still pre-warned them prior to appearing with the conscripts at people's doorsteps. Some said they wondered why Papa couldn't have first sent his kids out to inform the villagers beforehand. Nothing Papa said could pacify them not even his own question of how the conscripts knew where to find his house met an answer. He tried to convince them the visit took him as unaware as the rest of them but many were having none of it. There was also the argument that he didn't care whose sons joined the army as his own were underage. Mama sobbed uncontrollably, listening to the arguments and people talking over each other at the top of their voices. Even at that age I understood village politics enough to know why my parents were concerned.

They later decided at the meeting that the villagers should dig trenches for men to hide away at nights to avoid a repeat of what had happened. These were to be located in the forest away from the village living quarters. The men would spend the nights in the trenches and go about their normal business during the day. The villagers also decided to fix locked gates to the stream bridges surrounding our village, the Aku and two Ikwe streams. A rota was created to open the gates in the early hours of the morning and lock them late at night, putting the villagers in control of visitors. The youths were charged with taking food and drink to our village men at the trenches daily, before and after school.

We also had fun times when at the trenches. We sat and ran around while the men ate and talked about the war. They had quite a few radios with them that they listened to and on this particular morning we walked in on them discussing a speech by Lt Col. Odimegwu Ojukwu, the Biafra leader. I'm not sure how long the speech was aired for but they had just finished listening when the radio station began to play music. We all sang along with many of the songs playing on their radios like,

Unu si ebeyi Biafra (x2)
A gama rapu Biafra je Nigeria je biri (x2)

Translated:

Where are you from Biafra (x2)
I won't leave Biafra to go live in Nigeria (x2)

They also played the Death to Gowon song; the same song people sang welcoming us across the Niger Bridge. We were so hopeful, even in our impoverished state of hearts and minds, to win the war so that we could govern ourselves separately from Nigeria. These were emotionally loaded songs that we sang everywhere, young and old, as if to temper our suffering. Meanwhile, more stories went round of assassinated Igbo politicians in various regions, the Igbo business people who had their goods confiscated and they themselves were maimed or killed in the process. It was awful; a time to dare to hope to see the next day.

Then came the 1968 farming season when people cultivated their land, including their nearby gardens, to plant crops. People also took short-term farm work trips to other parts of the region to earn money. By now we were spending Biafran currency and we could only earn and spend it in Biafra. I had learned that Uncle Kevin took people on these trips and I thought about earning some money too to help my parents. He laughed at me and said that I was young and inexperienced in farm work. I was hellbent on convincing him to take me and decided to make my case that I had been home for long enough and learned all I needed to know about farming, from clearing the bushes to burning and raking them to ready the ground for ridging and planting of crops. I also knew how to sow from corn to okra, from cassava sticks, cocoyam to yam. To stop me pestering him, he promised to speak with my parents to ask for their permission to take me along. To my surprise, my parents did not hesitate to give their consent. I was happy to get away from the village for three months. I was getting tired of Papa's overdose of cultural and traditional etiquettes, telling me who to respect dearly, who to call or not to call by their names and who to lend support or care for in their homes. In fact, my parents bored me with explanations of who was who to me; my relationship to them and why I was supposed to be extra kind to specific individuals who were more closely related to me than anyone else in the village. Some villagers that lived alone also relied on youth support to live independently. We brought them firewood or did their washing at the stream, dried and brought it home to them. I was fed up running back and forth between our house and other compounds on top of all my responsibilities to my siblings at home. I was taking a break from it all and couldn't wait!

Uncle Kevin's trip was planned for Owaza in the south eastern region. I was more than ready to go earn Biafran currency and thinking of what I would do with my earnings. I couldn't wait for the date set for the trip. I was happy to say goodbye to my family on the day the six of us and Uncle

Kevin set off for three months. Our journey started with a trek to the federal road junction where we caught the first bus that took us to Anara. We then embarked on the Intercity bus journey to Owaza township for our final shuttle ride to the family home we were going to live and operate from for the duration of our trip. Uncle Kevin made this trip yearly even before the war. And so he had a longstanding relationship with the matriarchal family we had come to stay with. To them, Uncle Kevin was their seasonal tenant along with his crew he brought with him.

We got to the family home about 6pm and were well received. The mother whom we called Nne Boy prepared us dinner of crab, beef and rabbit soup and fufu. She had two sons and a daughter. Her husband must have been dead or something as there was no daddy around and we didn't ask questions. He just wasn't in the picture. The eldest son, Manny, was in the middle of medical school when the war broke out and his dream of becoming a doctor hung in the balance. The second son Kanu had been pursuing teaching studies and their sister and the youngest Kachi was around my age and, like me, also had her education put on hold. The four of them plus the six of us – Uncle Kevin, Paul, Cyril (CY and younger brother to Uncle Kevin), Kate, Emmanuel and I – shared two separate buildings in the compound. Manny and Kanu occupied the three-bedroom building to the right while we shared the four-bedroom building on the left with Nne Boy and Kachi. Manny was a tall quiet guy who smiled a lot each time you walked past him. He was charming and pleasantly spoken too. Kanu was also a fine young man who often hung around with my male teammates. They would pluck, break and eat coconuts together, chatting war politics while listening to the radio.

Our typical employment routine was to congregate at the town centre very early in the mornings where farm owners came to hire us on a daily basis. Sometimes we were lucky and all got hired by the same one farm owner, but other times we found ourselves split, depending on the amount of work to be done. In all cases Uncle Kevin negotiated our wages and agreed on it beforehand with farm owners. He was also responsible for paying our monthly wages to us. This was our daily routine except on Sundays when we stayed home to help our host family and attend to our personal effects like washing our clothes and plaiting our hair. We did have unlucky days when nobody hired us past midday and we returned to the house and spent the rest of the day with the host family, or we just did our own thing. I loved reading and listening to music apart from helping the landlady when needed. Nonetheless, we worked full days more often than not.

We had been at the town centre one morning carrying both our sharpened machetes and water containers, and luckily for us we were all engaged by one farm owner. We climbed into his truck and he drove us to his farm then he led our leader round to show him the boundaries of the farm. They both shook hands in the end and the farm owner got into his truck and drove off.

'Patie, you will work between Emma and I. The rest of you

take your position and let's get going,' Uncle Kevin instructed as usual. As the youngest, he would always make the special arrangement to accommodate my novice ol' self when working at the farms, to the annoyance of Kate.

'Alright for some,' she said as she walked away to take her position.

'What does that mean, Kate?' I immediately blared out.

Without looking back she responded, 'You do less work than everyone else but get equal pay. Somebody tell me how does that even work!'

Uncle Kevin would place me between Emmanuel and himself and both of them more or less cleared my own patch as we worked to the finishing line. They did this to ensure I wasn't left behind. Nonetheless I ran along in between the two men while others kept pace to the farm's finishing boundary.

But I would normally keep a look out for when the farm owner brought our lunch, to make sure I wasn't seen not pulling my weight like the rest of them. This was very important as I ran the risk of not being picked for work the next time and that would mean no earning for me.

Nearing lunch time on this particular day, I hadn't noticed the farmer's truck as he drove towards the farm site. I caught a glimpse of another driver at the wheel with the farmer's wife on the passenger seat, and I got going with work like I was told. I began to cut every stem and twig in my path while my two flanking heroes continued to cut down the thick and tall bushes in front of us. Emmanuel had a pole which he used as lever to heave up the bushes in order to gain access to clearing the bush undergrowth. I looked up at the pole in his hand and there was a twain holding the bushes to the pole, running up the small tree in front of him. I went to cut the twain to free his pole and lazily landed my freshly sharpened machete on his wrist. Two veins stuck out and there was blood everywhere!

'Run, run, run. Get me my muffler from my bag over there. Quick,' Emma shouted. By this time I was crying uncontrollably as everyone dropped their machetes and we all ran towards the cleared ground behind us where we left our belongings. Uncle Kevin held on to Emma's wrist to try and stop the bleeding. 'Steady, Emma,' he was saying as CY took the muffler from me and tied it on Emma's wound.

'Please, I'm sorry. I didn't mean to hurt you. Please forgive me,' I kept yelling in my perfect Igbo language. Uncle Kevin asked everyone to pack up; we were all going back to the house to see to Emma's wound. We had to go back and abandon our lunch that the farmer's wife had brought to the site as the driver rushed all of us as a matter of urgency back to the house. Manny attended to Emmanuel at the house and applied a proper bandage on his wrist before he was taken to the local hospital. Kate couldn't wait to take a swipe at me again as Uncle Kevin and Manny left with Emma for the hospital.

'Can we now eat please I'm starved? Please guys?'

I didn't say a word in response. I was having a very bad day.

'I had always said that Patie cannot farm, just because she is from same kindred with Kevin,' she said without looking in my direction.

Uncle Kevin, CY and I are from same family clan. Her unfair treatment claim made me feel even worse and I spent the rest of the evening crying my heart out and refusing to eat that night. I went into our room and sobbed till I fell asleep. I worked for two to three days a week from then on to stay behind and keep Emma company. He wasn't able to work again as he nursed his wound at home. I expected him to be bitter towards me but I could see that he appreciated it was an accident. On the days I stayed home I enjoyed the company of the guys in the house – Emma, Manny and Kanu. Kachi accompanied her mum to the farm or to the market most of the time. We would even have a couple of Manny's own friends join us and we listened to music in their quarters and ate whatever fruits like mango and pears they had, and the guys played draught board games sometimes. And when the rest of the household came back, I returned to our living quarters.

Papa stood with Charlie at our village T-junction on the federal road one afternoon. He crossed back to the other side of the road to head home when Charlie had boarded a bus heading towards Anara. Charlie walked into our Owaza compound and straight into our room, the girls' room, and said to me as I raised my head from the mat to look at him, 'Mama is dead!' He then threw himself on my legs on the mat and cried more.

'Mamam ooooh,' I yelled out of sleep and immediately felt the cold chill down my spine. I opened my eyes as I felt the ray of sun stream into our room from the open window. It was a Sunday so everybody was out of the building. I rushed into the kitchen for a glass of water and went back into the room to sit down. Thank God I was dreaming I said to myself reassuringly, but I was still shaken. The war had become so intense that even our host family were thinking about moving away for safety. It was time for us to end our trip and return home to our families. We packed up our belongings, said our goodbyes and Manny and Kanu walked us to the town centre. We were going home with what we had left of our earnings for the two months we'd managed to stay.

We waved goodbye to the brothers as we alighted from the shuttle bus to the town centre to catch the Intercity bus to Anara. And I began to think about my family and the awful dream I'd had that felt so real. Tears filled my eyes as I wondered what lay in waiting for me in the village that I was heading to. As I was the youngest, Uncle Kevin felt he had to deliver me back to my parents. The other crew members came along for the possible gossip, I suppose. Mama had just returned from the farm as we walked into our compound through the back alley. She was dropping the firewood bunch she was carrying on her head. She rushed towards me and enveloped me in her embrace, holding onto me firmly and started singing a folk song with tears rolling down her eyes: '*Ama m ihe nna'koro chi m o agara si na ngara ga onwu o*' (I wonder what I would have told my God if I had died…).

I straightaway knew they were tears of joy. I just held onto her tightly too. To the best of my knowledge, it was the first time my mother hugged me. It felt so reassuring and a closure to the horrible dream I never told to anyone until documenting it here. Mama had miscarried twins two months into her pregnancy while I was away. She lost the first one early in the morning and the second one past six in the evening. That was how long her agony in the absence of proper medical care lasted. I also heard she nearly died as she fainted a few times during the ordeal. I was convinced that was the reason for my horrible dream. I couldn't imagine Mama getting pregnant again after the conscripts' saga. I began to cry. I couldn't bear the thought of losing her, not to mention the burden that could have been on me as the first child and a girl.

Uncle Kevin and the rest of the team offered their condolences to Mama and I. Mama asked us to sit down in the living room while she prepared us something to eat. She stepped into the room to chat to us from time to time as she cooked in the kitchen. Uncle Kevin told her about Emmanuel's incident and he gave my mother what was left of my earnings minus the twelve Biafran pounds it cost to treat Emmanuel's cut wrist. Mama was very grateful nonetheless. She too told us about all that had been happening in the village since we left. There were news reports about how close the Nigerian enemy fighters were to our communities. She also told us about a number of villagers that had died. People of all genders and age groups. She then served us boiled yam with red oil and pepper and local spinach sauce which we enjoyed and thanked her for, before the team dispersed to their individual homes. I couldn't wait to see Papa who had gone to a meeting at Okwe town centre and was expected home any minute.

I looked round for my siblings and was told they had all left for Umuna the night before to spend the weekend at HRH's. HRH was my maternal grandfather. He married Oyiridie (my maternal grandmother) as a catholic man but they only had my mother together. To maximise his chances of having a son, my grandfather decided to change his faith to Protestantism. His thinking was that this would allow him to marry more than one woman, increasing his chances of having male children. I never met my grandmother, she passed away before my time but I met HRH in the mid-60s by which time he already had three new wives. When he passed away in the mid-80s he was survived by three sons, so I guess his plan worked.

By this time, some Umuna people were beginning to vacate their communities to get as far away as possible from the daily sound of shelling and bombing coming from Okigwe's direction. Some local soldiers were returning home with more terrifying news about the war and their friends or even family members who had died at the warfront or disappeared. They also told of parts of the eastern region captured by the enemy – the Nigerian soldiers. True or false, we in the villages were none the wiser. You needed to see my parents and other adults discussing the war raging at Uzuakoli war front, close to Okigwe township that is in turn close to my village junction.

Night was falling and I was the only child in the house. Papa, we were told, was back but had stopped over at a village compound to speak with the villagers. I said goodnight to Mama in the living room and went to unpack my suitcase of my clothes and belongings I'd brought back from Owaza. I sprayed our room with mosquito killer fluid before turning in half an hour later lying there and gazing at the ceiling. My mind ran through my journey home that day, remembering Manny and his family when they said 'Bye-bye' to us. I wished we could have stayed longer on the trip. Exhausted and still no sign of Papa, I slept.

Everyday became harder and harder to survive. Farm produce was difficult to come by and the farmlands were all drying up from being re-tilled with little or no gap for the soil to mature. Every corner of the village forest became a hiding place with dug up makeshift trenches for the men as well as bunkers and air-raid shelters for the villagers as we ran from the heavy gun and shelling sounds ripping above our heads daily. It was even harder to save crop seeds for the next planting season as people had to eat first, and so they cooked and fed the seeds to their hungry families reserving little or no hope for the next planting season. Malnutrition set in big time and families struggled to stay alive, including mine. It was mid-1968 and quite a large number of the villagers were by now suffering from kwashiorkor. Mama was selling her valuables to keep the family afloat, including her sewing machine that was the only treasured thing after her jewellery she brought back from Lagos. By this time the Red Cross and Akanu Ibiam charities were establishing feeding centres all over Okwe villages and beyond. And we had the choice of either a cooked meal or non-perishable provisions. We heard these were donated to us by a handful of nations, like Bulgaria, that recognised suffering in Biafra. People were beginning to rely on the relief food rations for survival. A lot of soldiers were visiting their families, going past my village into Alaocha and to Umumgbada. Paul, Jacob and brother Borny deserted the war and joined the village men's trench movement to avoid being picked up again. Our village square was getting busier with human traffic going to and from our federal road junction through to other Okwe villages and beyond.

I attended Akanu Ibiam's recruitment fair at Okwe town centre and was hired. The organisation, like the Red Cross charity, provided relief food to villagers across the town. I got to work in different villages weekly and was sometimes lucky to work in the company of my village mates so we came home together. But we were never deployed to our own villages, something to do with the organisation's policy for us to work objectively and not be biased when allocating food. And so one evening Mother asked Charlie and me to bring in some scotch bonnets from the back garden for her to cook dinner and Nelson tagged along. In between raising the candle I had in one hand and plucking a ripe pepper on a branch close to where Nelson stood, I noticed his feet were swollen. I knew it was not normal and knew about the kwashiorkor illness. I pushed my forefinger on the top of his left foot then the right and it sank in nearly half an inch each time. I called my mother who came rushing out of the house before I could drag Nelson to the back veranda from the garden. Mama repeated my test of his feet and I could feel what she felt just by the look on her face as tears rolled down her cheeks. I had to give up my Akanu Ibiam job to help care for Nelson. I was taking him to a doctor's surgery about four villages away once a week and it was hell most times! After taking him to and from the surgery for about five weeks, Harriet also fell ill. I was beginning to dread the surgery trip now that I had two siblings with me on the weekly ritual. Sometimes I wished they were both dead to relieve me of the dreadful task of walking miles on sunbaked sandy roads to the surgery. And no matter how early one arrived, there were tens of people and patients already in the compound. Some spent the night to beat the long queues in the mornings. The whole process of queuing and seeing the doctor took up to two hours.

Two months later, not much progress had been made by either of my sick siblings. Food scarcity had worsened. Both Nelson and Harriet were admitted to Okwe sick bay, a makeshift hospital with a long L-shaped ward in Ama-ikpa village close to Okwe town centre. This was a hell of a responsibility for my parents as they struggled to cope with us well children while caring for the other two at the sick bay. In the end it was decided that I would stay at the bay to look after them with Charlie relieving me as and when Mama saw fit. A typical day started with breakfast – relief food of porridge – followed by the morning medication round where a team of national and international medical staff walked from patient to patient to review and agree their further care plan. Lunch was either cornmeal or semolina and salted fish soup, all relief stuff. Dinner was dried or powered egg yolk and maybe shortcake and orange drink. Families who could afford it brought additional hot meals for their relatives while observing their medical dietary requirements. Over half the patient population at any time was suffering from kwashiorkor; the swollen bellies, feet, faces knew no boundaries in age or gender of the sufferers.

There was a constant ambience of crying and moaning by the sick and the dying. We had between two to five deaths daily in the ward, people of all ages and genders. Although I cannot remember the number of patients at the time, it was around fifty on each side. Each family had a mat-space on the floor so they could stay with their sick relatives. You were provided with the mat, a pillow and a pillowcase and the mat-sized blanket. It was up to you to provide more bedding for yourself if you liked. It was a horrendous experience each day seeing groups of men and women carrying their deceased family members back home and crying along the way till they disappeared from sight. No sooner did they vacate their patch than another family was admitted. We would watch them dash around to collect bay supplies and settle in their space. I often compared their sick relations to my siblings and wondered who might die first among them while at the same time remaining very hopeful for my siblings to get well soon!

The war was the last thing on anyone's mind at the bay yet we felt the wrath of sickness, death and misery around us 24/7 as the dead patients were being removed and the new patients admitted onto the vacated floorspace. To my annoyance, good ol' Mother was still getting pregnant. And according to some traditions, children could fall sick if they sensed another baby was expected by their mother. Was this why my siblings were chronically ill with the killer disease, kwashiorkor? Anyway, pregnant or not she still ran to and from the sick bay and my village like a yoyo, an hour's roundtrip at least. She usually walked or rode her bike if she was to go to Umuna to see her father. HRH fell very ill at the time but thank goodness it was not kwashiorkor. Without any knowledge of how old he might have been I would think he was past middle age in 1968 and was already walking with a limp slightly supported by his special walking stick. Hence, I wasted no time linking his age to his illness, as no one discussed it with any of us children.

I came home to the usual household chores whenever Charlie relieved me at the bay. Mama decided when it was appropriate for us to swap for me to be the one to take our dirty clothes to wash and dry by the stream. Or, when she would ask that I went in the company of other mothers to the market to sell and buy stuff for her. This was usually when she couldn't go to the market 'cause she had other engagements like visiting or running errands for her father for example. I always wished I was at the bay to avoid all those errands each time Charlie took over from me for a half or full day stay with Nelson and Harriet. And you could roast under the sun from morning till 6pm at the market and not a single soul would be interested in what you had to sell as, presumably, everybody else was trying to sell similar commodities to pay for their own individual shopping needs. In the long run you settled for half the price of the goods in most cases to get rid of them for the cash you desperately needed to buy your own stuff from the market. While the majority went to the market to buy and sell, we still had people begging for anything you could part with that they needed for survival. Those suffering with kwashiorkor increased in number everywhere you looked, including families that got told they'd have to wait for a vacated space at the bay.

I began to wonder why as Nigerians we were fighting each other and who were the brains that dreamt up the killer war in the first place. 'May they burn in hell,' I was repeatedly praying each time I remembered to pray! Soldiers returning home increased in numbers. There were still those men who operated alone or in small groups to terrorise local communities and these men neither joined the army effort nor struggled to survive like the rest of us. They were all out committing crimes against people and the public. The majority of these touts ambushed people at night to steal food and valuable belongings or whatever else they could from them. This went on around us in Okwe, Umuna, Okwelle and beyond.

The sight of wounded men in military uniform was almost normal, including some amputees catching their transport to and from the local and federal roads. We were all overwhelmed with the everyday war news on radio Biafra about soldiers being captured in this town or that town. And just as some men were returning from the war, we also had some who had grown more upset than others and ran away from home to join the army without telling their families. People began to see joining the army as an escape to sustain their survival. They considered serving in the army as a guaranteed way of catering for their wellbeing as opposed to living at home like the rest of us and struggling with the hardship we all were experiencing. Food shortage made this period the hardest I'd seen since the war began. And so many men would rather gamble on staying alive at the warfront and getting fed than dying of starvation at home.

Still in 1968, my two grannies fell sick and so did Auntie Chikanele, not forgetting the two patients already at the sick bay. And as if it wasn't enough that Mama was expecting a baby, so was my Auntie Julianna. We were virtually surviving on wild fruits from the woods and our back garden produce. Times were so hard that we normalised the chasing and killing of lizards for meat to add to our diet of snails and slugs that we cherry-picked from the back of cocoyam and cassava leaves. I was at the bay one morning after breakfast and Mama stopped briefly to drop us some home cooked meals on her way to her father's. We chatted about my sick siblings and I told her Harriet hadn't slept a wink the night before. She'd cried most of the time and as I struggled to deal with her incontinence the more she'd cried. Mama cuddled Harriet and Nelson one after the other and spoke to them about coming back as soon as she could from her father's visit. She then left us the food in the communal kitchen outside at the back of the bay and rode her bike to Umuna via Umudike, another of Okwe villages.

Back at the bay, the medical team doing their rounds got to Harriet and the doctor looked into her eyes, pushing down her lower eyelid each time. He asked the nurse to dispense some tablets to me for her. He only spent a minute to check Nelson over. As soon as they moved to the next patient, I went out to the kitchen to get a spoon and some water to dissolve the tablets in the spoon to give to Harriet.

I barely stepped back into the ward and Harriet was crying and muttering something. I felt she was hungry as she hadn't eaten much of her breakfast. I put everything down to go get her unfinished breakfast from the kitchen. Hopefully after eating that she could then take her medicine. And as I grabbed the porridge bowl I heard a very sharp cry coming from inside the ward. I ran back quickly and saw it was the young boy next to us. He was a little older than our Harriet, just gone past his second birthday. The boy was dying. His mother and a couple of relatives in the ward wept uncontrollably. I glanced at Nelson and he smiled at me showing his blacked-out teeth. He had taken so much medication and rarely did we let him chew icheku to clean his teeth out. Nobody cared. Our hope was to keep him alive any way we could.

Harriet on the other hand was gazing at me as if looking through me; I was used to her face not saying anything. She would sit or lie there and gaze in pain too with all her body swollen. I went to the kitchen and came back immediately with the porridge to feed her. Then I sat her up with a wrapper around her as all her clothes were soiled and dirty and waited for Charlie to turn up. Mama wanted me at home whenever she was away to look after things for her better than Charlie would.

I had started feeding Harriet when her crying tone changed all of a sudden. I looked at her and it was as if she could not see me even though her eyes were open and gazing into my face. 'Harriet! Harriet,' I was calling out to her while shaking her until I was screaming, but she was still gazing at me with a blob of porridge hanging on her lower lip. She started crying with difficulty. The woman opposite us asked that I put her down and stretch her out on the mat.

'Lie her down, my daughter. She's no longer with us. Sorry, my child.'

I ignored her instructions and continued feeding my unresponsive baby sister who was in fact dying. I didn't want to believe the possibility of my sister dying like other unfortunate kwashiorkor victims I'd watched come and go from the bay. And so I carried on feeding her but the food was not getting in. Her cry turned into a groan and she was dribbling like a baby, bringing up the little scoop of porridge I'd managed to put into her mouth.

The mother that spoke earlier got up and came towards me. About two other carers came along with her to take Harriet from me.

'Stop feeding her.'

The three women helped to lay her down, stretching her limbs and closing her eyes and one of them looked up at me and said, 'Girl, where is your mother? Go and get her quick. We'll look after your siblings. Go now and please be quick.'

I got up to look outside and saw Charlie coming from the village. I ran out of the bay to meet him with the horrible news. By the way the women dealt with me back there I knew Harriet was dead.

'Charlie, they said Harriet is dying, that I should go and get Mama or Papa to come and take her away,' I cried as I got to him.

Charlie dropped to the ground. 'Oh God, Harriet o!' he kept screaming as he cried and rolled on the floor.

We both raced back to the bay where the women stopped him from going any closer to see our baby sister's body. Nelson all this while was just sat there, watching all the drama unfold as Harriet's death kicked off the number of deaths in our family since our return from Lagos two years ago to the month of September 1968. The woman who spoke to me initially came to me where Charlie and I sat with Nelson on his mat.

'You're still here, daughter. Don't worry about your siblings. I will look after them. Go and get your parents as quickly as possible.'

'OK, ma,' I replied.

A nurse went round to check my dead sister out. A routine that I had observed often as it was happening to others in the ward. Now, it was my turn. I was to make sure my family signed off the register and Harriet was taken away on or before 6pm that day. I must also wash all bay issued bedding and plastic crockery and return them for other families' use.

'Charlie you have to go and get Papa and I'll head to Umuna for Mama. Don't worry about the dirty stuff, I'll wash them when I return with Mama,' I said to my brother who remembered to deliver our mother's message before she left for her father's. 'Mama said for you to bring back her kernel sacks from Kevin's mother from Amikpa on your way home. She's not returned the sacks since last Nkwo Okwe when she bought the kernels from us.'

And I said to him, 'You collect them on your way, OK?'

I was heartbroken by Harriet's passing. I was really hoping I could have nursed her back to wellbeing especially as Nelson who'd been suffering from kwashiorkor for longer was still alive and making progress. A week into Harriet's admission and she'd deteriorated far worse than Nelson did.

I sent Charlie to the village with the bad news while I made my way to Umuna trekking via Umudike to HRH's house. They were one of the handful of Umuna families yet to vacate their community to move as far away as possible for safety. People moved back into Okwe communities and beyond to stay as far away as possible from any federal roads. And these sounds and fear of the war filled our lives morning, noon and night!

When I finally arrived, Mama was holding her father's head, a native doctor had covered his face, arm, chest and belly with chalk-like marks and they sat on a mat by a big fireplace in his living room. I was still sobbing as I approached

HRH's premises. Mama could see me through the door that had been left wide open. She walked out of the living room to meet me before I could get to the front door and after I'd told her she was wanted at the bay 'cause my sister died, she asked me to wait for her outside. I saw her whisper to her father and the rest of the family members then I noticed HRH's two wives were also in the room. My mother came out and mounted her bike with me behind her on the passenger seat and we cycled away to the bay in silence apart from the cricking noise the bike made ascending and descending the hilly dusty Umudike road back to the bay. By the time we got there, my family had arrived and were talking with the bay staff about taking Harriet's body away. Uncle Vin carried her wrapped body on his head. Mama asked Charlie to look after Nelson and wanted me to go to the stream to clean out the bay's returnable stuff and our soiled personal effects.

Then Mama began to cry. She hugged the bedding that I had gathered for washing and danced about crying and clutching them to her chest. It broke my heart to see my mother burying one of us while still having more babies. It wasn't the time to be angry with her, not now. I just felt helpless that I could not do anything to soothe her pain let alone remedy the situation my family was in. I took all the dirty laundry to the stream and cried some more. I did the washing and returned them to the bay before relieving Charlie for him to go back to the village that evening. The next day Papa came to relieve me because he said my mother needed me at home; I assumed Charlie must be needed too for Papa to come and relieve me

– the first and last time that happened. The sick bay rota was between Charlie, Mama and I. Papa didn't get involved; he was the head of the house and wasn't to be seen caring for the children. That was the way I saw it then.

Sympathisers were coming in and out of our house when I got home. Some women were with my mother in my parents' bedroom, consoling her. I walked in and said my greetings to all in the room and Mama wiped her tears to talk to me. She said she'd got the message that HRH's health had taken a worse turn and that they would need to move him to Alaocha, his maternal home, for safety. I had to remind myself we were still at war. I had been so preoccupied with all that had been happening at the sick bay that I had not bothered about the war even though we constantly heard the shelling and bombing. What's more, I couldn't differentiate my war pain from my pain of my family's emotional crisis. And I'm talking about post-Harriet's demise. My family had eight members teetering on the brink of death even though Nelson was slowly but surely on the way to recovery. He was beginning to feed by himself and the swollen parts of his body had subsided dramatically. It was good news when the bay hinted at his possible discharge in a couple of weeks down the line. Early the next morning while Papa stayed with Nelson at the bay, Mama took Charlie and I to her father's compound to move him to Alaocha. Uncle Andrew, who was HRH's half-brother, had a Land Rover jeep which we used on the day to load up as many of HRH's belongings as we could to take him out of there. We packed what we could gather of his yams and livestock. War missiles were at their loudest as we were close to the federal road. We were panicking as we packed and loaded the jeep. Mama sat in front next to her sick father and Uncle Andrew drove. Charlie and I climbed into the back and we left for Alaocha.

Charlie and I returned home that evening while Mama spent the night at Alaocha. We woke up one morning to Uncle Vin's cry that his sister, Auntie Chikanele, was dead. Soon enough the village would be gathering at our house again barely a fortnight after laying Harriet to rest. And just as death was taking its toll on my family, so were many of my village families experiencing the same in the thick of the civil war, worsened by hunger and impoverishment, and of course the kwashiorkor illness was taking its toll on people too. It was horrendous to watch your parents go through that and not able to do anything about it. My step-auntie was laid to rest the next day. Death became the bogeyman that visited every other week to steal one of us. Next to go that same month was my sibling, Japheth, one of the three babies Mama had and delivered during the war. There wasn't much ceremony to this as he was very little and under a year old. He was followed by my step-gran, Iye Ihundie, and then another little brother of mine, Okechukwu, just nineteen months old. The latter had survived chicken pox only to die of slight fever. Okechukwu died a few days after Mama gave birth to the last baby, Ikechukwu, who also passed at less than three months old. You should have seen me; I almost lost the will to live. Everything around me spelled DEATH. In fact, I would stand at the back of the house and listen to the rain dripping from the roof onto the little pothole it made on the ground, wondering 'when will all this end?' I kept pondering, watching my parents in pain as they hopelessly continued to pretend they could cope. If only Mama could stop having babies at least. There were five of us alive, albeit barely surviving on one meal a day helped by relief food. August and September 1968 were months that nearly robbed me of the will to live. All my Owaza excitements vanished into thin air. I began to wonder how that family was coping in the war. I wondered whether they had been struck by grief like us? If so, who of them could have died? It was awful! I had enclosed myself in this weird ugly world in my head where everything in it was dead or about to die.

Chapter 3

The thought of death was never far from us as kwashiorkor continued to rage through our population, young and old. The village buzzed still with activities running up to Easter of 1969, when we had shows, religious outings and cultural add-ons in keeping with the festive period. It was during this period that I fell seriously ill; my immediate thought was that I was next in line to die when I'd gone for two days without food. I was breathing with difficulty and felt all energy zapped out of me but it wasn't kwashiorkor, thank goodness. Even as I was force fed by my parents and my uncle, I swallowed or held down little or nothing.

'You have to eat something else you'll die.' Papa's voice came through the parlour as Mama and other significant adults around tried to encourage me to eat. Regardless of how insensitive Papa sounded, you could see the pain written all over his face when he would just wander into the back to have a look and then disappear into his bedroom on the front veranda to reflect on how many of his family members he was having to bury during this punishing war. Everyone was worried sick about me. I constantly looked them in the eye, asking if they thought I was going to die at every chance I got with any of them. At the same time I couldn't help but feel for my family in thinking they were about to lose another. Every herbalist, or 'wise man' as they are called in the village, tried to heal me with their respective healing potions to no avail. I was throwing up after any food and still had the runs. I went through this agony until there was nothing left in me to vomit; I risked passing out which I did a few times so that Mama hardly slept! She was by my side in the girls' room as I teetered on the brink.

On this day while I was gravely ill, we had the village Masquerade Dance and all the youths were out running after the masquerades while dodging their whips. The masquerades would stop to do folk dances that wowed the crowd and were said to be spiritual dance moves only possibly done by immortals. I'm not kidding you, this was a very strong opinion, even though we recognised the voices. But we dared not to say who among our village men we thought might be inside. When the masquerade was about to dance it would say something in a muffled voice like, *okirikiri ka ana gba ukwu ose adigha ari ya elu* (you could only go around a scotch bonnet plant but can't climb it). We interpreted this culturally as meaning 'he' the immortal masquerade is so powerful that you could only come close but not overpower or overwhelm it! The masquerades would ramble out a collection of idiomatic phrases as they paraded the village showcasing both their dance and spiritual powers. I went along with the belief that masquerades are spiritual immortals and so should be feared and respected. It can be so mesmerising and scary at the same time to watch but very entertaining for sure.

I was too ill to join in the fun as I sat on Papa's reclining chair by my mother's kitchen who by now cooked separately from my grandmother and my Auntie Julianna's gang. Mama was worried and kept an eye on me as she rummaged in her kitchen on this late afternoon while my siblings had long joined in the village fun parade. 'Can I make you ukwa or yam casserole?' she asked not knowing what else to feed me.

'Nothing. Can I have water please, Mama?' I found that I could only hold down half glass of water and not more.

My siblings were gone for most of the day as they also attended the county building to practise their religious shows scheduled for Easter Sunday. Favour came to the back briefly to see me. '*Ndo Nwokem*,' (sorry my buddy) she said to me. I was avoiding her eye contact. I didn't want to acknowledge how bad friends and family felt I was getting. Before I could offer a seat she was already running off and taking the back route to catch up with the rest of the crowd. I craved for my mate's company but Mama was fulfilling all of my whims.

Favour's footsteps disappeared beyond next door's backyard and the coast was clear again – just Mama and I but I could still hear the noisy rant of the youths in the distance. I turned to look at Mama and asked in my faint voice, 'Am I going to die, Mama?'

Sitting close to my reclined chair she leaned over and enveloped my head and shoulder in her bosom. 'You're not, my grandma. You will be alright.' She reassured me even though her anguished face was saying differently as I lay on the chair pondering what would be.

A middle-aged man with a missing upper lip walked by our front yard as he was walking past our compound. He stopped briefly to say hello to Papa who was sat on our veranda. The man, Okwaranwune – a herbalist – was visiting from another village beyond Alaocha.

'Obi, what's the matter this bright day?' he asked my father as he walked into the compound towards him.

'Fellow elder, welcome. My eldest daughter is seriously ill and hasn't eaten for days. She has been seen by many local physicians but to no avail. In fact God brought you to Umuofeke village 'cause I was going to ask Augustine to come and get you.'

My parents had also taken advice from a few armchair physicians, one of whom gave them worm tonic to administer to me and I vomitted up to half a dozen round worms – like regurgitating a spaghetti meal, they fell out of my mouth and I was still sick. All this Papa was saying as the man listened while walking past him on the veranda and into the living room. He went out to the backyard and disappeared into the garden from where he picked specific leaves and reappeared towards Mama's kitchen. I recognised some of the leaves but not the majority of them.

'Our elder, you are welcome. How is the family? Hope everyone is alright,' Mama was saying to him when he gave the leaves.

'They are all fine thanks. Here, make her a light soup. You can add a bit of yam or cocoyam if you like and feed it to her,' he said to my mother and took his leave through the living room where my father was waiting to offer him kolanut and alligator pepper. Mama went in briefly to thank him again and shared in the kolanut.

'I've come to order a few gallons of palm wine from your kinsman for my grandchild's outing ceremony and then saw you almost not here with us,' he jokingly concluded before telling my parents, 'don't worry, she will be fine.'

Mama walked back to the kitchen.

'May it be well with you,' I heard Papa repeating to him till he left to continue his visitation on the other side of our compound. It took me that long growing up to recognise the significance of kolanut in my tradition in the absence of which an Igbo man would consider you as unwelcoming, regardless of the pomp and ceremony you laid on for them at their visit. Cultural tradition in Igboland demands that you offer kolanut first thing even if nothing else, it would suffice for a grand gesture.

Back in the kitchen and I could feel a wind of optimism in the way Mama got on with making the vegetable casserole dish for me. She had started to peel a piece of yam when she told me about Okwaranwune. A highly respected herbalist, a go-to when the chips were down, so to speak. Mama told me, 'Some soldiers thought to be missing in war action were returned by his power.' That was powerful indeed, perhaps I'd survive by his grace too. Papa came by the kitchen to see how I was doing with the meal Mama had now dished up for me. She nodded to him encouragingly. As I ate one spoonful after the other I felt a hot flush overwhelming me. The more I ate the more I sweated. I glanced at my parents' happy faces, got up and ran out of the compound to join the masquerade parade. I was healed. I was energised to run around the village with others.

I returned to work not with the food distribution team but with the medical unit. I worked as an interpreter at the medical walk-in centre opposite the sick bay. Our wages remained the same. I had the elementary 4 level of education under my belt before the war. My English mixed with pidgin was standard albeit not backed by a vast vocabulary, but it sufficed compared to many of my peers around at the time. And so I found myself in the interpreter role Mondays to Fridays from 6.30am to 5pm. In the mornings, patients queued outside the unit, along the corridor and into the consultation room where a white woman doctor saw them one after the other. The patient came into the room and I spoke in Igbo to them to find out why they had come then I relayed it to the doctor. She either wrote a prescription or gave them an investigative form which they took to another room where two nurses and their local assistants would carry out whatever the doctor ordered. I collected the patients' notes and returned them to the admin room by end of day.

I was coming home from work one day when I met two young men heading towards Alaocha. The one in army uniform stopped me and wanted to get to know me. He said they were visiting a friend in Umuchiri, a couple villages after Alaocha. He asked if I was from here, Umuofeke village, and I nodded.

'I'm the son of Ajah from Umuaaka in Okwelle and my name is Daniel, you can call me Dan.'

'I'm from this village,' I replied and continued, 'I'm Obijiaku's first daughter.' That was us finished with our introductions. You were someone's son or daughter those days first and foremost. And your surname sufficed in many cases to identify you especially where you lived in close neighbourhoods. He told me him and his friend would come by on their way back to see my dad.

'Why?' I muttered to myself as they left me, as if I couldn't guess why a man would want to visit a thirteen-year-old's parents. Why else would he want to see my father other than asking for permission to marry me? And so when Daniel said they would stop to see my father that was surely what he meant. He was good looking and had a wound dressing on his left ankle. And how did his indirect marriage proposal make me feel? I was not sure what I felt or ought to feel. I just went about my village life and thought no more about it. I still helped Mama with the daily house chores when I returned from work. Either I went alone or with a group of mates to the stream to process cassava for fufu, wash and dry our clothes, or rags more like, as well as dishes at times. And depending on the time we would swim afterwards before we packed up and returned home. Adults would warn us to be careful not to stray beyond the parameters of the three streams circling our village so we wouldn't get kidnapped or have conscripts follow us home to hunt our young men for soldiers to join the war efforts.

Mama took anything sellable to local markets for cash to buy foodstuff that she didn't grow i.e., beans. We still cooked without salt and families were still living with and dying of kwashiorkor. The Obijiaku family you could say had had our fair share the year before burying my step-gran Ihundie, step-auntie Chikanele, my siblings – Japhet, Okechukwu, Ikechukwu and not forgetting Harriet that opened the death floodgate.

Nelson was a lot better by now and had since been discharged, giving us cause for a family celebration. We prepared plenty of fufu and vegetable soup cooked with game meat to go round the villagers and our distant relatives that came. The game meat was Papa's hunting spoils on the occasions he went hunting with friends. We would cut and roast the meat in pieces to preserve them for prepping meals at later dates. Nelson's 'welcome home' feast was one such occasion. Adults had palm wine and local gin with their meal and the children made do with water from our streams.

As we got busy clearing up after the party early in the evening, Hope looked up into the living room and turned to me to announce we had visitors. Dan and his entourage appeared at our house. One of the two men with him was the friend he was with on the first day we met that he never introduced to me. The second man was elderly and spoke when the family assembled with them in the living room.

'My brothers, you are welcome,' Papa said as he raised the bowl of kolanut, garden egg, peppered peanut dip and alligator pepper which he handed to his brother, Uncle Vin, to present to our guests.

'Our brothers, you are welcome. Here we have kola to welcome you and to pray we eat these for good health and prosperity. And our visitors will spend time with us and return home in peace just as they came. All these we ask in Jesus' name.'

'Amen,' by everyone present.

I listened from where I was with my siblings by my grand's hut while Mama and Auntie Julianna were in Mama's kitchen prepping food for our guests – African salad and vegetable soup for swallow food afterwards. We could hear the eldest visitor speak from the back for what seemed a long time and people laughed at intervals as he told jokes as well as indicating why they had come.

'We've come about your beautiful eldest daughter as wife for our son here. Since Dan saw this Umuofeke gem, he has lost his sight for every other woman. So we asked him to take us to where he found the gem and here we are...'

This was followed by a roar of laughter. I could just imagine him pointing Dan out to my significant adults sat around with them. I began to wonder how they could have just turned up unannounced.

'Mama, why did Okwelle people turn up without—'

Before I could complete my question, Mama smiled before bursting into laughter joined by Auntie Julianna and said,

'They told us at the last Ekego market. We wanted to surprise you.'

A little while later I was sent for and after I had said my hellos, I stood close behind Papa. Uncle Vin and Uncle Alphosus, the most senior to Uncle Kevin and CY, were also present in the room. I deliberately didn't make eye contact with Dan but could sense his eyes all over me.

Papa began to tell me what their visit was about and pointed out to me everything they'd brought with them. 'They have brought all these with them to ask you to marry their son Daniel here,' Papa said, pointing him out. 'He's also asked that I give you this soap and if OK with you they will then name the day to come and formalise their wish with our Umunna.'

Umunna is a collective name for the villagers that literarily means our kindreds. My people referring to the visitors as brothers meant that no relationship had been formalised in which case they would become in-laws.

I accepted the soap and the jubilation was all too surreal. My parents, my uncles, brother Goddy and everyone else was happy. I was happy alright but for a different reason – the soap was the Sunlight brand I was used to in Lagos. I went to the back and didn't have to say a word for my mother and Auntie Julianna to express their happiness too. They wore these huge smiles, beaming at me as I approached them.

All I could think of was a long bath with the Sunlight soap at Aku or Ikwe stream as well as using it to wash what was left of my inner wears to sustain the floral scent – to relive the freshness I was used to in Lagos. The black soap we'd been using since our return was homemade and still in use today. To this day I've never tried to find out what it's made of as there was no alternative. With the Sunlight soap tablet in my hand I was all too excited. I used to love the advert and sing along to it when it came on the TV at No. 4.

'Mama, it is Sunlight, the same as we use at home,' I said excitedly to them holding out the soap for them to see.

'This is home,' Mama replied with a smile. I ran off to my room with my soap in hand and the song sprang to mind:

Sunlight soap is good for all washing
For happiness and laughter and (unintelligible
something, something) too.
For all washing, Sunlight is best for you.

I was a five-feet tall, flat chested teenager but my parents were comfortable giving me away into marriage. I wasn't fazed either. I was just happy chatting about the possibility and making my family happy. Favour and I would swap sleeping arrangements to chat more. She spent more nights at mine than I did at hers so that I didn't leave my sisters sleeping on their own. She had two younger brothers, all living today. We talked about the kind of married life we wanted and hoped for. Our expectations like how many children we would love to have and how we would raise them. Favour already had 2lb-size breasts and of my age group in the village only a handful of us were flat chested. And then we learned about a bug-like water creature that never gets wet; they buzz around in groups on the water surface by the stream banks. It had been rumoured that these water-loving species aid breast development by biting on your nipples from time to time. We used to hold them up to bite our nipples each time we went to the stream. It was madness and we didn't see anything wrong with this healthwise, but needless to say our breasts didn't develop spontaneously. These water creatures are black with a thin white stripe on one side of their shell-like tops. How foolish a reasoning in hindsight. Our hope was huge to say the least for breast growth.

A couple of months later, Dan and his people came as promised. They met with my villagers who were gathered with Papa at home to welcome them. It was a feast day for everyone. I had a fantastic time with my friends and was the centre of attention for once during my miserable war child life. It didn't matter that the war was still on, I was getting married to a soldier and it didn't matter that he was home for such a long time either on leave or absent without leave. I'd no idea and I didn't ask. My parents were happy about me getting married – that's all that mattered. Nelson was growing from strength to strength despite the food shortage, and for the first time since our return my parents seemed truly happy. And so began my traditional culture of keeping up appearances both at home and at Umuaaka, Dan's village in Okwelle.

I did house chores at both ends. My short stays with Dan's family usually lasted for no more than a week at a time. These visits were to give his family and villagers the opportunity to assess my 'wife-material' worthiness. More often than not families based their judgements or decisions on the village gossips about the girl. Remember, family name was paramount and you worked really hard to protect it. They judged you by how strong you were to farm, how you could run a home, how you greeted people, how helpful and respectful you were and how well you got on with the villagers especially members of your would-be family. My immediate problem, however, was the double chores which were killing me as I dashed from my village to stay a little at the Okwelle village.

My village's main source of income was and still is palm oil. The villagers tracked palm trees in the forest once a month to chop down ripe palm fruits to be processed into red oil. Households would cut these down from as many trees as they could find on the given harvest day. Some were skilled in the use of a special climbing gadget called Ete to climb up the tree to cut their own palm nuts. Ete is a heavy-set twain that the cutter wears around their waist, enclosing them and the tree with a lock mechanism that aids their flight up and down the tree. The unskilled villagers contracted experts to do their cutting for them. My parents would always contract a palm cutter to avoid my father risking doing it himself.

On this particular month's harvest day, my parents had hired one of the renowned cutters from Umudike Okwe, who would cut down double or more palm nut heads than any other cutter could manage. They had gone into the forest with him early in the morning in search of palm trees with ready nuts while the rest of us still slept in the house. The cutters are then paid and given a take home present usually a fresh or cooked food item like a chunk of meat or stockfish. People headed back into the bush after eating to complete what they started – gathering their palm nut heads and bringing them close to their living quarters and away from the forest. Still at war, but now we were beginning to eat with salty sea sand which was still expensive even though it wasn't real salt. This didn't bother us, as long as it tasted salty we used it like that.

My gran Anyamnele had fed us breadfruit porridge the night before. She loved having us around to eat with her even though Mama would cook for us and caution us from time to time about spending time with her. She would do anything to discourage us going into her hut let alone eat with her. Gran had been experiencing some growth in her palms for over a year and already had one bad eye that they couldn't or hadn't bothered to treat, a white patch covering her iris that could have been cataracts. Mama quarrelled with Gran any time she caught or saw us coming out of her hut. She would yell at her at the top of her voice to stop encouraging us into her hut. Mama explained to us that she feared we might catch our grandmother's diseases – the moles on her palm that no one named to us. One day our granny was upset and reported Mama to Papa and all hell broke loose. It was one of the few times I could remember my parents raising their voices at each other and neither listening to the other. I also noticed this only happened whenever Mama wanted the kids to behave in a particular way and Papa would rather deal with it differently. Both my parents punished me nonetheless and so I related to them equally.

Mama hadn't spotted us on this very eve of our palm cutting day when we enjoyed ukwa with Gran. Then came the day itself when I was looking forward to returning to granny's to warm up the leftover breadfruit in her clay pot and eat it with her. For some reason I found breadfruit tasted more delicious the day after than when freshly cooked. Perhaps the clay pot had something to do with it. I don't know and never really found out. So my parents had left very early with the cutter and while my siblings slept I left for my gran's hut. She was lying flat on her bamboo bed with one hand on her stomach and the other on her temple. I rushed in as usual calling out her name with my morning greetings.

'Iye, good morning,' I said to her. But no response. Not only was she not responding, she made no move to acknowledge my presence in the room which was unusual. She just lay so still that I had to bend over and touch her arm to try to get her attention. But she was as stiff as a tree. Fear overwhelmed me and I screamed and ran outside. An elderly village man walking past our compound stopped by to find out what was wrong with me. I was still crying as I announced that my Iye was dead. The man placed his hand over my mouth to stop me crying and asked me to go and stay with my siblings inside while he handled the situation. He also warned me not to talk to anyone about it. I got my siblings, who were now awake, together in the living room and then went and stood by the back door watching the man go inside the hut for a few seconds and come out closing the door behind him. He walked back to the road and as he disappeared, I felt a chill run down my spine with the thought of another funeral in our compound!

My parents were home within half an hour. Not sure how the old man managed to reach them while not knowing their whereabouts in the forest, but I was relieved they were back. I could see the pending agony in my parents' tears, albeit subtly, as they wept. I felt their anguish and pain as they met with the villagers trooping into the compound to offer their condolences to us yet again. With the support of the village elders, Papa laid his mother in state in the living room where more people came to offer their condolences. My siblings and I were asked to spend the night next door at Uncle Willy's mother's hut. Mama was with us while Papa slept in their bedroom. My parents brought food over to us next door while they were joined by groups of people including those from neighbouring villages that had heard and came to offer their condolences. I was beginning to identify many elders of my family clan as a group of them headed off to Papa's maternal village, Umuduru Egbuaguru, with the bad news as tradition demanded.

The sky let rip with rain as soon as those digging the grave had finished at the backyard. The grave was filled with water when my parents' entourage returned a few hours later with many of Papa's maternal kindred: tens of them, men and women. They sang and danced along from the village square into our compound. They went into the living room where Gran was laid, cotton buds in her nose, her face powdered and one of mother's wrappers thrown over her from her neck down.

Umuduru kindred claimed the heavy rain that filled the grave was them shedding tears ahead of their arrival to our compound for the loss of their daughter and big sister. The rain stopped about twenty minutes after their arrival before the ceremony began. Some of the men drained the grave and my gran was laid to rest after which our villagers joined in the cultural funeral songs and dance ritual. People chanted as they ran around the village and let off many gun salutes at the compound. My gran went to her grave with my mother's wrapper. The one covering her from the neck down. Her people refused to let us retrieve it because they said Gran had told them how cruel my mother was to her when she was alive. She had told them several times about how she wasn't allowed near her son and grandchildren. For them, burying Gran with our mother's wrapper served as a punishment and also to get back at her for not taking good care of Gran as a good wife should. I felt sorry for my mother who was now left with just one wrapper. As much as I was not mature enough to understand the politics of such a feud, it was easy for me to take sides considering all that I had seen and was still witnessing Mama go through at the time. 'May my future husband's mother be dead by the time I meet and marry him' became my constant prayer and my number one marriage life wish! Harsh but that was how much I felt for my suffering mother.

Gran's kindreds then demanded an arm and a leg for all

the traditional burial requirements, which my parents I'm sure must have gone a-borrowing to be able to afford. They demanded much more after the burial, including live goats and fowls, yam and corn seeds for planting season. Our mother was managing with one wrapper for days on end, having sold all her possessions to feed us. Every other day, she would wash this remaining wrapper and spread it to dry overnight for use the next day. Papa still had some shorts and his white hospital overalls, about half a dozen of them, that he had brought home with him from Lagos. You could see they'd lost all trace of their originality but he had change of clothes all the same, which is more than Mama did. She made us shorts and dresses with multi-print materials that she had spent hours stitching together to provide us with clothes on our backs.

Meanwhile I was still back and forth between my village homes doing everything required of me from sweeping the compound, fetching water and firewood for Dan's mother through to babysitting his year-old niece. His mother was tall and skinny and liked to show me off to visiting villagers. She would send me on errands in and around the village so that I met people and introduced myself to them. Dan and I enjoyed each other's company. He would even snitch on his mother whenever she complained about me to him. Her and another village woman reckoned I was talkative and would rather spend time with Dan's male friends than with the village girls who would specifically come round to spend time with me, 'their new wife'.

I must admit this was true of me; I preferred spending time with the guys rather than the girls, especially when they told me about their war and love life escapades in their local community. With the girls, I was quizzed about marriage dos and don'ts and that wound me up. Dan's mother's killer punch was that I wasn't behaving like a girl. She claimed that I was too vivacious and flat chested, all of which in her book spelled infertility on the horizon. When Dan told me this I pondered over it for a while on my way back to my village one day and wondered why had I not menstruated and barely had dots on my chest for breasts. I immediately decided I wasn't going to marry Dan. I needed to concentrate on my development as a woman first. I was a pretty girl, people told me again and again, but with my flat chest and no 'menses', as we referred to women's monthly bleeding period, what was the point of my prettiness? Favour, Nkechi and the rest of my friends had all experienced theirs. I needed to concentrate on that and not getting married to a man whose mother disapproved of me. I told my parents and they invited Dan on a day I wasn't going to be around to call it quits. I was later told Daniel was almost in tears as my parents relayed my message to him.

Papa wasn't one for farming. I worked that out a few months into our return to the village. He would come along but spend the morning trying to organise us while Mama, Charlie and I got on with the farm work, much to our mother's annoyance. He didn't find cutting grass or tilling the earth as easy or interesting as operating the hospital's heavy-duty washing machine. He would rather risk going hunting with his mates at night instead. Mama had forced him to come along one day and I stayed home to watch over my siblings and fetch firewood ready for cooking our dinner. I had my day planned out. If I was lucky, Favour could come with me into the newly burnt clearings to fetch as many dried tree stubs for firewood as possible later. Meanwhile, I was going to get on with my school assignment. A number of us were to produce half a dozen bunches of broomsticks for school on Monday. It was a makeshift school, with no grading or age specifications involved. It was just a place for all school kids to go in the mornings and during the day while the adults went about their business. On this day, I sat at our front veranda processing palm leave stems or sticks for broomsticks. The classes took turns to produce these brooms at given times for the school to keep the environment clean. Producing broomsticks and sweeping the school compound were routinely done by the pupils otherwise you could be asked to do any of them as a punishment.

There I was sitting on the veranda prepping my broomsticks and CY, Paul and Kele had come round. We were joking and laughing out loud as we would normally do.

'I'm coming,' I said to them as I got up to take a pee in the back garden. I returned two to three minutes later and sat back down to continue with my broomsticks. I looked up and every one of them was chuckling, especially Kele, trying to suppress his uncontrollable giggle. Not sure I was in on the joke. I looked behind them and Auntie Julianna was veering into the compound when my friends all took off, deepening my confusion. It couldn't have had anything to do with my auntie's return as they would often come to the house as members of my Okoro clan where they would be asked to run errands by adult members of the family.

Auntie Julianna stood still to watch them rush past her. She looked enquiringly as she watched them disappear out of the compound.

'Why were they running off like that?' she asked me, still carrying her cassava basket on her head. I told her I hadn't a clue. She had started walking to her hut when she said, 'Have you gone to fetch the firewood I heard Mama ask you to this morning?'

Even without a wristwatch I knew it would soon get dark, but I had a particular spot in mind to fetch them. I still needed to have the firewood at home before Mama returned. I decided to suspend my broomstick processing and go straightaway – I wasn't even going to bother about getting Favour to come with me. I stood up and arranged my unfinished work not knowing she was looking on. I became aware of her glare when I saw her hastily put down her basket. She grabbed both my shoulders and said, 'Turn around.'

Whatever she saw behind my dress. There it was, I was menstruating! My dress was massively stained behind me. It dawned on me that was why my village brothers were giggling earlier.

'Come with me.' She took me through the parlour and to my room and all I could hear was her soliloquy. 'Right, where can I get a big and small piece of rag? Which is your clothing box?' She was picking and dropping clothes in the room until I opened up my box for her and stepped back. Grabbing hold of my old worn out school uniform she tore it with such precision that I was in some form of nappy before I could blink. 'You are now a woman and must mind not to be seen with boys again else you will get pregnant. And so stay away from boys.' As she was delivering this becoming a woman sermon she was jolting me back and forth to put finishing touches to my stray nappy – a stringy piece around my waist and the neatly folded bigger piece tucked into the string both front and back. 'Right, run along and fetch the firewood. Mama and Papa will be home any minute now.' As a younger wife in the family and despite how many times she fell out with my parents she referred to them as Mama and Papa as cultural tradition demanded.

I left home with my basket and machete and went to the nearest clearing by the village county building to get some firewood. I kept checking the padded cloth between my legs in the woods and couldn't believe how much blood was coming out of me. Each time I struck my machete on a dead wood stub to break and collect it into my basket, I could feel the blood spew out of me. The more dead the wood stubs the easier I knocked them off. I got home at almost the same time as my parents returned. I put the firewood down and headed for my room. I was exhausted and went to the utility room for a cup of water where Mama cornered me and let rip with her own sermon about me staying away from boys to avoid unwanted pregnancy, which was one hell of a taboo culturally.

I pretended to understand what they both meant about the ban from boys or men but really never had the bottle to ask for clarification.

'What about Charlie and Nelson, my brothers?'

She looked up at me with a screwed face and said emphatically, 'You must not let any boy sleep with you.'

'Yes Mama,' I responded. I never repeated my question about the ban again. Somehow, I felt like the adults knew something more about menstruation than they were letting on.

I held up a big piece of broken mirror in the bath to look at myself and realised my breasts had grown and my nipples were darker than the rest of my skin. I had grown alright! I was now a woman. If not for the war I would have loved to have finished my education, got married and had children, but not at the rate my mother was breeding though. Four died and the miscarried twins plus the five of us alive made a total of eleven children. That was too many. My dream was to have four children, three boys and a girl. Drawing from experience I promised myself I wouldn't want the girl first because I wouldn't want her to go through the dogsbody lifestyle like me. Neither did I want her as a last child because I didn't want her to turn out to be a spoilt brat. I would just like her anywhere in the middle.

Chapter 4

It was late afternoon on Nkwo Okwe day, running up to the second week of January 1970. Mama was preparing for Ekego market the next day. We were both at Aku stream processing the breadfruit she would be taking to the market. I was going to go with her to help carry some of her goods. For over a week, my siblings and I had been cracking palm kernels each day when we came back from school to fill a 50kg bag. While Mama worked on the breadfruit in the water, she asked me to go and look round the nearby bush for some dry firewood. Together we headed home afterwards, Mama carrying the processed breadfruit, and I the firewood. Papa and some elders were relaxing on our veranda drinking palm wine with calabash funnel cups, like they did most days. They often met when the women and children had all dispersed to work, market and school. And that was aside from going hunting at night, monitoring their bush traps and tapping their palm wine mornings and evenings.

Everywhere they were gathered the men talked about the

war while women mostly chatted on their way to the market
or farm about putting food on the table and the usual gossip.
This was how I perceived the adults around me at the time.
On this evening their chat wasn't sounding optimistic like
before. It was no longer 'we will kill Gowon tomorrow' and
the rest of it. They were recounting the number of eastern
cities that had fallen into the hands of the Nigerian soldiers.
Mama and I came into the compound and disappeared to the
kitchen to prepare dinner after we'd said our hellos to Papa
and his friends. The rest of my siblings were in their rooms
and within an hour of returning, our yam casserole dinner
was ready with my help in the kitchen. Mama dished it as
usual and I ate with my younger ones. Mama took care of
Papa's dinner when the last of his visitors ate with him before
he left to go home. After spraying the mosquito killer in our
rooms, it was time for us to go to bed; we had the busy market
day ahead of us. Mama was also taking two heads of green
plantain to the market for sale. A heavy load indeed but she
looked forward to selling all these to buy the stuff she needed
from the market.

Mama woke me up very early and took me to the back
of her and Papa's bedroom window where she had already
placed a bowl of water on the house skating board. She made
me stand on the opposite side of the bowl and splashed a little
water on her face at the same time looking at me and saying,
'Owaa.'

I replied, 'Owa a gbakwara gi.'

It was a traditional practice we believed in that still

survives to date. This meant as a 'clever and intelligent girl' or person, people sought your best wishes before they went to the market to hopefully improve their chances of lucrative transactions – whether they were buying or selling. I liked the idea that I was always singled out to do this, which massively boosted my confidence to be considered a clever girl and perhaps, magically endowed. But it still didn't excuse the errand girl I was turned into as a girl and the first born. No household chores were too much and that was on top of looking after my siblings.

It was a different atmosphere as we set off for Ekego market that morning. Mama and I left the compound and headed to the village square where some villagers were already ahead of us while people were passing us and heading in the opposite direction towards Okwe town centre. It looked like the people ahead of us were cheering as they hurried along. But we couldn't hear what they were excitedly chanting about until we came closer to a number of them still climbing up the hill away from Aku bridge. And then we heard them: 'One Nigeria, Long live Nigeria!' They chanted repeatedly as I looked up at my mother and she was in tears but laughing. I had never seen her like that before. I ran to catch up with the people ahead of us for some form of validation of what I'd just heard that evoked Mama's emotions. I increased my steps to catch up with a couple of the women ahead and chanting as they hurried on.

'Mama Louisa, good morning. What am I hearing? Is it true?' The two women stopped to talk to me. Only they weren't talking. They were chanting and managing to nod their heads to the chant of 'One Nigeria o. Long live Nigeria o'.

And Mama Louisa said to me, 'Look,' pointing to the small vehicle convoy approaching us, 'it's the soldiers in those jeeps that told us the war is over. They said we should tie yellow palm fronds on our wrists too.'

I was far too excited by now but had to stay put while the women walked along so Mama could catch up with me. She went to help me bring down my load and I was looking at her when she said, 'Put it down and help me with mine. I want to go into the bush for some palm fronds for us.'

She already knew. Mother and I assisted each other to bring our loads down. Within minutes she was out with yellow palm fronds as people had pulled much of it off the agriculture palm trees nearby and left them lying around on the ground.

'Give me your wrist.' She tied one of them on my right wrist before I helped with hers. We helped each other again with lifting our loads back up to our heads and off we went with the villagers still streaming towards the junction. Our village road by now was teaming with people and the happy 'hurray the war is ended' noise was permeating the air as we came closer to the main road junction. We could hear the sound of vehicle horns bellowing ahead of us and the celebratory mood was felt by all of us as we all jingled and jangled along together.

It suddenly dawned on me that the war had really ended. We can't all be crazy and the soldiers couldn't be lying to us. The war had ended indeed. Trailers and tippers and gwongworos, the kind that brought us home three years and four months ago, were zooming past on the federal road heading towards Okigwe. The majority of vehicles were filled with military men in uniforms, shooting their rifles into the air at random as their vehicles whisked past us. The noise was deafening as we merged with Okwelle people to our right and Ezelu people to our left. The crowd kept swelling, increasing the chant as the military vehicles rolled along. We were all so very happy to comply with their instructions, especially as they also rewarded our obedience with goodies they threw at us from their vehicle: mini Nigerian flags, biscuits, milk, sugar and coffee sachets, mini pots of fresh milk, chewing gum and lollies, you name it, all the goodies I was forced to leave behind years ago. It was such an exciting time. For that brief moment I was alive again. I had branded biscuits and chewing gum in my hands for the first time in years since coming back from Lagos. It was brief but it was all the moments I longed for rolled up into one. The nasty war had ended. For me the war ended on 12th January 1970. I still had two more years to finish my primary education by the age of fourteen. At least the war did end and from that day forward I was alive to sojourn. I was alive to finish my education and get to that disco with the multicoloured lit dance floor and dance in a flared skirt like I used to see on TV at No. 4… I was alive to daydream again.

Life improved. We returned to school, and this time we attended our proper classes. I attended in my elementary class to continue from where I stopped in Lagos. It was almost at the end of my elementary 4. The school year was from January to December. Mama continued to be engaged in her farm work and her stall at the village square. We were back eating with salt again. Auntie Julianna had had another daughter and now had a total of four daughters while Mama looked after the remaining five of us. Papa went back to his routine of waking us up for school like he did at Modile Way except that we had no live-in maid and Papa was unemployed. Before I knew it, my parents were discussing the need for Papa to move to find work and they agreed he should make the journey. Papa left for Enugu and asked us to behave ourselves and look after our mother while he was away, but he didn't tell us when he would return. He also reminded us to go to school together and come back home together now that we were all attending school in Okwe town centre, the very school my parents attended prior to Papa's move to Lagos. I was back at school with my siblings. Hope, Rose and Sunny attended St Michael's primary school in the village, while Charlie and I went to St James' at Okwe centre. Both schools were Church of England and are still operating to date. HRH was also now back at his Umuna compound. We had since visited him a few times since the war ended now that he was well again.

Our school Vice Principal at St. James' decided that a number of pupils had potential. This was the first time I'd heard the word. The school had decided to move us up a class, trusting that we would get excellent grades in our final results. That was how confident he was! We would skip elementary 5 to join the final year pupils. The VP asked to see our parents to tell them about the school's decision. I told him my father was away and didn't know when he was returning and so only my mother would be able to come. He asked if there was another male adult in the family to come along with Mama. I had long known that important discussions or decisions were made or taken by men and not women; even in their absence a woman would not be allowed to make decision for them. And so, when I told my mother and Uncle Vin, it was no surprise that he was glad to come along to represent my father.

My uncle went along with Mama to the VP appointment. The Principal himself, who had a sister in our group of potential students, was also present. Mama was excited but she was also concerned about what Papa would make of it. Uncle Vin decided they would agree provisionally, pending Papa's return, before they could give a concrete answer to the school. I was very excited and full of hope to finish my education as quick as possible and move on to secondary education the following year. After all, I had wasted so much time during the civil war; three years to be exact. I should be half way through my secondary education by now. But looking on the bright side, I was alive and had survived the civil war!

To say Papa didn't like the idea of me jumping a class into my final elementary school year was an understatement. He desired things to be in order like his white boss had imbued in him. And so, he insisted I must finish elementary 5 before moving to 6 to stand a better chance of coming top of the class. Making good school results was his thing and he was always pleased each time. Although he acknowledged the reasoning behind me moving a class ahead, he did put his foot down. I remember coming third in class before in Lagos and he was mad at me.

'I take it the father of the first in your class raised his child better than me, or has he two heads? And why leave the second position land in the third place? You might as well had carried last!'

'Papa baby, what now? Why don't you become the teacher to make sure she comes first?' my mother asked.

'I'm not a teacher but also a civil servant! Why don't you keep quiet if you don't have anything to say?'

As much as I hated seeing them in disagreement, Mama's intervention at these times was usually a blessing for me to just walk away from it all.

'Spare her your drill and congratulate her for passing in the third place out of a class of over thirty.'

'Leave her alone. What about those that failed?' she would say.

Papa's response was as always, 'The father of the first child is not better than me.'

I continued to hear them argue as I begrudgingly walked out of the compound.

Come the appointed Friday evening to visit our VP for Papa to hear the school's recommendation first-hand, Papa was reluctantly getting ready and barking at Nne baby not to hold him up.

'Let's get there on time and get this thing over done with,'

Papa said as he stepped out of his bedroom and onto the front veranda, his travel strap bag under his left armpit. I was doing everything in the parlour not to come out to the veranda even though he knew I was coming along. I had returned from school about three hours earlier but was eager to accompany them in the hope that Papa would give his approval after hearing the VP explain it better. That would make my day, I was thinking to myself as I put my shoes back on in the parlour and waited for Mama to lead the way out of the house. I stepped out as soon as I heard her voice at the front.

'Let's go. I hope you keep your cool and listen when we get there. Don't be in a haste. Remember he's the teacher and knows what he's talking about...'

'Let's go please. I want to get back before dark,' he said and began to lead the way out of the compound.

'The school has decided but oh no Christopher, or shall I call you Thomas (as in biblically speaking), you insist on doing it your own way. The last time I checked you were not a teacher and know nothing about teaching,' Mama was saying to him as we walked along to cross Ikwe bridge.

At the VP's house, he narrated everything he had said to my uncle and Mama verbatim. He didn't mix his words even though he repeatedly expressed how happy he was to be talking to Papa.

'I need to finish confirming the list of students before the next staff meeting.'

Papa didn't appear to be moved by the urgency. 'I don't think it's worth risking her opportunity to be better prepared the year before her final year exams. But I will get back to you on Monday,' I heard Papa say, but his face told more than I needed to know – that Papa was not buying it. The thought of not moving on with the selected few was killing me as we walked home almost in silence with a good distance between us, with me ahead of them. I couldn't get home soon enough to have a good cry! He will get back to the school by Monday? How? And why? The thought of him handing me a refusal letter to take to school on Monday was tearing my heart.

Back at home nothing more was said till Saturday morning. Before we could get to sweeping the compound, Papa summoned me into their bedroom. Mama was already sat next to him in bed.

'It's true your school VP thinks highly of your academic ability and reckons that you'd do very well as a final year student. I also believe deep down that you are the cleverest of my children...' I was really wishing Papa was going to come round and as he spoke I was full of hope of him agreeing to the idea until he said, 'But like I told the VP, you need to finish elementary 5 before moving into your final year. That way, you'll pass out with flying colours.' I couldn't believe what I was hearing.

Mama interrupted him only as a point of correction to reiterate what he'd promised the VP. 'But you told the VP you'll get back to him on Monday and not just say no to the whole idea.'

Mama's intervention wasn't doing me any favours this time around. I wanted to protest but Papa was looking me in the eyes throughout the bedroom meeting. That stare of his that meant either to instruct or tell you off. He never listened to what I wanted! It usually was his way or no way.

'I would like to be done with my elementary school this year, Papa. The war is over. I can now go to secondary school next year.' I heard myself starting to respond to Papa for the first time in my life! And I even managed to speak with a frowned face.

'And where do you suppose I would get your school fees from next year when I have only just started working?' he asked with stern voice. 'You will go to secondary alright but finish your elementary properly first. That the VP thinks you will succeed doesn't guarantee you will,' Papa concluded and almost convinced me of my limited chance of making it if I defied him. I stayed in my room all day and night. My siblings were serving me as usual but I was beside myself. I thought so much about how to change Papa's mind but to no avail. I decided there and then that I would run away from home. But where? I will run to HRH's home. I loved spending time at HRH's place in any case as there I did nothing but eat with him and play outside with the villagers who all knew and regarded me as their grandchild.

Very early the next day I packed my little bag with everything precious to me and slipped away through the backyard, and taking the back alley I headed for the federal road T-junction. I couldn't care less about going to school on Monday and I made sure no one heard or saw me leave the house. I got to my maternal home later that morning and two of HRH's wives were there with their children, but he had left for some meeting, I was told. I was to stay there for nearly a term. Papa wasn't coming for me and neither was my mother. According to our cultural tradition, HRH's authority overrode anyone else's including my parents. Not only this but it was considered a cultural taboo to turn away a grandchild at their maternal village. So although HRH was the only person who could make me go home, the tradition of almost worshipping a grandchild and protecting their freedom (which still exists today) also worked in my favour and meant that HRH was happy for me to stay... for now anyway. I went everywhere with Umuna youths. During school days I went foresting with them. My best buddies were boys because the majority of the girls my age were married or less sociable. I walked through the bushes and rode motorcycles with the boys on both the main and narrow village roads. I wasn't being told off like I was used to at home and I did little or no house chores. HRH's wives looked after their respective children and still took turns to feed HRH whom I ate with all the time both as his first grandchild and his reincarnated mother – I was lapping it all up. It reminds me of the saying that your parents will love you unconditionally but your grandparents will be on your side unconditionally. HRH let me get on with my life until one day when he returned from Afo Ezuru market he asked me into his parlour. His children and I loved to gather round him whenever he returned home from the market, forest or any other outside engagement to share whatever presents he brought home for us.

'*Nnem*,' he began to say to me after giving us *agbara ti* that he got for us from the market. *Agbara ti* is fried up mashed watermelon seeds. This was the equivalent of bringing chocolate home for the kids. He reminded me that he wasn't the one paying my school fees and to go against my fee payer's wishes wasn't going to work in my favour, and so he advised that I return home to get back to school before it was too late.

'You know your father knows what's best for you,' he reminded me. He spoke gently and quietly even when he was telling you off or appealing to you to see his point. It wasn't difficult for me to understand what he meant about completing my education. By telling me to return to school, I was beginning to see that it wasn't just to please my father but also to follow my dream to get an education. But I now had two school terms to perform magic in and prove Papa wrong. I went to talk with the VP from Umuna and I convinced him that my father had agreed at last – I had my parents' blessing to pursue the goal he was setting for me to complete my primary education in 1970. I also lied to HRH that the reconciliation with my father went well and he had agreed that I could attend school from Umuna, if I desired. Umuna was double the daily journey to school but my stubbornness got the better of me. I was making new friends, particularly the Ezelu and Umudike students that I walked to and from school with. The VP gave extra support assignments to the eight of us who had now joined the final year class to give us a better chance of passing our final exams. The exams came and went and I passed with a distinction. Papa who was now living and working in Enugu was both pleasantly surprised and happy for me, even though he took his defeat on the chin as he replied to everyone that congratulated us.

'I knew you were going to make it,' he said to me. I was beaming when I saw his reaction to my final results. It was the first time I had seen Papa concede to his original objection – he glanced at me and called out my pet name, '*ogom nwanyi, I gbalia la.*' (Well done my mother-in-law.)

My parents couldn't wait to revisit the VP and thank him for believing in me and for all his support and encouragement that enabled my good result. Papa had come home specially for the visit, and we left to see the VP via the Sunday service at Okwe town centre. St. James' school was opposite the church with teachers' quarters adjacent to the row of classrooms and the school management office including the Principal's office. We brought a keg of palm wine to the church service which we left in the backroom to take with us for our VP's visit.

My parents mingled with other adults for a while after the service while I collected the palm wine keg from the backroom, and we started to walk across to the teachers' quarters. We arrived as they were returning from church service too. While the adults chatted, I was spending time with the Principal's sister, Ada, in their yard. We talked excitedly about what secondary schools we were considering as she sorted her dirty clothes ready for washing. After a while the VP came outside and told me my parents were about to leave and wanted me to come back inside. He congratulated both of us again as I ran to where my parents were still standing near the front door and chatting with the VP's wife. Mama had the empty keg in her hand and one lonely glass of palm wine sat on the table with a couple of flies buzzing around the spill on the table as well as around the glass. Out of my excitement, and without asking, I picked up the glass and drank the wine in one take. Only Mama's eyes caught me putting the glass back down on the table. I had no prior experience of being tipsy or intoxicated; ever. I'd always been hyper without any catalyst, so drinking palm wine was still my happy expression that my life was on course after all. I had no clue what to expect when I downed the glass of palm wine. How naive I was.

I ran like crazy on the way home through Alaocha village towards Ikwe bridge while carrying Mama's handbag and she had the empty keg. Papa would give me that angry look each time I fell over and got up running again until we got home. I was feeling so dandy that I had no room to ponder any impending punishment for taking alcohol. Somehow, I wasn't frightened as my head was spinning. Punishment was the last thing on my mind. I was tipsy and loving it.

And then came the question of me going to secondary school. I had no clue how much Papa was earning as to whether he could afford my school fees. I sat my common entrance exams to attend one of my three chosen secondary schools, Ezeoke Girls, Ehime Girls and Madonna mixed secondary school. I got into the former and my parents were happy to send me off to Ezeoke Girls in Mbano in January of 1971. I was optimistic that with Mama's financial support in the house, Papa was up to the task. I was headed for my secondary education. We already had an Okwe girl from Umucheke village schooling at Ezeoke. And gosh, did Lucy look after us three Okwe girls that started at the school in 1971 – myself, Mary and Sarah!

But before I began my secondary education I had to prepare. I had to look the part of the first Umuofeke girl to attend secondary school. First and foremost, I needed a pair of glasses to look academic. I used to admire secondary school girls who wore glasses that made them look more intelligent than those who didn't. For the first time I was free from Papa and Mama's shadows. I could now make decisions that only I was responsible for. I got me a pair of face furniture in a speech bubble shape that made me look pretty with a 60s feel. I don't even think I had any idea why people needed to wear them. For me it had nothing to do with correcting bad eyesight but for accentuating my facial beauty.

I was going to Ezeoke Girls where I made do with just girlfriends. I read a lot and played a lot too. I belonged to every other group or society going in school including the dramatic society, performing arts, debate society, etc. My public speaking ability was recognised and that led to my Shakespeare performance as Brutus that we later performed to the whole school at the end of my second year. It coincided with the end of school year for our final year students – the pioneers of the school and the first set of students to sit their WAEC (West African Examination Council) exams in 1972. I was close to two of my school mates then. Adaku was in the same class as me while Patience Obijiaku, my namesake, was a year above. She also had two senior sisters at the school, Precious and Vivian, all a year apart from each other. Vivian was the school prefect and my 'school mother'. She and her sisters were kind and protective of me. And Vivian didn't have me running around every minute for her like I saw some other senior students do to their school daughters, plus she gave me provisions and money at times. However, my namesake and I had a personality clash now and then 'cause we were one and the same character-wise even though we were not in the same class. She was a year ahead of me and we happened to have many friends in common and we both were popular. But in all, it was a fulfilling experience schooling away from home. Living in the dormitory with tens of other girls of my age and older. Lucy took care of me and my town's girls too. We spent the weekends either visiting home or staying behind in our dormitories. We sometimes visited other schools to see our friends. I was growing into my own person and Mama visited once every so often bringing me foodstuff and provisions as well as pocket money.

Every now and then we would suck up to the rich girls for any handout going. I would even offer to cook for them so that I could feed myself also to tide me over till my mother next visited with supplies. And as a fresher, you were almost guaranteed to be one of the dogsbodies for the girls above you. But I was so lucky to be the senior prefect's school daughter, which counted for a lot. That alone was my umbrella to shore off any senior girls' heavy handedness towards me and made my first year interesting and enjoyable. I also loved sports, long and high jumps, track and field events. Catch me at dance and drama class and I was present and a good dancer, people told me all the time. I was enjoying school so much until Vivian finished her final year and then my problems began. I was no longer as secure as I was before. I was bullied by some senior girls who just didn't like my vivaciousness and so would ask me to run errands for them, failing which I got beat or punished to do chores for them. It happened to me once and so I started to fake chest pains.

With Vivian Obijiaku out of the way, enough senior girls were after me and I ducked and dived from them, hiding behind my chest pain claim. I didn't feel like having a school mother anymore. It got to a point where I wasn't enjoying school at all. I would prefer to do my work in the dormitory and hand it in through my mates. I was turning into a recluse and spending all my time inside the dormitory rarely attending any event in the school other than my class lessons. I made do with my book of songs and the ones I was compiling since being in secondary school. I would listen to the latest pop songs on a loop until I had written as many lyrics as I could understand and sang along as they played. It was that serious that even my namesake couldn't cheer me up. I wanted to leave so I wrote to Papa constantly asking to be moved out of my present school. I started bugging my parents about my fake chest pains so much so that they decided to let me change schools and move to Enugu to live with Papa. I was pleasantly surprised when I read from him that he had spoken to a teacher at Okunano Girls secondary school in Enugu about my possible move to the school. He also enclosed my transport fare for me to come down to Enugu and meet with the teacher as soon as we broke from school.

It was the end of my second year at Ezeoke and I couldn't wait for Mama to come and get me out of there. I had some preparations to do to attend Okunano Girls in Enugu. This I broadcast to all my friends on the last day at school as we exchanged contact details. 'Don't forget to keep in touch,' we all said to each other. I wasted no time giving out my future address, Papa's address at Onu-Asata in Enugu, promising to write to them too. I had spent the night repeating the address in five rows on clean ruled sheets of paper carefully cutting them ready for handouts to friends. So proud I was to be going to a school long established before my present school Ezeoke, which had just clocked up five years in 1972. Back at home still on holiday in the village and it was all about my school transfer to Enugu. But hold on, Nwokem asked me, 'Have they enrolled you yet?'

'Yes,' I heard myself utter the lie. 'Papa has already met the Principal and put me down on the class 3 register.' This was the next class I was moving on to. A little lie wouldn't hurt and at least I was going to Enugu for a fact and Papa would do the rest. Who better to win this for me than Papa who had lived with and knew the ways of the white man to convince people? He would tell them how clever I was and how it would be good for the school's profile to have a student like me. I was daydreaming again as I had always done when in pursuit of something I desired.

Papa's Enugu yard was one of those 'face-me-I-face-you' oblong buildings with an equal number of rooms on either side of a long corridor running through the middle to the backyard; his room was the fourth on the left-hand side. Papa worked at the teaching hospital as he did in Lagos. Through networking, I suppose, he was able to privately offer his services to individual professionals i.e., nurses, doctors and teachers. This was how he came to know the Okunano teacher I was to take his introductory letter to regarding my admission into the school a few days after I had arrived in Enugu.

The room before ours was occupied by another Okwe town family. Their daughter, Pauline, who was near my age and in the same school year with me, had other younger siblings. The family was from Alaocha village and we were very close in Enugu. Our parents would convey messages home for one another when they travelled to the village and helped each other out any other way they could. The rest of the yard occupants were from in and around Enugu and we all got on well generally. Papa had already bought me a new mat, an extra bucket and towel for my use. And we had a cotton drape separating his bed from the rest of the room where I put my mat down to spend the nights. This same space doubled up for our living room to have our meals morning, noon and night, to receive and entertain visitors.

The separated bed area had the food cupboard at the foot of Papa's bed. The whole yard was fairly clean and tenants took turns to tidy communal areas – the shared kitchen, bathroom and toilets. With the war just ended, Papa could only afford the single room living space. You had your stove stand in the kitchen while most of your foodstuff was kept indoors. You opened your bowels into designated bins which were emptied by night collectors. We called them *Agbe poo* in Yoruba and *Onye Oburu nsi* in Igbo, meaning faeces waste collector. They take them in a truck to go dispose of them. The drum usually sat under a wooden deck with a central hole that we squatted over to ease ourselves; far from the cistern water system we enjoyed in Lagos. Same as the bathroom which we filled buckets with water from the main yard pump and took to the bathroom with your toiletries to have your bath.

Although not quite the Lagos system, it was still preferred to wandering into the bush in the village where you were mindful of all sorts. Once I was dying to go and I dashed into the bush. I stood on a cluster of dry bush and pulled down my pants to do my business and immediately felt a slight movement beneath me. I glanced down and couldn't notice anything and so thought nothing of it. I felt the heave once again and I looked down to realise I'd squatted on the bushes obscuring a folded brown and beige snake as I frantically searched for the particular bush leaves to clean myself up. The snake's head was raised to start moving away when I stepped off the bushes. I was close to being killed by some snake I staggeringly thought. Scary, but it somehow didn't deter me from using the bushes as I had no alternative while in the village. We peed anywhere, even close to our living quarters, unfortunately. But with all we had to contend with during that war, sanitation was the least of our worries to stay alive!

Now post-civil war, we were moving on and life was returning to normal as fast as possible. We danced to the likes of Aretha Franklin, the Jackson 5 and Donna Summer. I looked forward to getting into Okunano at the beginning of term. Then came the registration day when I was supposed to take Papa's introductory letter to meet this teacher. I was hit by the chaotic atmosphere at the school as soon as I entered. Crowds of parents and their children were everywhere right up to the school administrative building. With the letter in my bag, firmly on my shoulder, I headed for the office block. I stepped forward parting the way through the sea of people before me to the building. And then I heard the announcement.

'The intake exercise is now ended. Could you all please leave the school ground. New admissions are closed.'

A woman standing next to me looked at me in despair. She turned round and firmly holding her teenage daughter's hand they started making their way back out of the school and towards the gate. I felt deflated; I only had my return bus fare on me and I was beginning to feel hungry. Then I listened to all the chattering in the school grounds and heard some people talking about the admission exercise happening at Queen's College that morning too. I followed the crowd streaming out of the school gate as I contemplated what to do next. I was already making up my mind to go to Queen's to try my luck even though I had no introductory letter to rely on this time. But it was closer to home than Okunano, I tried reasoning with myself still very much aware that I was punching above my social class to even dare to head to Queen's.

Consumed and overwhelmed by my disappointing news, I had completely missed my bus. Realising how long I had been walking I was very hungry now, so I decided to head home and wait for Papa with my heartbreaking news that I wasn't getting admitted into Okunano Girls as we had planned. Nearly half an hour later as I neared our yard, still hungry but somehow energised, I veered off to Queen's College. The atmosphere was different there. There was the one-arm gateman lifting and lowering the bar to let vehicles and visitors in and out of the college grounds. I walked through the long school lane to the front of the admin building. There I spoke to a lady. I told her I had come to apply for admission into class 3. She looked at me and then pointed to the chemistry lab where she said the class 3 intakes were sitting some tests. I rushed off to the direction she signposted and into the long corridor where school bags, books and pencil cases left by the candidates inside the room all laid everywhere on the floor. Without thinking I opened up an exercise book and extracted a double page from the middle, picked up a pen and ran into the test room where everyone was quietly doing their English language test.

The female invigilator standing in front of the class said to me, 'Hey, where do you think you are going?'

'Sorry I'm late,' I replied. 'I didn't know when…' I was mumbling as I adjusted myself into an empty seat with the test paper on the table.

She looked at me for another second and said, 'You've only got twenty-seven minutes left.'

'Thank you, ma', I replied and opened up the question paper. I marked a number of the questions I knew I could start on before tackling those requiring me to read and decide what verb was appropriate for the sentence or to spot wrong spellings, and so on. Time was up on the dot twenty-seven minutes later and the invigilator collected in the test papers.

I was beginning to feel very hungry now at around two in the afternoon so I decided to tag along with a group of the girls that were in the test hall with me, but I wanted to listen to their conversation first to make up my mind. They seemed to gel with each other and nearly every one of them had a sibling or friend already at the college. Then I thought about the school's reputation and social status. Queen's was deemed a college for rich kids from Christian family backgrounds. My parents were neither rich nor were we avid religious practitioners! Considering all that, coupled with the fact that I was late for the first test, I mean, what were my chances? Then I stopped to buy me two bananas and a pack of roasted peanuts with what money I had left for my fares home. I stood there deliberating whether or not to go home after I'd finished eating. There was no point banking on getting admitted if I was late for the first test and who knows what I might be able to do with the maths test that was to follow. As I walked down the long school lane to the gate, the one-arm gateman shouted at me to get back.

'No student allowed through the gate until 3.30pm.'

I took a step back as he yelled at me and a few other

students trying to leave. He didn't give us time to explain or I would have informed him that I was not yet a student, so I just did a U-turn with the rest of the people.

My test group were all disappearing back into the test hall and I started to run back as fast as I could to join the last few candidates entering the hall. I borrowed a clean sheet this time from one of the girls to do my rough calculations first as the test sheets required that you showed both your workings and answers. There were thirteen minutes to go when I finished and handed in my papers.

'You came late for the language test – are you sure you are finished?' the invigilator asked me as I let go of the paper and walked out of the room.

I wandered round the school corridors looking for a tap on the grounds and I found one right at the end of the chemistry lab block. I opened the tap and let it run a few seconds before running it onto my cupped hands and drank a few times. I looked up and saw my group members coming out of the exam hall some in twos and more. And as I watched them, everyone was headed to the front of the admin building, then my self-doubt kicked in again. What were my chances of making it even if I did well in the maths test, as much as I loved maths then? What chances were there for me to beat fifty-one other candidates to make the three positions that the school was offering to class 3 intakes? I quickly followed the crowd.

The school was finished for the day and students poured out from the buildings, those that knew some of my fellow applicants headed towards us as the lady began to speak.

'There are three of you selected to start schooling with us. Please proceed inside the office as soon as you hear your name called.' She adjusted herself and then continued, 'In no particular order.'

The first girl to be called, wearing a small black bow pinned to her blouse, stepped onto the pavement and shook hands with the lady before disappearing into the office behind her. There were sighs for her by many of the girls as we waited to hear the remaining results. A voice from the crowd said that she had recently lost her mother. The reason for the black ribbon on her blouse, I thought. Her mother must have brought her luck that afternoon, I reasoned, as we do believe in such spiritual connections. She was very lucky indeed. No sooner did she disappear into the office than the lady called the name of a second girl. A very slim tall girl walked up for the handshake and into the office she went. And then I heard my name.

'Patience Ifeoma Obijiaku.'

I couldn't scream excitedly enough as I rushed up the steps to shake hands with the lady and hastily disappeared into the office too. Another woman ushered me into an inner office to meet with Reverend Sister Agbasiere, the Principal who was sat behind her desk, her white head cover immaculately tucked round her chin and wearing gold rimmed glasses. She smiled as I walked in front of her desk, shook my hand and gave me a school welcome pack. She welcomed me and asked that I report to my class block on the first day of school. I had started walking out of the office when I saw and heard the rant brewing outside.

Many of the girls were talking at the same time as they gradually but reluctantly dispersed. And then I started listening and they were rebuking my admission. Some claimed it was fraudulent seeing that I came late and didn't even do all the tests to have passed. A couple of the girls shouted after me as I quickened my step to leave the premises. They wanted to know if I knew anybody at the school particularly any member of staff.

'Why do you think you made the list, ee-rh, if you don't know anybody at the school?'

Without a word, I walked straight out of the gate with the gateman nowhere to be seen now that it had gone past 4pm.

I had a spring in my step walking home and got back before Papa. I gave him all my news that had kicked off badly at Okunano Girls through to gaining admission to Queen's College.

'What?' His eyes wide open with disbelief. Once again I was overjoyed to see Papa happy again about my academic performance. 'Did you see Mrs. Robinson at all?' As he began asking, I was reaching for his letter in my school bag and handed it back to him. By the time I finished with the whole day's gist, he was so happy, and I mean smiling, that he didn't bother about the leftovers we were supposed to have for dinner that night. He changed his clothes and out he went to La Ronde Hotel opposite us on the other side of the main road facing our yard. The hotel was owned by an Okwe man who had returned from Ghana with his family and had managed to reestablish his hotel business in Enugu after the civil war. I warmed up and had the left over rice and stew in the house. Papa returned a few hours later quite tipsy. I was beginning to reflect on the times I had seen him in such a mood to realise that it was the only time you knew he was happy; when he was in that merry mood and would sing acapella to Obey's songs – that was usually him in celebratory mood.

Papa sent me to Ogbete market the weekend before we resumed school to shop for all my school needs and to buy supplies for a party later in the evening to celebrate my college admission. He had invited his friends mostly Okwe, Umuna and Okwelle community families living in Enugu including Pauline and her family and all the yard neighbours. Papa and I even did our round of commercial laundering this particular Saturday to be delivered to his private customers on Monday. Other than this one party I can never remember Papa hosting any form of event on my behalf in any shape or form in my life. I was the happiest girl on the planet that weekend in any case. Already, the news had trickled down to my village. Papa had sent the message to Mama via an Okwe brethren. Already I wore glasses, and now I needed to think of how I could up my social status to match Queen's College studentship, whatever that was.

Papa and friends chatted, drank and ate my party food of fish pepper soup, jollof rice with goat meat! Kelechi, the landlord's son, supplied the music and we set the party table in the long corridor through to the back. I had met Kelechi on only one prior occasion the year before when he was at home on vacation from college and I'd been visiting Papa. He didn't pay me much attention then, but now that I was joining the Queen's College rank, I could sense he couldn't hang around me enough at the party offering to DJ for me and even brought in some spirit drinks of his own that he shared. It was a fun night on the whole as I was free for the first time to have a natter with all the yard boys especially, without so much as Papa frowning at me.

I was a day student and made friends with both live-in and day students, a number of whom I walked to and from school with. Papa would leave for work nearly an hour before me in the mornings at 7am and Pauline and I walked to the bottom of Ogui Road where we parted ways to our respective schools. This was in the early 70s. Also thrown into my new 'high-class Queen's scholarly status' was me coming into my own when I wore platform shoes and flared baggy trousers. As a girl I was allowed to put on trousers even from early age, although I'm not sure why I didn't get told off or banned because the majority of my village girls never wore them except for returners from abroad like me. I suppose our abroad status exempted us from being banned like our village counterparts, but no one spoke to me about not wearing them. I needed the funds to afford these and other fashion accessories I was craving so I decided on part-time employment while I schooled. By this time I had my buddy school friends to work with. In fact it was Amaka that introduced me to buying and selling bread in the evenings. I became friends with Josephine who was already Amaka's friend from their primary school days. I knew both girls from Queen's and we were tight!

We would go to bakeries straight from school to buy up their rejects, burnt or otherwise, in all shapes and sizes. These we sold along Ogui Road to people during rush hour any time from 7pm till late. We would get home with our goods, have something to eat and meet up on Ogui Road to display our bread for sale. We used to make good returns as people stopped to buy one or more loaves at half price, even less depending on the condition of the loaves they were buying because we also sold stale ones at further discounted prices. All the buyer did was scrape off the dead bits and consume the rest. We even had to do the same ourselves when we took home some left over stale ones for breakfast the next day.

School was fun again and I was doing well and Papa was happy with me but remained his old commander in chief self. He would return from work angry. I knew this as soon as I said my greetings and got a question in response.

'Papa *ilola*,' (welcome Papa) I would say to him and the next thing would be either, 'why is that there?' or 'did you remember to fold the clothes I asked you to?' This was quite an indication that something was bothering him and may not necessarily have anything to do with me. On this day, Papa came in thinking aloud as he opened the door. I hurried over from the kitchen to greet him but had to wait for him to finish talking aloud to no one in particular.

He abruptly glanced at me and said, 'Why are you standing

there looking at me? You had better do well in school not like Charlie, your brother. I'm not slogging myself at work to waste on school fees.'

I didn't say anything as I could sense what he was upset about. Apparently he had heard news from home that my brother didn't do too well in his term results. My first end of term results on the other hand were good so Papa was pleased, but not as in to hug or kiss me to share the feel good factor with me. My parents didn't express their affection in that way.

Chapter 5

I had come a long way from Modile Way; I'd lived through a civil war and was in the third year of my secondary education. At seventeen, I had so far remained what my people liked to refer to as a 'good girl' that stayed in school, got my first school leaving certificate and beat forty-eight candidates to gain admission into Queen's College. I was yet to give my parents any cause for alarm – no 'girl/daughter' problem such as getting pregnant or eloping with a lover, or worse. Many Igbo teenage girls were said to have eloped with Nigerian soldiers immediately the war ended – marrying and having their children.

I can remember witnessing the kidnap of some of them during the Attack Market after the war. I think it was called Ahia Attack because it was a black market – as I'd heard – where we bought goods smuggled into the eastern region. We risked the long trek to Okigwe township to buy and sell and it was usually a night trip to return in the early hours of the next day as soon as we were done with our transactions. Mama and I made the trips carrying baskets of breadfruits, gallons of palm oil and anything else she had for sale to buy the likes of life's little comforts we were used to: tea, sugar, tinned milk and salt.

Women and children, mostly teenage daughters, made this journey and were stopped at checkpoints by men in Nigerian military uniform for whatever reason. We had to pass through a few checkpoints on our way to the Attack Market. You stayed close to your mother and did as you were told on the journey and would only get a break to pee or do your business by stepping a little into the roadside bushes when your mother saw fit for safety purposes. The men in uniform would shine their torchlights all over us as we approached the checkpoint and one or more of them could have even started walking towards us. You wondered what next and all I could hear on several occasions were girls screaming for their mothers as they were bundled away into the bushes by some of the uniformed men. My first experience of this was when two of the men walked up to me, lifted my right arm up and flashed his light at my armpit before tossing my arm back down and moving to the next person. I was more frightened than I was bothered about what he was doing to me or why. I had never been that close to an 'enemy soldier' as we still regarded them, especially on the market trips.

Other women consoled the kidnapped victims' mothers as the group continued the journey. These mothers cried uncontrollably, while some returned home leaving the rest of us to carry on. A number of them completed their journey regardless in the company of fellow women sharing their pain, and those parents whose daughters had not fallen victims, like Mama, consoled them along the way. From the conversations during and after the kidnappings, I was able to conclude that the uniformed men, the kidnappers with their searchlight on us, were checking our maturity to determine their spoils. My mother later confirmed that the men were more interested in teenage girls – the reason they looked for hair in their armpits of those they stole. I had a pound or two weight of breast on my chest but no hair under my armpit, thank goodness – I wouldn't be ME today otherwise!

And so, here I was in my secondary school days striving to make my parents proud still. I was very much aware of how lucky I had been, considering.

Every so often Papa, like he did when we lived in Lagos, would travel to the village to spend part of his annual leave. He would take on more private work running up to his travelling week and that meant work for me too, assisting him so that he made extra money for his travel. I had free time when he went off to the village for four to ten days at a time which meant little or no house chores for me during that period. I lived on mama-put cooked food (take-aways). I would also buy knick-knacks from Baba Aneke's kiosk outside the yard's frontage. Baba Aneke was a very friendly guy who was kind to the neighbours especially those that shopped on credit from him and owed him till next time, including my student old self. All of us paid him back by given dates or on pay day for those that earned. My days were spent visiting my girlfriends or playing music as well as dancing in the house. I rarely read or did any serious college work. Perhaps only when I was studying with my friends at theirs but hardly on my own at home. I just made sure I kept the house the way I knew Papa would like to find it when he got back.

The year was 1975 and my third and final year of study in Enugu. I had returned from school one day to find Mama was visiting us. I nearly dropped dead realising she was heavily pregnant, again! After my greetings in my pretend happy face to see her, I went to the backyard and Baba Aneke's wife who was also pregnant was congratulating me on Mama's expected baby. Birth of a baby was and still remains a blessing culturally that people laud no matter the circumstances surrounding the pregnancy. Your social, financial or class status didn't come into play when we talked about a new baby on the way. A birth of a baby as far as we were concerned was a gift from God. Once a baby is on the way, legitimate or not, it was and still is always welcome news. I asked Baba Aneke's wife whether my father came home to let my mother in and she said that he had left his house keys with her husband at the kiosk. I went back into the house to ask her about my siblings. I walked into the room and she had dished up oha soup and garri. This was heaven come down for me. I hadn't eaten this delicious soup in ages and now that she was here and went the mile, the meal was enough to forget about my angst. I mean, the special meal was enough incentive to welcome our mother's last pregnancy and birth of my last sibling the year that I finished my secondary school education. She will survive I heard myself say in my mind.

Months down the line, in July 1975, Henry Anayo (late) Obijiaku was born. Could you believe that? At my age I had a baby brother but I wasn't marking myself down to help Mama this time as I was job ready with 5 O levels but no English or maths. Papa was so disappointed in me, and Charlie's poor elementary school results back home was no consolation either. It was disappointment all round for our hardworking father. Soon enough Mama had to return to the village with Anayo, while Charlie was dying to attend secondary school with all his primary mates. Papa was holding his ground based on Charlie's latest poor final primary results. He said he wasn't going to waste money sending him to secondary school.

'Look what Patience came out with after all that!' he would say in response to any further pressure put on him to send Charlie to secondary school. And he would always drag up his objection to moving me to my final year in primary school. 'If you had finished elementary 5 before 6…'

I was getting frustrated from reading my brother's crying letters that he wanted to go to secondary school like all his mates. I had to do something. Amaka, Josephine and I remained best of friends still and would go miles for each other. I no longer had to live by Papa's rules now that I was a college graduate, so my friends and I embarked on expanding our business. We weren't just buying and selling night breads, we were also dealing in cosmetics, fashion jewellery, ladies' bags, shoes and other fashion accessories. We would go to Ogbete market in the early hours of Saturday mornings when Okirika wholesalers received and sold their bails of second-hand clothes from offshore Nigeria. We were making enough to buy our own brand of gear for nightclubbing whenever we could. We eventually joined the ranks of the girls-about-Enugu-town. My interest in music had gone full blown by now from reggae, disco through to highlife. I was a walking boom box for both religious and commercial songs.

I was pretty determined to get Charlie into secondary school, and so I transported him to Enugu and hid him at Josephine's when the time came for him to sit his common entrance examination. He did the exam and passed. I couldn't be happier. I was doubly sure Papa would change his mind now that he had proved himself to be ready for secondary education. Papa's response to my excitement was, 'Whoever paid for his exam may as well pay his school fees. If he didn't do well at elementary level what chance has he got at secondary level?'

There and then I decided that I should be heading back to Lagos to find a job to at least pay my brother's fees. I would be returning to Lagos as an adult and no longer a child like I was under my parents' care before the war. Plus I had enough relations living and working in Lagos so I wouldn't have any problem residing with any of them. What's more, Victoria was now living in Lagos too. I knew Victoria from my secondary school days. She was an Okwe girl like me and I loved and adored her. I was one of a handful of people in our town that really knew her. I still think she was very much misunderstood as she turned out to be one of the warmest persons you could ever had met. Rest in Peace (RIP).

I returned to the village to tell my mother about my decision to go back to Lagos. She seemed pleased with the idea and so a of couple days before my planned journey I said, 'Mama, are you sure you can pay the first fees? When I get to Lagos I will send it back to you.'

'*Nne nnam*, I know you will. Of course I will. God will continue blessing you and provide for you to look after your brother in Jesus' name,' she replied and I knew she was pleased. She was working as hard as ever while still nursing Anayo and keeping up with her farm produce – not to mention her village kiosk and generally managing the family home. An incredible woman she was.

The next day while in the kitchen she said, 'I've got ugba and dry shredded cassava for you and Victoria for when you get there.' She was showing me these four parcels she had packaged in a big cement bag with rope tied round to secure them for my journey the next day.

'Mama, thank you,' I said.

'Please be careful when you get there. Lagos they say is rougher than it used to be before the war. Make sure you stay wherever Victoria asks you to. Respect your elders and remember the family you're coming from.' She read me the Be a Good Girl sermon that I'd heard on several occasions from her.

'I'll be alright, Mama. I'll locate Victoria as soon as I get to Lagos, otherwise I could stay with Uncle Rowland and his sister Esther.' I tried to reassure her. My Uncle Rowland is from Umuchiri Okwe village and a distant relation of mine on my father's side. Both Victoria and Uncle Rowland lived in Orile Iganmu, Lagos. Until you are old and grey, I don't think your parents could ever finish telling you about the last of your relations. I would normally simply nod to all the explanations they gave when introducing me to yet another relation upon relation.

'When you told your father you are going to Lagos what did he say?' Mama asked.

'Nothing,' I replied. I hadn't given it a thought till then why Papa had said nothing to me when I told him about my Lagos plan. 'And I also told him I was coming to the village first to see you before leaving for Lagos to look for work.' Mama looked at me as if to say that it wasn't a good sign that he'd said nothing. 'What was I supposed to do, then?' I asked rhetorically as if to break the silence that persisted.

'He knows and he's OK with you going to Lagos, but I'd ask you not to pay a penny of your brother's school fees without telling him first, OK?' Mama said, wagging her forefinger emphatically so that I heed her warning.

'I hear you, Mama.'

I thought I'd said it aloud a few times in Enugu when Papa was refusing to sponsor Charlie. Obviously he must have heard, seeing that Mama heard too when in our Onu-Asata with baby Anayo. I got the message. As a daughter I mustn't take such a responsible step without Papa's blessings; I got it and I made her the promise to write Papa each time before sending fees to Charlie at Okigwe National Secondary School in Umuna.

It didn't take all day to pack my few belongings and the foodstuff that Mama had put together both for my consumption and the ones to be gifted to my would-be host when I got to Lagos. I said my goodbyes some days later, and I was off to Lagos, journeying to Anara in the early hours of the morning to catch an Intercity bus to Lagos, the land of my birth. For the first time in a decade I was moving away from what was left of my siblings. I was optimistic of getting a job to make good on my promise to sponsor my brother's secondary education. I was ready for the world of work and adulthood in the real sense and was walking away from both my parents' care and authority and fending for myself in Lagos. Ready as much as I could be. I was heading to Orile Iganmu where the majority of our town's people resided and still do today.

I wasn't short of takers to live with when I arrived in Lagos by February of 1976. Like I said, Orile Iganmu is an area in Lagos that boasted of my community members. My first accommodation was with three of my village brothers of the same age group. They were Christian, Edwin and Dennis (RIP). We shared a room in a boy's quarter in a long winding yard facing the main Orile Iganmu road. As brothers they respected my privacy and all but one, Edwin, were my seniors. This is hard to believe now but it was something we did without any thought of how we all managed in one room. Apart from the saving from not renting rooms individually, the overall goal was to be able to afford living expenses in

Lagos while still having a little left to look after our folks back home. It was neither frowned upon nor rebuked as we saw ourselves as brothers and sister trying to live life as much as possible and cater for our families back home at the same time.

We set off each morning to work on weekdays and spent the weekends playing music and doing our individual chores as well as organising our house chores among ourselves. It didn't matter that I was the only girl, we all did the tasks accordingly including cooking and washing dishes although I ended up with more of the cooking. However, often we had one or more of their lady friends join us and they would help me with the chores while I enjoyed their company. My room mates and I got on very well and we shared same taste in music. Fela, then 'Ransome' Kuti, reggae from Mighty Diamond to Bob Marley through to Jimmy Cliff. Our disco favourite then was Chris Okotie's *I Need Someone* and *Carolina* and the rest of his first album. To think he's now a gigantic church leader beats me a wee bit! Our loud music disturbed no one as we lived in the boys' quarters a few yards away from the main building facing the main road.

My first employment was as a bus conductress with Osondu transport; Mr. Osondu the owner was from Okigwe. He had a handful of Intercity buses within Lagos city. I couldn't wait to get started on this job. I was very determined to foot Charlie's school fees as soon as I could earn a kobo (our equivalent of a penny which has since been dropped from our currency but was still in use in my time). And so, I didn't have the luxury of seeking out an office job, I just took what was available. Earning my keep to pay my brother's fees came first; I couldn't disappoint Charlie. So I took on the next best thing: conducting on a bus from one area of Lagos to another. I was the first employee for the new Lagos city buses, and I wore Osondu's company apron over my clothes and strapped the ticket machine to my waist, operating it while the bus was on the move. I was getting a 2 Naira daily lunch allowance aside from my monthly wage and sent half to Charlie every day.

Mama and I agreed that she would pay the first fee for Charlie which she would discuss first with Papa and inform him that I had promised to start paying the rest of the fees. I was happy and quite proud nonetheless to be doing this as I saw it as a way of supporting my parents to cope with raising the rest of my siblings at home. I now was in Lagos and Charlie schooled at Okigwe National in Umuna town. As time went on Charlie's termly results were improving and Papa began to show interest. Charlie attended college as a day student from HRH's compound where he lived and walked the distance to and from his college site. A few months down the line I had moved in with my cousin, Columba, in Lagos whom I called and still call 'Uncle Soko' today. His mummie dearest was HRH's sister. I used to spend time at their place in Okai village in Umuna. He was single and working full time in Lagos while preparing to leave the country for the United States. He would leave home before me to go to work while I took my bus ride to connect with my bus driver. Together we began our shift each morning from the office depot on Kirikiri Road. My driver would complete the paperwork to pick up his bus while I collected petty cash from the office to start the early morning shift before we took the bus out onto the roads.

I got to the office one day and my driver and I rode off on our early start. On our return trip from Lawanson, I got hungry round about 8am. We had stopped for passengers to both get on and off the bus. I bought me a sausage roll and a chocolate milkshake and tucked into my breakfast immediately as my driver pulled out to drive off. I was feeling sick after a few bus stops and needed to find a loo or I felt like I would pass out. I'd never felt anything like it. Five minutes later, I felt the discomfort in my stomach. Luckily I spotted a colleague of mine off-duty who hopped onto my bus at the stop opposite the Iddo train station. I begged him to finish the trip for me while I went to the loo. The plan was for him to hand over my bus on his return trip and he was happy to help out. I tossed the ticket machine and money bag to him and flew out of the bus and into the station.

I was coming and going back into the loo as I struggled to contain the runs I was having. And each time I managed to look out of the station to see if I could spot my bus, I was forced back into the loo by the need to go again. I thought I was dying! Not one person that brushed past me at the station knew or sensed what I was going through there. I spoke to no one as I went back and forth to the loo, cleaning myself up with water as is common where the toilets are built into the ground. And I refilled the little plastic kettle each time I used it from the stand alone tap by the loo entrance. I eventually saw my bus the nth time I managed to come out of the station and I just waved it to carry on. I never saw my bus again and left the station so very late that evening that, unusually, Uncle Soko was home from work before me. When I got home, Uncle Soko couldn't believe the state I was in. Like life was drained out of me. He helped me out of my clothes and told me to go have my bath. The next morning he went with me to our head office where he explained to my line manager why he thought an alternative job position was needed for me. He did not think I could handle my current conducting position that in his view was more a man's job.

'She's a clever girl and will do well working in the office,' he concluded. My office manager who was also a relation to Mr. Osondu promised to talk to the boss. I was sent home and informed by my driver who came visiting me over the weekend that I was to start working as one of the office clerks the following Monday. I was thrilled.

My new job was to handle the transport revenue from the bus operators as well as take in their expenses' receipts for fuel for example or toll charges. I recorded the entries into the ledgers and bagged up all the monies in wallets ready for pick up at close of business by Mr. Osondu's driver. I enjoyed working in the office environment in the company of five or so male colleagues. We had conductors and drivers coming in and out of the office in the course of their normal daily routine. My monthly salary had increased slightly too and so

I raised Charlie's pocket money aside from his college fees. As friendly as the office environment was, my manager was strict in his supervision of the tasks we needed to accomplish daily. He couldn't stress the need for accurate accounting to us enough.

'You know the boss will kill us all if he had anything happen to his money,' he would say.

We all got the message quick time and remained very much fearful of the overall boss, Mr. Osondu. This was General Murtala Mohammed's era as our national head of state. Life was almost back to normal from the civil war. We had food, shelter, clothes, and we played and listened to music. Most of all, I was employed. Life was nearly like it was before the civil war except I was now an adult catering for myself with the rest of my family on my mind all the time.

I'd visited Umuofeke village a few times since returning to Lagos including spending what would have been my first Xmas in Lagos, since we first left. I spent the Xmas with my family and brought everyone presents too. But having dinner a couple of days before the new year, I noticed Charlie wasn't looking happy despite ukwa porridge and roast bush meat being one of our treats. I pressed him to talk to me.

'I don't want you to tell Papa and Mama.'

'What is it?' I interrupted, searching his face for some response.

'I'm not happy at school. Granddad's house is too far to attend college from. And I hate to study alone in the house when all you hear are the sounds of all sorts of animals in the dark environment. It gets too dark and spooky when everyone is asleep.'

'We must tell them so we can find another relative where you could move to be close to your college.'

'No, sister, don't.'

'But you must, you never know, they might have a better idea,' I said as I got up and asked him to follow me to the parlour where our parents were having their own meal. Papa looked at us as we approached them, Charlie almost hiding behind me.

'Papa,' I began to say, 'Charlie is having a problem with attending college from Grandad's house. He said it means walking home alone and finds it difficult to study at night when it's just him and he has his lantern on...'

'Get lost both of you,' Papa snapped, thrusting his spoon at Charlie that narrowly missed his left shoulder. 'Didn't you choose to go to secondary school? All of a sudden you are having problems like all of your academic hurdles. It's either you man up and stop pussyfooting or declare you are not up to the task. What a nonsense!' You could feel his rage even from where we stood as he got up from Mama's side and off he went to their bedroom, muttering, 'Useless thing,' till he shut the door and there was a brief sense of calm even though we had Charlie's problem still to solve.

Mama took a deep breath and adjusted herself on her chair. 'Charlie,' she called out. 'Have you said anything to my father?'

'No,' Charlie replied before saying, 'I sometimes stay

behind with my mates in their dormitories rather than returning home late alone. The last time I returned very late was worrying for Granddad and the whole family. I don't like upsetting him.'

Papa opened his bedroom door and walked right back into the parlour not minding he had been listening to us. 'That's why I never wanted to send you to secondary school in the first place until you were man enough...'

I was so vexed by Papa's comment that I turned back to Charlie and said, 'Nna don't worry. I'll come with you to see what can be done. Let's go and speak with some of your mates living close by the school to see if one of them could help in any way.' I could see his face brighten up a little, and somehow I was optimistic I could resolve the problem.

My brother and I left for Umuna after the new year celebrations and stopped at one of the bars along the federal road that the students frequented. Charlie introduced me to a few of his mates, including a guy I was told was one of their lecturers. David was his name. I ordered a round of drinks and we all chatted about Charlie's accommodation problem for the next five minutes or so. I then appealed to them for any help they could render; if they knew of any students looking for a roommate. And then David offered to take Charlie in to live with him. I was surprised alright but happy and pleased with myself that I was going to be able to solve my brother's problem. The students cheered at the lecturer's offer and I couldn't help placing another order for a round of drinks to celebrate. I was pleased for Charlie and hoped for the best.

Charlie and I couldn't wait to return home with the good news, to say the least.

David was a tall, gentle guy who looked intelligent. It wasn't until Charlie's move-in day when David made a pass at me that the surprise hit home. To be going out with a lecturer with my 5 O levels wasn't so cool I thought. His teaching job was to buy time he said, to gain university admission. Our love affair remained mostly through correspondence, nonetheless. Charlie improved academically and I sensed in his letters to me that he seemed happier. He told me so much about his 'master' David; how kind he was continuing to be towards him. He would give Charlie the bus fare for his weekend break to the village where he spent time with Mama and returned to Umuna with foodstuff and pocket money that she would give him.

And then it came to the time Uncle Soko was ready to leave for the United States and we had his sending off party in our yard. I had no idea what state he was headed, I just knew he was leaving for America. That was enough for me to invite my work friends to come to our party. We ate, drank and danced all night long. I had to move in with Uncle Rowland and his sister a couple of days before he left. I was back again living at Orile Iganmu. I would daydream about if and when I could join Uncle Soko in the United States, but life was good in Nigeria. All I needed to do was start living in my own space and possibly buy me a car: a Volkswagen Beetle. So I moved out of Uncle Rowland's and rented an unused garage space still at Orile Iganmu. I needed to start saving so I opened a bank account. Everything was going fine until a military coup threatened to disrupt my life again. I was in Lagos far away from my family this time around. What do I do? The plotters were tried and sentenced to death. They were to be shot dead at some spot on Kirikiri Road that was a walking distance from my office. I had never seen anyone killed before not even during the civil war.

I was determined to go to the rally to witness the killings. The nation had unanimously condemned both the coup and the plotters so much so that our reigning Igbo Highlife band, Oriental Brothers, made a meal of it with a song:

Muritala Mohammed (x2)
Muritala kere Anambra State.
Muritala created Imo State
Muritala ekecha State nwu o
O Dimka, Uwa o!

Translated:

Muritala Mohammed (x2)
Muritala created Anambra State.
Muritala created Imo State
Muritala died after the State's creation
Oh, Dimka, what a World!

The day came and the excitement was huge for those going to go see the sorry event live. The crowd streamed behind the big vehicle taking the culprits to their final destination and their convoy went past my office. I quickly finished bagging my cash into about seven wallets and off I went with some of our off-duty bus drivers and headed to the spot. There were cement filled drums with metal poles in the middle onto which the men were strapped; their legs also tied together at the front bottom of the pole while their hands tied behind the poles. Their necks were tied loosely, allowing the movement of their heads a little. It was a hot late afternoon. Standing on the outside of a sea of heads in front of me, I couldn't see a thing but I heard the voice of the commanding officer instructing the would-be shooters. All I could see of the condemned were their heads. The crowd swayed from front to back and left to right as the noise increased. Someone must have come with a dog that appeared behind me; I hated dogs especially ones as big as this so I felt it was time I left as I wasn't seeing any action anyway. When I got back I found out I was in trouble no less. Mr. Osondu had sent for the collected monies and they couldn't find the wallets, I was told. I started blaming myself for not securing the wallets in my desk lockers out of excitement. Besides, I thought none of my co-workers was a thief, so how did the wallets disappear. But my manager was all out to make me feel there was the possibility of a thief among those people that went past our office to drop by and nick the wallets. That was it for me!

I felt a cold chill down my spine as I considered the possibility of having misplaced these wallets and without even getting any joy from the firing squad I went to see. The thought of losing my job gripped me because I had recently increased my financial responsibilities to Charlie and my mother back home. Just when I felt I was living and managing my finances alright, this had to happen!

It would be a step back into hardship, something I never want to do again in my life not after the starvation and hunger we suffered during the war!

Our office manager handed me a week's suspension letter signed by the boss before I left for home that day. I was to report back to the office on Monday week for the verdict. The threat of losing my job became all too real and I cried myself silly when I got home. I was fixing my lunch when Uncle Otti, Innocent's father from my village, came walking past my house. He stopped briefly to ask after my wellbeing and wondered why I was at home that time of day instead of at work. He said he was on leave and was headed to his wife's second-hand clothes shop on a main road patch. With no reservation I told him the whole missing wallet story for which I'd got suspended. While feeling sorry for me, he informed me about a recruitment event that Monday at Kingsway's store in mainland Lagos close to where he worked at Leventis. I remember Papa used to brag about the Peak milk, a specific brand which was regarded as high quality, and other provisions he bought from there. I was so hopeful for the job that I too shopped at Leventis store. My daydream raising its ugly head again!

I walked into the air-conditioned store and couldn't believe how many of us had come after the five customer service positions. Kingsway's store was a massive retail shop with departments which sold all sorts of goods and accessories. We were taken upstairs to a room and handed the aptitude test papers; we put our names on the answer sheet and waited for the start time to be announced by the invigilator in the room and we were off. After we'd finished, we went into their canteen where I bought a Wall's chocolate ice cream while listening to Elton John's *Goodbye Yellow Brick Road* being played via the tannoy as I relished the idea of working in a musical environment. Fifteen minutes later, we went back and I was one of five candidates chosen. The five of us were then told the working week started on Thursdays and ended the following Wednesday to aid their accounting system at the time. I couldn't wait to look my Osondu colleagues in the eyes when I countered their suspension verdict with my resignation to start my new job. And moving into the new job meant yet another increase in my earnings, in fact such a substantial increase that I felt my 'working girl' status in Lagos was certified.

I stepped into the Kirikiri Road office on the Tuesday, as opposed to the day before when I attended my Lagos interview.

'Sorry I couldn't come yesterday,' I said as I entered the office being my exuberant self while showing my excitement.

Our manager was sat behind his desk in the far left corner of the room with a couple of colleagues missing from their workstations. I was bursting with the urge to scream out about my new job; a better one for that matter I thought as

I walked towards his desk. But I thought it better to have a little patience to find out what decision awaited me first. He asked me to go and sit down, raising his hand to signify my workstation as I approached his desk and then he got up and followed me with an envelope in hand. I was now more than eager to know this verdict. I sat on my chair and put my handbag down still in control of my urge. A little more patience won't hurt I told myself, before slapping them with my good news. At last, the good old rejected 'cornerstone' as they biblically say, was at play here. I had come to rely on the very christening name Patience, that I renounced for my Igbo name during my secondary school years, back in 1973.

And the manager began to speak as he stood in front of my desk and handed me the envelope, saying, 'This is for you. Oga decided you come back to work.'

'Thank you, sir,' I was obliged to say in response, glancing round at my colleagues all who appeared to be happy for me that I'd been pardoned.

He continued as I tried to open the envelope to read the letter.

'Your punishment for your carelessness is the loss of one week's pay. You're not getting paid for the week you were suspended. And you must write me a brief note on the lesson or lessons you've learned from this.'

He walked back towards his workstation. Now that I knew the verdict I wasn't feeling the vindication, not when I was being recalled back to work with no explanation as to whatever became of the money wallets. None of these thoughts mattered anymore. Either way, I was on a winning streak, a new job in Lagos Island as opposed to working in urban Kirikiri Road.

I reached for my prepared resignation letter in my bag, stood up and followed him as he sat back behind his desk.

'Thank you, sir,' I said, trying really hard to feel happy about news he'd just delivered to me, 'but, I was going to hand in this. I'm starting a new job on Thursday.' I gingerly left my resignation letter on the edge of his desk while managing to avoid his surprised face by looking away at colleagues as if to ask them to note they were there as my witnesses. Our manager joined in congratulating me on my new job by the time I'd finished telling the whole office about the aptitude test story that got me the job.

'I've always known you are a go-getter,' he said. 'You wait till I tell Oga that you really are leaving us.'

Was I going to wait? I don't think so. I had my handshake with the last of my colleagues in the room and exited the office to go back to Orile to prepare for my new job in three days' time.

I was able to replace Mama's Singer sewing machine, long sold during that war to fend for the family, but not before I had gotten Papa's permission to buy and transport the machine back from Lagos to the east for Mama. In Papa's reply to me when I wrote him about this was the beautiful Igbo adage that says *Ebe nwa siri lo uwa, ya biri* loosely translated as regardless of the origin of a newborn the goal is for the baby to live and/or survive. Everyone was happy, including Papa.

I was now a fully fledged bread winner not just for myself but also for the family. I was able to pay Charlie's school fees through to his final year plus his examination fees. I was living large by all accounts. Although I didn't get to buy my dream car, I commuted to and from work in yellow taxis. That meant a huge status. I was enjoying a new salary scale and was so happy with myself and doing so well with both my work and responsibilities until I had the hiccup that cost me my beautiful job!

As shop floor staff we also operated the tills. I had a surplus of N100 at the close of business on a Wednesday evening and that spelled trouble. I had been working there for over a year and knew as rule of thumb not to be caught in such a situation that would call for an investigation. I'm still not sure to this day how I managed to balance my till without spotting the N100 surplus! I worked in the Children's Wear department and served middle and upper-class Nigerian families. Unable to explain how my accounting discrepancy came about that end of week, I got the sack and this was particularly painful as I now had to struggle to keep up with my new social status while taking care of all my responsibilities. I wanted to return to the village as soon as I could. I couldn't face living in Lagos unemployed.

And so, to the village I returned feeling completely deflated. But I wasn't going to let it show. I needed to think and act fast in deciding where to go from here. My siblings, who were duty bound to serve me, were at their wits end each time they encountered one of my crazy outbursts especially in the absence of our parents. I would bark in place of talking to them even though I was asking for favours, ordering them about or hitting them for no reason. Probably for just looking at me, even. That was how bad it got. It was madness. Uninvitedly one morning, I decided to help out with the house chores and went and sat with Hope and Rose, my sisters, round the wooden block to crack palm kernels for one of Mama's market days. But I was miles away even though I was listening into their conversation.

'Sister, are you going to spend Xmas with us?' Hope's face lit up as she asked. I could see that she was wishing it more than she was voicing it. Something kicked off inside of me. She became all my frustrations personified as I deliberately lifted the baby stone (what we called the stones used to smash the kernel on the wooden block) and rammed it on the back of her right hand! All you could see was the bruising, but to say I didn't smash her bones would be a lie. I saw a red light flash as I blinked to realise what just happened. I could hear Mama's racing footsteps through the parlour upon hearing Hope's almighty scream, while Rose stood up – her still gaze at me was painful. I will never forget that look in her eyes as Mama reached out and pushed me aside to tend to Hope who was now crying in pain on the floor.

'Sorry, there's no blood coming out. You'll be alright. OK?' I repeatedly tried to make her stop crying.

Instead Mama, who was wailing more as she applied *ori* (shea butter) on Hope's hand, was cursing me and calling me all the demonic names she could muster.

'Since you brought back your useless self, we've known no peace.'

Leaning on the building wall where I'd stumbled from Mama's push, I was feeling disgusted with myself but still feeling my own pain that no one could imagine. My heart was broken by my job loss and the fear of not being able to care for them like I used to. I've lost all respect from them this time, I admitted to myself. I could feel it and saw the unspoken disappointment in Rose's eyes.

Mama invited herself into my bedroom one early morning to have a word. Whenever she corners you like that 'a word' usually takes more than an hour – an hour you have to just listen without uttering a word.

'It's not a pretty sight to see you frustrated and taking it out on your siblings or anyone else for that matter,' she began, perching at the foot of my bed and looking me squarely in the face. She was no longer angry but I could feel her despair between the two lines above her eyebrows as she continued. 'It hasn't been a fortnight since you burnt all Charlie's clothes and shoes 'cause you bought them for him. Thank God for Vincent who wasn't amused when he saw you going after your brother and chased you away. I'm very upset that you don't listen to me. I don't know who should talk to you for you to heed advice. I'm asking you to return to Lagos where both your friends and our community people could support you back into another job. OK?' She begged of me one more time to do this instead of remaining spaced out in the village and a pain in the necks of family members. 'Even the villagers are starting to gossip that you couldn't hack it in the city that's why you have returned to remain a lay-about in the village,' she said as I sat up on the bed while she continued. 'No one around you is safe from your crazy tantrums; you are no longer a child. Neither is your father amused. You know him well. He was more concerned with giving you away into marriage and ridding everyone of your trouble. And I know you will reject his proposals, and so you people might as well kill me here.'

This was preferable for him than wasting time on disciplining his grown woman of a daughter, I thought! Mama was getting up as she said, '*Nne Nnam* (my grandma), it would do you good to return to Lagos, OK? You need to trust in God and by his grace you will secure another job in Jesus' name we pray.' After nearly an hour, 'a word' had a prayer closure.

It was a huge step down for me to have worked my way up to that employment status and fall right back down to returning to the village. It was really sad indeed! Suffice to add that I was sick and tired of the marriage preference by my parents. It was either I succumbed or went back to the city.

It was becoming difficult to live in the village as many of my age group were in cities living and working to look after themselves and their home folks. Even Nwokem had left for Lagos where she lived with Lambert her younger brother, while I was stuck with my misery in the village. I then got a letter from Victoria saying she'd been looking for me and had heard that I had since returned to the village. She was an air hostess with Nigerian Airways and wanted to get me back to

Lagos as soon as possible and even enclosed my fare in the letter sensing it might pose a problem for me to be able to come immediately. She was hell bent on getting me to work with the airline. Not only was she my senior, but also my role model regardless of whether she considered herself to fit both roles. Victoria was every girl's wish for a big sister – she was very caring and would go miles for you if she believed in you. Mama was very happy about the news and she gathered my skinny body into her embrace when I told her I was returning to Lagos at last. She particularly liked the idea that I was returning to stay with Victoria. I packed up and headed back to Lagos the second time.

Victoria was living with her uncle at Orile Iganmu in two rooms similar to our Enugu yard. In the boys' quarter were three rooms, a bathroom and toilet at the end of the row. The next weekday, Victoria took me to see the Airways Personnel Manager (PM) who appeared to be expecting us.

'My cousin, Ifeoma, I told you about, sir,' Victoria said to introduce me. I was admiring the plane models on the table and framed company pictures hanging on the walls when Victoria turned to me and said, 'Ify, stand up and hold up your dress to knee high and walk round that table. Pretend we are not here.'

I got up and began to do as I was told around the table, or what I would call a stool, in the centre of the room's sitting area while she and the PM looked on. I went around the table full circle and stood there waiting for the next move I'd be asked to complete. Instead, the PM started clapping and said to Victoria, 'I think she's good to go and will grow into the job. Let her apply.'

Quickly I interrupted. 'What job?' I asked in slightly raised voice.

Victoria explained as I hastened to sit back down. 'Air stewardess,' she said.

You would think they'd given me the start date for the job the way I felt. The job offer wasn't for me 'cause I'd always been afraid of heights.

'I don't want a flying job,' I heard myself say in response to both enthusiastic professionals.

'What type of job do you want to do, then?' Victoria asked, staring at me as if not believing I could turn such opportunity down out of ignorance.

'Clerical work that I'm used to like I did at Osondu before my last job,' I replied.

'In that case,' began the PM as he reached for the writing pad on his table to scribble down on it. Carefully folding it into two, he handed it to me and sent me across the road opposite to the Engineering department. 'Give this to Mr. Williams when you get there. Tell him I sent you to join them.'

Dismissively, Victoria waved me to run along. I left the Personnel Office and walked across to the building where I saw a man with a bunch of papers in one hand and directing people into the building with the other. Mr. Williams himself waved me in giving me no time to explain how come I was there. I followed the group into the building, thinking his disinterest in what I had to say was weird but I didn't care.

I might not even be the first the PM had referred to him, he may even be used to it, I thought. I was here now to get a job; an office one that's all that mattered.

Inside the large hall, around thirty or more of us applicants, men and women, were yet again put through English and maths tests. I got hired to be deployed to the newly refurbished Airways Catering Unit as store clerk. We were to start at the beginning of the following week. The whole process took about an hour and a bit.

I rushed back to the PM's office with my exciting news.

'Vicky left a while ago to catch some sleep before her evening flight to the UK.'

I wasn't listening as I kept thanking him. 'I got the job. Thank you, sir.'

'Congratulations, young lady,' he replied. 'Have you got transport fare to go home?' Before I could reply he dipped into his trouser pocket and gave me N50.

'Thank you, sir. God will bless you.'

I was sprinting to the bus station to connect my rides home, thinking welcome to employment once again, Ify. I was feeling very optimistic that working with the airline would be the kind of work I needed to regain my confidence. I took my first bus from Ikeja and was looking forward to breaking the news to Victoria. She became the older sibling I never had from then on. My role model she was, passionate about life and fun loving in the little over a year I spent with her and her uncle before she too left for the UK.

The news that I was working with Nigerian Airways was

music to my parents' ears. From then on, I lived with Victoria and her Uncle Ben for the first few months in my job before I moved into my own one room – a sort of studio apartment by local standards where the room was divided well enough so that I could even do my cooking on my stove indoors, and I shared the bathroom and toilet with a couple and their two kids in the same block. I had never been happier. Many of my community people came by for some of my airline food giveaways and others I sold to them for cash – fresh fish, beef or tinned vegetables, peas, sweetcorn, etc. Getting these for free or paid for didn't matter to them perhaps; they did not want to jeopardise that privilege or opportunity of rubbing shoulders and remaining friends with me.

Mama had visited me in Lagos to remind me of a family event for the Easter break. A special celebration of our own to look forward to. Hope was getting married to Donatus, who was from a couple villages behind Okwelle called Ezike. With my airline employment under my belt I was all for enjoyment galore. I had plans like my mentor, Victoria, and the rest of the airline crew who were already going places that I could only dream of, like visiting London, New York and other United States destinations. I was ready to fly even though this scared me a little. My parents were happy for me for doing well in my new job but really bothered that I wasn't still giving marriage a chance. To them, I didn't seem to be ready to settle down.

I returned to the village for Easter as I had promised Mama and was introduced to my future brother-in-law and his relations. A mini eating and drinking event was put on to celebrate my return, even though it wasn't me getting married. My family had done this to cheer me up, I guess. Papa also had a separate agenda on top of this as I had always sensed he would. He was using this opportunity to make it up to me for marrying Hope off at that tender age that he knew would wind me up and we had argued about it in our recent correspondence. She hadn't even finished her elementary education yet she was considered ready for marriage. Earlier in the year I had arranged for her apprenticeship with my hairdresser in Lagos. I had paid a N200 deposit for a year after which I would pay up the balance of N200 when she'd completed her apprenticeship. I felt it my responsibility as the first daughter. Anyhow, Hope was happy, Papa and the rest of the family were happy too and so it didn't really matter what I thought. My baby sister was married and I returned to Lagos. On my next short visit to the village she was pregnant and nine months later she had her first baby, my nephew, Kelechi Gerald Ejisimekwu, while I still worked with Nigerian Airways and continued romancing my dream of travelling. As Nigerian Airways staff, my discounted ticket would cost me next to nothing.

Chapter 6

As a member of the Nigerian Airways staff, and Victoria's cousin, I was rubbing shoulders with all the airline crew. Gradually I stepped up my social and personal outlook in terms of the clothes I wore and the friends I made. I continued to bring food home and would go days without lighting my stove to cook, especially weekdays when I returned home late in the evenings 'cause of the traffic from Ikeja to Orile. I ate what food I brought home, listened to music and turned in for the night. Victoria brought me gifts as she flew in and out of the country – from neck scarves to perfumes, blouses, trousers and fashion jewellery. She made a point of making me feel and look like a 'Lady' as she would always say to me. I also wore quite a few of her classy hand-me-downs that I couldn't afford in the shops. And then she dropped the bombshell – she was getting ready to leave for Britain. Why was I being left behind by everyone I looked up to? Uncle Soko had left and now Victoria was flying away too. Saving for a Beetle car was not cutting it like the opportunity to fly out of the country. The dream of travelling abroad was never far from my mind as I pondered over what to do with my savings.

My annual leave had to take a backseat for a senior staff member to take theirs before me as a matter of urgency to do with some personal matter. Meanwhile, I got busy putting my travel documents together. I obtained my passport within a week through people I knew at the passport office. I had up to N1k saved to obtain my basic travelling allowance (BTA). You were only allowed that much to travel abroad then and I was ready and waiting for my leave date to fly out. My dream to fly into the sky and above the clouds to London was now so close that I could taste it whether or not I had a vertigo problem! I did get an invitation letter from my godfather, who was and still is living in the UK, to show the immigration officers at the border as proof of my reason for travelling to the country. My godfather, Uncle Godwin Offomata was getting married in late August 1980. The plan was for me to attend their wedding and return to my Nigerian Airways employment. I spent all the money I had, including my September wages that I had taken in advance to prepare for my trip, aside from my N1k travel allowance. I was buying toiletries mainly and would buy clothes and shoes when I got to the UK, where rumour long had it the roads were paved with gold particularly the streets of London! And so for my trip, I packed a set of African attire, my makeup and toiletries.

Dressed in a silk blouse over my beige jeans, I parcelled myself up to leave the country. Little did I know how long I was going to be gone for even though my leave was for less than three weeks. Already I had the plan to provide sick notes to my unit manager weekly while out there to both delay my return to work and to buy me time to extend my stay in London so that I'd have time to shop and buy plenty of goods to take home for sale. It was all about making profits like all my flying crew friends were doing as well as all the gifts I could get for myself. I had everything ready; the last page of my passport was stamped to detail the £998 I got for my N1k BTA exchange. I also had my yellow card stamped with my completed vaccinations. I then needed to go home and tell my parents about my plan for the coming September. I would have to travel to Aba to visit Papa where he had since been transferred to continue his line of work at the General Hospital.

'Papa ilola,' I greeted him as we met halfway before I followed him to the house. I could tell he was pleased to see me.

Similar to the apartment we shared in Enugu, he lived in one room divided into living and sleeping areas; this time to serve just him. Rather than have his clothes thrown over the dividing curtain, he now had a clothing rail in a corner where he'd arranged his clothes on hangers. His room was ordered and had some ironed clothes heaped on the ironing board. I remembered us two washing, ironing and delivering them to his private customers in Enugu back in the day. Seemed he had continued the same thing in Aba to make a bit of extra money to top up his civil service pay cheque. Who could blame him with several mouths to feed even on top of all Mama's endeavours?

Papa wasted no time enlisting my support to prepare dinner.

'Right my in-law, go in there and get the big pot out. It's already washed. You will see the yam tuber by the floor there, bring it and let's peel some and prepare casserole. I hope you still like it?' He chatted with me as he took off his outer clothes to put them away.

'Yes Papa. I'm always cooking it for myself.' I finished peeling the yam and placed a bucket of water in the communal bathroom for him to have a bath while I prepped the ingredients for the casserole.

And we ate together like old times.

'You said Goddy has sent you an invitation letter?' he asked, looking up in between eating as we talked.

'Yes Papa, their wedding invitation.'

'I see, where is the wife from; do you know?'

'No Papa but I understand she's Igbo and not Oyibo,' I replied, feeling that would be pleasing to him somehow seeing that he was one of those with the notion that you can travel overseas to study alright but must return to take a wife.

He finished eating before me and stepped outside the yard for a minute while I cleared up after I'd finished.

'Papa thank you, sir,' I greeted him as he walked back in and sat in his reading chair. He was scanning for a radio station on his wireless when I walked back into the room with the cleaned dishes to put away.

'Let's see your passport and travel documents,' he turned to me and said.

I dashed for my bag to bring them all out; knowing my Mr. Orderliness – I was happy and proud I had everything on me to show him.

'This is the invitation card and Uncle Goddy's covering letter he said to show them when I get to their airport. I'd also taken it to their embassy for my visa.' I continued speaking as he tried reading one of the documents silently after a good look at my passport.

I was feeling all grown up and very optimistic of Papa's approval.

'Well done, my in-law. When do you fly?' he asked as he rummaged in his work trousers on the rail and got his wallet.

'An early morning flight on the 28th. A week today.'

'Add this to your spending money. I pray you go and return in peace, my in-law,' he said as he handed me a fifty naira note. 'Make sure you stay close to Goddy and Donatus over there and give them my regards. Tell them I would love to read from them to know how they are doing.'

Papa pulled out a mat from behind his headboard. 'Here, spread it out there and here is a pillow.' He handed me one from his bed. 'Let's pray,' he said and I knew to close my eyes and join in. His prayer touched on mostly my trip and how I would return a better person and grow in my airline job... I was filled with gratitude that he was treating me like an adult now, different from how it used to be.

We left the yard early the next morning for the township

where we parted after he had waited for my ride to Aba branch to leave. I sat near the window and Papa touched my right shoulder through my open window and said, 'Take care and remember, I don't want you going to England and forgetting about us. Do remember whose child you are and where you come from. My message for Nne baby, don't forget. God be with you and guide your journey.'

I waved him bye and off I went to see Mama and my siblings in the village. And I was not likely to forget the N100 he gave me to give to Mama.

A couple of days later, everyone said their bye-byes and I left for Lagos where I prepared to host my send-off party to embark on my trip to Europe. It didn't matter whether I was travelling for business or pleasure – no one asked and it was no one's business. My send-off party at Orile Iganmu was the place to be on this day particularly for my community people. It was attended by the majority of them and their families and people from the neighbouring yards too. I had so much support from friends and family members to provide my party food, the music and buy the drinks too. I got nearly N500 in gifts altogether from my guests on the night. My travel date eventually came and I embarked on a Nigerian Airways flight to London Heathrow airport on the morning of 28th September 1980. My return ticket cost N3!

I boarded my flight and everything was as I had expected. I was on the outer seat next to a young man seated by the window. He must have sensed I was nervous as I constantly sought the attention of the cabin crew from helping me fasten my seatbelt to switching off my overhead lights for me. I was getting ready for when we entered the clouds and crossed over to England while at the same time shaken by the thought of being suspended mid-air. This was it! The real thing. I was prepared for the life changing experience of visiting the white man's land beyond the clouds in the sky. But I was not prepared for the frightening experience I had with the plane taking off and reaching its height before my fright evaporated.

I let out a mumbled scream each time I felt the aircraft jolt in any way as it leaped into the air and continued to climb up. Slowly but gradually, we were reaching for the clouds above us. The guy next to me sought to calm me down from time to time. My new friend had been doing his best to make me feel comfortable all through the journey. He must have known this was my first flight to anywhere. I had told him my name when he asked earlier on as he continued his comforting. And even though he told me Ogbonna was his first name, I was far more concerned about the immediate threat I was facing mid-air.

At last I could feel the plane descending. There didn't seem to be any panicky passengers on board that flight but me, I mean visibly panicking, and I had to pull myself together every now and then. The tyres touched down and the plane raced for what seemed like miles and miles before slowly taxiing to a halt on the tarmac close to the gigantic spread of the airport building that one could make out on that autumn evening. As we walked down the steps of the plane, the cold September wind felt like all the harmattan I had ever experienced put together! My jeans and silk blouse were both inadequate and far from the winter clothing I was supposed to have had on. Even Ogbonna had a massive suede coat on; I nearly didn't recognise him as we made our way off the tarmac area. I had only brought what I was wearing for my maiden London trip. How wrong I was! My good friend became my guide as I dragged my one and only piece of hand luggage and walked briskly to keep up with him. From then on he communicated with me in Igbo. He must have sourced it out from my surname. He asked me for my destination and I handed him a scribbled piece of paper from inside my diary with my godfather's Forest Hill address. We walked into the airport building and through to the border checkpoints with the rest of the passengers.

There we all split into queues with the information hanging above us, all of which I didn't pay much attention to as long as I was with Ogbonna. It was such a blessing my guide was on hand that day as I could hardly understand the Englishman at the border desk. He spoke so fast, albeit softly, that I could neither make out a word of what he said nor was I able to assist him to help me. My guide was my mouthpiece who informed the officer of the reason for my visit. My passport was stamped and my guide waved me to come with him as he too finished and collected his passport. We collected his two suitcases which he stacked on the trolley and off we were again through the Nothing to Declare route and out into the arrival hall. The lack of noisy atmosphere that I was used to back home plus the chilly weather reminded me I was in a completely different territorial part of the world. We walked with the trolley, this time with my hand luggage thrown on top, as some of our fellow passengers on the same flight hastily breezed past. I couldn't help wondering what spot on planet earth this must be where no one looked at or spoke to anyone other than who they were with, something I'd never experienced before and didn't get it at first quite frankly. I felt like an alien as I walked hastily side by side with my good Samaritan pushing our trolley.

Approaching us as we emerged into the arrival hall was a lady looking all excited. She was stood with other people behind the barriers. Some were holding up placards with names on them as we came out.

The lady hurried to Ogbonna, embraced and KISSED him. They took their time kissing and as I looked around I spotted quite a number of people doing the same almost: hugging and chatting cheerfully with each other. There were men, women and children everywhere. I had begun to loosen up seeing how relaxed and cheerful people were all around me and nobody seemed perturbed by what I was spaced out about. It was a rude awakening to say the least.

'Ify, my girlfriend, Chika.' Ogbonna introduced me before lowering his head to Chika. 'Honey, this is Ify. We flew in together. She's from Okigwe and works with Nigerian Airways.'

Chika and I shook hands. 'My sister, you're welcome. How is the family over there?'

'They are fine, thanks.' I replied.

'Darling, I got you a ticket.' She got it out of her jeans pocket and showed my guide and we started to walk, with him still pushing the trolley. And then there was silence except for sounds of people moving things around and the airport announcements at intervals. Even the air-conditioning was starting to get to me. I was feeling differently indeed.

'Ogbo, Ogbonna,' Chika called to get my guide's attention who was a few steps ahead of us with the trolley. 'Hold on, let's get Ify's ticket.' Chika went off while we waited for her. She walked back and gave me the ticket. 'Put it away to show the ticket collector at London Bridge.'

'Thank you,' I replied.

We went up and down the stairs of the winding corridors to get to the airport train station. Underground station, Heathrow underground station, I was reading the signs on the wall as we waited.

'We're taking the train home. We'll change at Green Park for the Jubilee line to London Bridge,' Chika was informing me, still in Ogbonna's embrace.

The train was jam-packed with passengers. We managed to get on with our luggage but all the seats were already taken. And so, we stood in the aisle with other people, holding onto the rail handles for safety.

And my new friends were still regarding each other like they had been apart for centuries; still hugging and kissing even more as the train screeched and crept along the tracks. They kissed each other without a care in the world!

And these are my fellow Igbo brethren living in London, I thought.

Some forty minutes or so into our journey, the train came to a halt.

'Get ready to get down, Ify. We going to change here,' Chika said. One by one we brought out our luggage. We got on the second train and six or so minutes later, we arrived at London Bridge station.

Ogbonna got out the paper I'd given him with my uncle's address on it and said, 'I'm going to call Mr. Offomata when we get home and tell him I'll put you in a taxi. Forest Hill is a bit far from our house in Tooley Street.'

'Alright, thank you,' I replied as we moved along till we got to the foot of an escalator.

'This is the way out of the station. Come on,' Chika was saying to me.

'What about our luggage? And I'm afraid of going up those moving steps.'

'Don't worry, we'll come back for it. Let's take you up first,' Ogbonna said.

My eyes rolled into their sockets each time I tried looking up the escalators. I can't imagine why I never associated the escalator with those in Kingsway stores where I once worked. I never once got tempted to ride it. I would buzz around the environment watching people go up and come down as I listened and hummed the songs playing on the tannoy.

It took us more than five minutes to go up the escalator.

'I'll call your uncle as soon as we get home,' Ogbonna

reassured me as we dragged our luggage out of the station. 'I'll tell him you're with us. So not to worry. Let's have dinner first then we'll call you a taxi.'

I felt so much at home seeing that they were Nigerians and Igbos for that matter.

We arrived at their building and took the lift to the second floor. I was glad to finally sit on the couch after the whole journey. Chika wasted no time serving the meal she'd already prepared before coming to the airport. It was interesting to eat exactly what I would normally crave for back home. We had egusi soup with stockfish and assorted meat including shaki (tripe) and fuku (lungs). The couple's dinner table chat trailed off beyond me as they talked to catch up for however long they'd been apart, while I enjoyed my food.

'Didn't know you could buy egusi and bitter leaf here.'

'We get them from the local markets. They sell everything there,' Chika replied.

I also noticed that the room was warmer than I'd felt outside since my arrival and was shown the radiator which was on and heating the room. Wow, I remembered when my granny died and we had to sleep away from home on a raised wooden bed at Uncle Willy's mum's. We had a fire underneath to keep us warm in the mud house in the harmattan season. This was different.

I was fed and watered and I couldn't be more grateful. Ogbonna had called and spoken to my uncle's wife who thanked him and was at home waiting for me. They put me in a taxi at about nine o'clock.

'I can't thank you enough for everything especially for Chika's delicious soup. I will visit from time to time, I promise.'

'You're welcome, my sister. Do call us to let us know how you're getting on,' Chika said as I got into my taxi.

When I got to the address, the front door had a note pinned on it saying *I'll be back soon. Gone to the telephone booth.* I was so happy to have reached my final destination as much as I was cold in my flimsy wear that night. And so I put my suitcase down on the front steps and sat on a lower step to rest my head on my luggage. Not sure for how long I had been there waiting, but I must have dozed off to sleep. A shiver from the cold wind suddenly woke me. A light had come on in the house opposite so I picked up my luggage and quickly walked to the door. I braved the dog barking inside as I pressed the doorbell. A middle-aged white woman opened the door. I pointed out my uncle's house and said that there was nobody at home except for a note on the door and what it said. I also told her they had been expecting me since a month ago. She asked me in, shoving the dog along to make way for me, and closed the door behind us.

I sat on the settee while she disappeared into what I sensed was the kitchen then emerged back into the living room carrying a small tray with a cup of tea, biscuits, sliced tomatoes and cheese.

'Make yourself at home,' she said. 'Mr. Offomata is our good neighbour and his wife, Doris. She'll soon be back unless she's gone visiting her aunt. He works nights, she sometimes goes to her auntie's to stay there,' she continued as she poked the fireplace. I wrapped the provided blanket tightly around me and moved close to the fireplace to keep warm.

The whole place was quiet not even a sound except for vehicles that drove by and I slept like a baby till morning. I folded the blanket and listened to the distant rushing sound of morning traffic. About twenty minutes went by and my host walked in with my uncle behind her. I was very excited to see him.

'Good morning, Uncle.' I rushed into his embrace.

I turned to my host and said, 'Thank you for having me.'

'Doris was telling me Ify never did arrive. I wondered 'cause we spoke the day before to confirm she was travelling yesterday. We didn't know she was here. Thanks a lot, Mrs. Hart,' my uncle said.

'You're welcome, Mr. Offomata.'

Uncle picked up my suitcase and we went home to their ground floor flat. I had informed the border agent via Ogbonna that I was there to attend their wedding. I was still granted a six months' visiting visa even though the wedding had taken place the month before and I carried the expired invitation letter with me but was not asked to produce it.

My uncle and his wife took me everywhere: Brixton market, Trafalgar Square, Piccadilly Circus, Buckingham Palace, you name it. We went to Ridley Road market in Dalston on the day he bought me my first winter coat running up to Xmas of 1980. I let Uncle in on my plan to work and live in London and not return home. He was not happy and told me he felt things would be difficult for me to remain in Britain. He didn't think he could give me any more support than he had already done by agreeing to be my Home Office (HO) guarantor, something I didn't quite understand but probably meant he had been contacted by HO upon my arrival to discuss my visit to the country. This made perfect sense.

I was living the dream I'd nurtured from watching TV at No. 4 Modile Way. I watched Top of the Pops once a week in the evening and had access to a variety of food options so I never went hungry, unlike back home. I could never starve here, not if I had at least 10p to spare that could buy me a bag of chips with ketchup on it. I also met some of the Nigerians who had gone through the 'Johnny Just Come' (JJC) stage I found myself in and they all sounded hopeful to make it in London without proper legal documentation. I too was determined to achieve the same. Any lifestyle I was experiencing was better than the one I'd left behind in Nigeria. But my uncle didn't agree with me. He felt the hardship I would face in London was going to outweigh what I was imagining my life to be if I returned to Nigeria, especially since I wasn't going to get my proper papers to remain in the country as a tourist. This begged the questions: a) what would I do for money both for school fees and upkeep? and b) On what grounds was I going to apply for my legal status to remain in the country? He and his wife continued to strongly advise that I return to my job with the national airline. That I would be better off than ducking and diving to steer clear of the law in London. I began to hang out with my Nigerian friends and going to work with some to find out how I could join their ranks to work illegally too. This put a lot of strain on my relationship with my host couple. To my uncle, I wasn't listening to his advice both as my senior and as representative of my father at the time. Most importantly of all, as someone who knew how English law worked long before I arrived, he couldn't persuade me enough not to become an overstayer in the country.

I decided to move to my maternal uncle's, Uncle Donatus, who like Uncle Godwin had also been in England long before I came. Uncle Donatus was HRH's nephew and Mama's cousin. Both my uncles were supported at some point by my parents in Lagos prior to their travel to England before the civil war. They had both lived briefly with my parents prior to locating to their respective Lagos residences. You could then say that culturally they had equal responsibility for me in London. And so it wasn't a big deal for me to move from one uncle's house to the other. As soon as I moved in with Uncle Donatus's family I met with more young Nigerians and a few that attended the Centre for Business Studies college in Greenwich. Chima, Uncle Godwin's family friend, was in support of me staying put in London. He advised me to go and enrol at the college and get on with my studies which should stop anyone pestering me about returning to Nigeria. By this time I had a little over £900 left of my BTA and I went ahead and paid for my whole year's fee of £900 to study business administration.

Even though I was living rent free and paying nothing towards food, I still needed money for transportation and other sundries. This was when I had to take the leap of faith as advised by Yemi, one of my classmates at the college and a Yoruba guy. He told me to go out there and find me a part-time job. He drilled me through how to speak to employers and said that I should always claim that I had bags of experience of the job each time I was asked. I rang a cleaning contractor telling them I had long been cleaning offices, small and large, and was a good time keeper who could get to work for six in the morning. I was hired and told to report for work at the Bank of Illinois building in Blackfriars, starting Monday week. They told me to head to the top floor and ask for the supervisor the first day I got there. I was earning £11 a week. Yemi became my new guardian so to speak who went everywhere with me after school especially getting to know London; Uncle Donatus would be mad at me whenever I came home late from college. He would complain that I ought to know to come back early to help out in the house. My persistent lateness apologies were weighing me down so I began to toy with the idea of finding a place of my own but wasn't sure if I was capable of moving into my own space just yet. I also felt it would offend both my uncles to think that they had homes and I couldn't stay with either of their families. As a family tradition you just didn't do that.

Uncle Godwin visited me regularly at Uncle Donatus's nonetheless, asking after my wellbeing and how I was getting on with my studies. He would at times give me pocket money when he visited as I was seeing him off.

I mentioned my desperation for a place to Yemi and he was on it like clockwork. He was in the middle of moving himself and had just found somewhere. But as soon as I told him about my problems, he let me take the place he'd found. He could find another, he'd said.

'I'm not desperate to move yet, you are,' he said to me each time and insisted that I moved first. While still pondering on the move to my own place, I was feeling the regret of leaving my uncle's where I had no food or shelter bills to worry about – all of which I would have to pay when I moved into this my own space. Meanwhile, I would go to Liverpool Street and Aldgate East markets at the weekends with friends to shop for clothes, the type my friends and I bought and sold in Enugu. I decided I would go and live at the Herne Hill ground floor room Yemi had found. It had no central heating and so I borrowed a Valor heater from my uncle and also used it to warm up my food each evening when I would I return late from college via work and I found entering the kitchen was too cold for my tired old self. Although my uncle never liked the idea of me living on my own, he nevertheless helped me out with not just the heater, he also put me in a cab to take it home with me.

It didn't come as a surprise that Yemi, my best friend and chaperone so to speak, started hitting on me, but I was surprised he didn't mind that I was an Igbo girl. I on the other hand did mind as it would be a relationship I wouldn't know how to explain to my parents.

I returned from work one night to find I had run out of paraffin and the nearby petrol station at the top of my road was shut by that time. I got into the house and thought of freezing to death as the place was not just cold but the walls towards the kitchen past my room had mould on the skirting boards. My landlord, Mr. Agbaso, was often away from his own area of the house. He occupied upstairs and had shown me round the house the first time I moved in, but he was away on this particular night. I was hungry and had to eat my left over jollof rice meal cold. To pass the night in that freezing cold I used a kitchen knife to prise out the nails holding down one edge of the carpet. I laid flat on the carpet and holding on to the edges I rolled it round me and kept rolling till I hit the bottom of my bed. There, I spent the night. I hated the cold from my early morning cleaning experience when I would hop from one building to the other and from floor to floor to empty trash bins, dust tables, wipe telephones and hoover the whole place. At times I even had to wash dirty mugs and saucers in the sink and wipe down the kitchen work tops. Every household chore I had my siblings to help with, I was having to do in London to survive illegally in the country.

The next morning, it was an experience I couldn't wait to share with my friend; my best friend and confidant, Yemi.

'You won't believe my nightmare last night.'

'What happened?' Yemi asked, looking worried.

'Got home yesterday and the petrol station had no paraffin and I had none at home. I slept rolled up in my room carpet. Still was cold but it could have been worse.'

He was beginning to laugh but quickly realised I wasn't amused and said, 'Oh my God that must have been awful.'

'It took me forever to eventually fall asleep. I want to go

back home; I don't think I can deal with this hardship, God help me!'

Yemi wasn't having it. Given the chance, it seemed he would do anything to knock the idea out of my head of returning to Nigeria.

'You know I'm leaving the bingo. Why don't you come and get my operator's job there? You'll have enough money to fill your heater at all times. You can't be living on just your cleaning job. You may even give up cleaning if you get this one.'

'I don't know, o! That's if they take me, Yemi,' I replied.

'One hundred per cent. You're smart and that's what they're looking for. You'll get it if you follow what I tell you.' And he promised to be with me when I called the employer for the job. Anything was worth trying as far as my survival was concerned. His determination instilled the courage I needed to give it a go. They could only say no and that would be it. How I craved to earn more while still attending my college.

The day came and Yemi and I were leaving college.

'Let's take the bus to Elephant & Castle and get the 53 to Hackney Road.'

As he rushed for the bus, I followed. We alighted and giggled into the telephone booth right in front of the bingo hall entrance.

'Can I speak to Mr. Lloyd please?' I heard myself saying down the phone, Yemi quietly standing by me.

'This is Mr. Lloyd speaking.'

'I'm calling for a floor operator job, sir.'

'Have you any experience? Can you come in tomorrow at 5pm? OK see you then. What did you say your name was again?'

'My name is Ifeoma Obijiaku,' I replied before putting the receiver down and looking at Yemi. I couldn't help hugging him and we giggled out of the booth and rushed off to catch our respective transport home. But not before I gave him a real hug for the first time since I had known him.

'*Ose gan ni*, Yemi' (Thank you very much, Yemi) were my parting words.

'Say it again,' he joked and we left.

I was now looking forward to earning a total of £44 a week with £33 coming in from my part-time bingo operator's job and £11 still from my early morning cleaning. I was beginning to save up for my next year's college fee, Home Office willing. They must have been looking for me to remind me to leave the country seeing that I had long past my visa's permit!

Chapter 7

By 1981, I'd been living abroad for nearly a year and had had little or no contact with my folks back home. This was heartrending, especially when I felt homesick on festive occasions and each time I struggled with the cold weather. I'd been sick one morning and unable to go to my cleaning job so Mr. Agbaso offered to drive me to the hospital. Fearing I had no leg to stand on legally, I insisted he drive me to Uncle Godwin's instead. If I was going to get worse or even die let it happen with my uncle present; I didn't want to risk the Home Office picking me up from the hospital. He drove me to my uncle's in Forest Hill and I shivered in the car waiting for my landlord to go knock. I saw Uncle come out of the house and the two men faced each other for about a good minute chatting, before they both walked towards me to the car. And all I could hear as they approached was, 'Aaah long time indeed, and how are you?'

I felt like shouting to remind them that I was dying – experiencing a fever like never before. Not even my masquerade illness during the war could compare. I had energy alright but whatever I was suffering from was pushing up to my heart plus the physical cold on me was making it worse. My uncle helped me out of the car and we headed back quietly to the house. The men continued to reminisce on the friendship they had during their study and work days together. My uncle's wife joined in as she prepared a hot lemon drink for me. The men exchanged phone numbers as we all got ready and out of the house. My uncle and his wife drove me to the hospital by Camberwell Green while Mr. Agbaso drove home.

My weekdays started with my morning cleaning job then off to college in Greenwich for 10am and off again to start my bingo job in the evening on Hackney Road before heading home for 11pm. My life was on the straight and narrow at least now that I earned a little extra. I had done two terms at my college and didn't want to think of what would happen after my first year without a proper visa. Yemi and I remained friends both in and outside college. I couldn't thank him enough for giving up his newfound abode while I was still resisting all his advances. Courtship with another tribe was not spoken about let alone imagined for me culturally, and so I was sure he understood that as much as he thought he loved me. And then he dropped the bombshell. He was returning to Nigeria having finished his studies. It felt like losing one of my limbs to have to continue my diaspora journey without my best friend and confidant. I regularly called and visited all my uncles and families, but nothing compared to my relationship with Yemi; caring and supportive of me all through this time irrespective of our non-romantic relationship. A week later he was gone. I didn't visit or see him to say my goodbye. I knew he had left when I received a parcel through the post containing a pleated skirt and a jeans jacket with a note saying goodbye from him. I secretly mourned him alive and I sincerely hope he gets to read this book as I would like to take it as an opportunity to truly thank him for all his kindness and support he gave me those years in my early wilderness in London.

Hackney Road's Top Rank club employees were comprised of mostly Nigerians at the time, one of whom was Oye who had tribal marks on both sides of his cheeks. He had a good sense of humour and made everyone laugh, making certain noises on the game floor as we worked. I got to know my colleagues at work within a week of starting. They were Mama and Papa Bisi and Kemi who is the youngest sister to Mama Bisi. There were Joseph, Emmanuel and Karen(RIP) his wife, an English lady from Liverpool but they lived in London. All of us worked the place except in the cashier room where we had two English guys, whom I barely knew. We only interacted with them to hand them customers' winning dockets which were used to pay their winnings when they attended the cashier booth. Some of us sold bingo booklets while the rest gave out change in exchange for currency for customers to play the slot machines downstairs. We would call out the winning numbers on the slot machines while we did the same for the booklet winning numbers aided by the overhead projector (OHP).

Joseph (Joe) and Oye would usually work on the first floor during bingo games while I worked with the rest of the staff on the ground floor – about seven of us, men and women. The ground floor also had a bingo area separate from the slot machines. Oye was absent on this particular day and as we got ready for the first game, there was an announcement. Mr. Lloyd, also the bingo caller, was standing behind the ball machine. He looked in our direction by the slot machines and said, 'Could any of you join Joe to manage upstairs? Oye isn't here today. Ify, if you would please, thanks.'

People began to head upstairs for the bingo. I felt a bit uneasy that Mr. Lloyd called me out, one of the newest staff. Why didn't he ask any of the old ones who had used the OHP more times than me? I went upstairs and positioned myself on the opposite side of the floor to where Joe stood and Mr. Lloyd started to call out the numbers. As luck would have it, the first three winners upstairs were on Joe's side but I had no problem writing out the winning dockets, which I took downstairs and submitted to the cashier's window where the winners would go to collect their winnings.

I went back upstairs after taking the last winning docket down and Joe was chatting with a mother and daughter at their table. I decided to walk up to him.

'Don't know about you, but I think a thank you is in order, don't you?'

Joe leaned away from the customer's table and smiled at me; he was about to say something when Mr. Lloyd started to call the next lot of numbers for 'Shoreditch Bell'.

A few minutes later a customer yelled, 'House,' waving their winning booklet in the air to indicate where they sat. She was on my side. Here we go, I thought. I went round and collected the book and headed for the OHP to read the winning numbers out. I finished reading, and by the time I took the book back to the winner, people were already going downstairs for the machine game. Joe was already giving out change to customers playing the machine as I went round to the cashiers to pick up my cash tray. Winners of the machine games were paid by a separate cashier seated in the area.

Joe would deliberately stand next to me with his cash tray in hand each time I called out the winning numbers. I could feel him silently breathing by my shoulder as I read the numbers. I wasn't keen on his show of interest. For a start, I already had assumed he was different, possibly from east or south Africa or even Jamaica, while the rest of the shop floor staff like myself were mostly Nigerians who I was more interested in making friends with considering how mindful I was about my stay in the country.

There was no denying that being different made him more unique. He got on well with many of the customers and each time he smiled he revealed his gapped teeth, which where I come from was symbolic like a 'beauty spot', not sure if that's still the case today. He was quiet, easy going and his timekeeping was exemplary. And yeah I liked him but he was too smooth for me to interpret, or should I say understand. He was liked by everyone especially Mr. Lloyd himself, and that somehow made him a person to go to in terms of work – for example, he would pick out uniforms for absentee colleagues if they were unable to come collect it themselves. And if you were not looking good or being yourself he would always want to find out what was wrong and whether he could help. But then, how come he didn't have a girlfriend? I'd only just joined; who was he pestering before me and how could he come after me out of all the female colleagues at work?

It was time again for another game of bingo so we returned upstairs. But not before Mr. Lloyd announced, 'Ify or Joe, could you take the Shoreditch Bell winning docket to the cashiers? The winner has gone to collect their winnings, thank you.' They hadn't collected their winnings because the docket hadn't reached the cashiers yet.

'So you didn't write out the docket even though I wrote three of yours? Aren't we supposed to work together?'

Unfolding his arms from his chest, he just smiled tauntingly as if to say do you like my gap teeth; as much as I was annoyed it was all I could see. I headed straight to the winner's table, apologised to the customer and completed the docket. I went with her to the cashier's window to collect her winnings and we both came back in time for the start of a new game.

A few minutes into the game and we had a winner again upstairs this time, nearer to Joe. I started an impromptu chat with the customers sat on the table close to where I stood – can't remember what we talked about but enough time had passed when I saw Joe go collect the winner's book and head to the nearest OHP. I finished my chat but was determined not to lift a finger to help him. Revenge was sweet as I poised to get my own back at him. 'Do me I do you God no go vex,' I mumbled to myself, a Nigerian masterpiece saying for retaliation.

He was finished confirming the winning numbers and, as if he knew, he walked back to the customers' table and started writing out the docket himself. I watched him walk across the floor to pass by where I stood. 'Can you take this downstairs f—' I heard him say as I felt a piece of paper swipe across my face as he went past me and kept glancing back for my reaction on his way downstairs to submit the docket and winking at me. I didn't know whether to get angrier or just stop speaking to him totally. Still musing on how to handle the situation and he was on his way back up wearing the same annoying smile – his gap teeth on display yet again as he walked straight to his side of the floor.

Closing time and I was in the ladies where we took off our work clothes.

'That Jamaican Joe got on my nerves today. I don't think I want to work with him again.'

'Who, Joe 90? He's not Jamaican,' one of my colleagues said.

'Who cares? Jamaican or West Indian. Everything is a laughing matter to him. I don't think I want to work with him again.'

'What? He's Nigerian, a Yoruba guy that you are calling Jamaican.'

'Seriously?'

'Yeah, ask Kemi.'

No wonder he was catcalling me. Who wants to go out with a Yoruba guy, anyways?

It was love in Tokyo for Joe and me. It didn't seem to bother him that I was Igbo. He fell head over heels for me as I did for him. Whenever I jumped on the bus to go home after work, he would jump on too just to hang with me to aggravate me and he did this for a couple of weeks on end. We play-fought on the top deck of our journeys from Shoreditch to Camberwell. I loved sitting on the upper deck for the long journey to Camberwell from where I either walked the short distance home or took a bus another couple of stops to Herne Hill. Plus it was high time I started being myself, sitting upstairs and having a cigarette! A habit I'd managed to keep under wraps while working at the airline. I was in London where no one cared if you smoked twenty cigarettes a day. I couldn't smoke while living with my uncles as I didn't want them to smell it on me and with all I was facing in everyday life, cigarettes were the last thing on my mind until I got the chance to smoke in my Herne Hill room. I still kept it secret as much as possible while some of my college friends smoked around me.

Joe would jump on the bus with me after work and we would sit upstairs so that we could smoke. Numerous times we play-fought all through the journey to Camberwell even as passengers were moving back and forth by us. We would do this a little noisily at times until we got off at Camberwell. He would then return home to Turnpike Lane, north London.

This became somewhat of a routine Monday to Saturday as we met up at work and travelled home together.

'I pray my landlord don't catch a glimpse of you, you know. Remember he's my uncle's friend,' I said to Joe one Friday evening when he came with me to my street.

'We ought to be careful then so that he doesn't see us,' he replied, catching the bus rail as he hopped on to sit beside me for the short ride. It was madness! I knew I was falling in love, but I never stopped worrying about how the mixed tribe relationship was going to pan out. We spoke Yoruba commonly; you'd think there was no divide between us.

'When are you going to start teaching me Yibo?'

'It's not Yibo it's Igbo, 'Laitan,' I interrupted him one day. 'You're not serious?'

'Why not? What makes you think I don't want to learn? If you're going to be my wife, what's wrong with me understanding your language, or don't you want to teach me?'

'I said you're not serious. All you want to know are funny stuff. That's not learning Igbo. If you like I'll write out the alphabet and even get you the book.'

'No, I want you to teach me it not from a book.'

We both got lost in giggles. I was seriously in love with him, I kept hearing in my head.

In the meantime, Joe wasn't happy about my living arrangements. He expressed his dislike for me living in the damp and cold environment and on my own for the majority of the time.

'You know you can move in with me at my uncle's. I've

talked to him and he doesn't mind. We can come and get your stuff this weekend,' he was saying to me on one of our bus rides to my home one cold evening.

'You can't do that without telling me. Even though I don't have to ask my uncle, I still have to tell him I'd moved from Mr. Agbaso's.'

'But you can't stay in that damp alone you'll catch pneumonia! You said to me you nearly died once. My uncle doesn't mind at all,' he kept repeating to me.

The relationship was moving faster than I could think. Colleagues were beginning to notice at work that we hung together. He was at the time studying a foundation course to an architectural degree at Tottenham college while I was at CBS doing business administration. Colleagues who knew him before me teased me at every opportunity they got. I would go pick up my cash tray from the cashiers and one of them would say to me,

'Why are you left to carry that? Where is he? He shouldn't let you go get it yourself.' As if I was carrying bars of lead. Without naming names, I knew who they meant. And we all would laugh at the joke of getting a helping hand for a silly little tray of cash – my colleagues' way of making me aware that they knew Joe and I were becoming an item.

And I would say to them, 'God forbid. We're just friends.' Swinging my right arm over my head and clicking my fingers away from myself – to indicate my objection to their premonition – going out with a Yoruba boy for real. But deep down I could feel it. I could feel I was lying to myself;

I had fallen in love with him. Little did I know some of my colleagues actually were his relations and they all lived at their uncle's in Turnpike Lane.

Joe had prepared to spend the weekend at mine. Mr. Agbaso was away outside London and we were on the bus going home from bingo.

'Have you thought more about my suggestion for you to move in with me?'

'I'm still thinking about how I'm going to tell my uncle. If I complain about the dampness, I know my uncle; he will start looking for another place for me. And I don't want to put him through that again. He worries over me – you know he still gives me £10 every week towards my rent, even though he knows I work.'

We got off the bus by my street junction and Joe went into the phone booth on the other side of our road. I crossed over with him but waited outside.

'Who were you phoning?' I asked as he stepped out and joined me to walk to the house about four minutes later.

'I told Uncle not to expect me the whole weekend. And he was taking a jab at me.'

'What did he say?' I asked as I unlocked the door and we went inside. 'I can't move in with you just yet 'cause I still need to tell my uncle.'

'By which time you could have been dead of flu,' was his reply from where he sat by my reading table. Still resisting entering a real relationship with him, I couldn't bring myself to say no to him; I was really relaxed and could be myself in his company. My long vanished exuberant self came alive whenever I was with him. He made me feel my good old self again like when we lived at Modile Way among all tribes. I was realising he was no different from an Igbo boy except for the language, which wasn't a barrier luckily enough for me as a Lagosian born Igbo girl.

'Do you know what Uncle said to me? He said enough of my frequent "phone home" exercises that I should bring you home.'

'Bring me home as what? I told you I'm not going anywhere with you until I can figure out how to convince my uncle.'

'About what? About moving in with me?'

'I've already told you,' I replied.

'My uncle said "this particular girl" in my life that has been keeping me away from home – that I should bring you home.'

I didn't want to believe him; coming from his mouth that his uncle said all that about him. I wanted to test the truth in that. I couldn't tell you why then and still can't tell you now but I felt comfortable and confident that I would be able to find out if I saw the uncle and I would be in his company still.

Uncle Henshaw was married with three children all of whom were back in Nigeria at the time. They lived in a three-bedroom terrace flat situated next to all the amenities in Turnpike Lane. I went home with Joe the following weekend and met his uncle and the rest of the household. There I met Mama and Papa Bisi, my colleagues at the bingo club including Kemi.

'Welcome home, our wife!' Mama Bisi started the taunt as

I knelt down to greet uncle. We all laughed and joked and he offered me a welcoming gift – a bottle of Cinzano Bianco. I started spending time with Joe and his family and one weekend we moved my belongings to Turnpike Lane where I shared Joe's room.

It was a full house for all of us when I moved in barely a month later. I was getting used to the family atmosphere that I long craved for since arriving in the UK. Uncle Henshaw was one of the kindest men I had ever come across my whole life. He made not just me but everyone else feel at home. We all sought his advice from time to time and loved to spend time with him and his friends who came visiting every now and then. They would sit around, we'd cook and we would all eat and drink with Uncle's oldies playing on the loop, most of which we all were welcome to dance to. We were one family and it was fun! You couldn't get a better family house. Although I never asked, I was sure Joe was contributing towards the rent and utilities for me. I just shopped and cooked with everyone. I'd finished my studies months ago and was now working hard but madly in love with this Yoruba guy. It was the worst scenario: an illegal immigrant in the country in love with another illegal immigrant, as I later on found out. Love knows no rules and regulations as they say and so it didn't bother me much. We both avoided discussing our legal plight and just tried to live together.

Joe was outgoing and streetwise, even for an illegal migrant, but a quiet and gentle guy. He was what I called a smooth operator. He regarded everyone around him, nonetheless. People trusted him and I admired that about him. Nothing was too much trouble to help friends or anyone out and he was good at putting things together, from laying carpet through to assembling furniture. He was passionate about friendships and associations but would let you have it if and when you crossed him. He never let me forget at any point that I was his girlfriend. Controlling may be, yet I liked the quirky streak in him regardless. After nearly a year or so into our stay at Uncle's we received very bad news from home – Uncle's youngest child passing in Nigeria. The whole house shook with grief and Uncle made the decision to bring his remaining two children, a son and a daughter, as well as their mother back to the UK. This meant Joe and I had to find a place to live, to make room in the house. And so began my journey with Joe as an item.

Joe found a one-bedroom basement flat owned by a Nigerian in Newington Green. It was a self-contained one bed with kitchen, toilet and bathroom. We were set to move into the flat when we received a phone call from Nigeria. It was Joe's mother informing us that Joe's dad had just passed after a brief illness. He was fifty-three. I'd picked up the call not knowing who was on the line. As she started talking my heart was racing as to how to introduce myself should she ask. But she said she was hoping to speak to anyone else but Joe and that I should give him the news and the specific message for him not to return home as a result.

'Tell 'Laitan to please not return home for the funeral,' she warned sternly over the phone. She said she believed the

'Daddy' was mysteriously killed following a religious feud at the church he had founded. Her conviction was so real that she could not stress the importance of her message enough for him not to come back home and risk the same spiritual or voodoo affliction. The call ended and I didn't have to introduce myself, thank goodness. Perhaps she mistook me for Kemi whom she may have spoken with on other occasions.

By the end of our phone conversation I was frightened about how to relay all that information. I braved it and went upstairs to tell him. Without uttering a word in response, Joe and I were ready to leave the house for college and work. Quietly we left for the bus stop to catch our ride, but to my surprise we alighted on Kingsland Road in Dalston. I just followed him, determined not to ask any questions. I didn't want to rub him the wrong way seeing as he hadn't said a thing since I relayed his mum's message to him. We walked into Ridley Road market and shopped for food until we couldn't remember anything else to buy. We then met a friend of his dad's visiting the UK who also happened to be shopping. They stopped to exchange pleasantries and I heard the man say he'd heard that Joseph Snr was rushed to hospital and hoped he'd recovered. Joe filled him in on the latest news and the man couldn't thank him enough. It wasn't until we returned home that Joe broke down. We met Uncle in the house as we offloaded the shopping into the kitchen. Joe dropped the bag and screamed into the living room; Uncle was startled and couldn't console him enough. I had long admired how Joe regarded his dad's airmail letters and couldn't help feeling sorry for him. I couldn't imagine how he must feel to lose his dad especially as he hadn't seen him since leaving home a year before me.

By 1982 we had moved into our new place and we found out I was four weeks pregnant; we'd barely been at Albion Grove a month. It couldn't be helped. Compared to every man that had wanted to marry me in the past, the father of my would-be infant was young and would readily pass his creativity and thoughtful genes on to my baby, and babies if I decided to have more. I was a bag of mixed emotions by now, realising the task ahead of me to inform my people about my predicament both at home and abroad. Perhaps postponing telling them might just do the trick till it mattered no more. But first I had to get through the morning sickness. Something no one told me about or prepared me for. It was awful.

I had Joe position bowls of sand strategically around the rooms to catch my never-ending spitting. Gosh it was an experience like no other and hell in summer. Winter was even worse; it felt the same. By this time I had little communication with my London relatives. I relied on friends and all I could read up on from public libraries to inform myself on my condition. Joe was excited and still at college while working at the bingo. Although we loved each other dearly, especially now that we had a baby on the way, I was still really worried about my parents disowning me. I wasn't only going out with a Yoruba guy, I was also pregnant and would have to explain all that to my uncles in the UK too. Both of them travelled frequently back to Nigeria on short trips to visit their old folks and for their respective housing projects. They were bound to see my parents who would pay them visits to find out about me. I got the chills each time I imagined my parents' anger when they found out what my life had suddenly become.

Joe was hardworking and committed to our relationship and was already hoping for a boy. He was beginning to exert himself as head of the would-be family we were both establishing and would insist I do as I was told regardless of all the affection he lavished on me while I carried his first child. Once again in my life, I was having to rely on someone else to tell me what to do, this time in a foreign land. Joe had been here for nearly a year ahead of me and so he knew best and he would go out on a limb to instruct and educate me on western lifestyle – preceeding almost every interactive sentence you said to anyone with 'please'. I struggled sometimes to adhere to his advice as I felt I had my own personal goals to discover things for myself. But nothing dogged me like the hurdle I needed to jump: the inter-tribal relationship I'd gotten myself into in the UK.

Joe wrote to his mother about us and the baby on the way. We asked her to travel to the east and break the news to my parents, and knowing there was the possibility of my parents providing her with a marriage list we filled her in on what to expect where marriage to an Igbo girl was concerned. We felt this needed to be done before the baby came along or else I would be prolonging my punishment for when the time came for my parents to eventually find out. Joe's mother made the trip with a male relative companion in the absence of Joseph senior. She did us proud as expected. When they got to my village she footed the bill to cater for the food and wine used to entertain the villagers for however many days she spent in the east. Some of my village friends wrote to me in London about the feasting period. How Joe's mother travelled first to Aba to see Papa before they returned to Umuofeke with Papa to have the ceremony – the introductions and bride price event rolled into one. I was more than pleased with the news when Joe's mother's feedback got to us stating that everything went as planned and both my parents and villagers were welcoming and very happy.

I was into my eighth month of pregnancy and still working at a clothing factory on Shacklewell Lane in Dalston close to where we lived. I even walked home at times when I felt like it. Joe encouraged me to apply for my national insurance (NI) number now that I'd been in London for nearly two years and had a paper trail of my employment history and a permanent address. As luck would have it this was posted to me weeks later. Joe already had his NI number, so together we applied to go on the council house waiting list in Hackney. While my heavily pregnant self stayed in the council's temporary place in Hackney Wick, Joe spent time at friends – going to college and work from there and would come by to see me and stay till late at times. Sometimes friends drove him down to visit and took him back to spend the night at theirs. It was thirteen days to my due date when we moved into a two-bedroom sky-rise building on Bath Street in Old Street. It was in a block of flats, the 100th flat on the 17th floor, but it was ours. By this time Joe had abandoned his studies for full-time employment now that we'd got a place and the baby was nearly here. He moved into a full-time job as the warehouse manager at Crusader Margolis, a furniture company on Shepherdess Walk, a stone's throw from our new flat. I had also jacked in my cotton cleaning job obviously as soon as I moved out of the temporary accommodation.

Joseph Olaitan Adenuga Junior was born on 19th September, a week short of the day I clocked two years in the country. Everything was fine now. I had my flat, my baby and baby father who was working tirelessly to provide for us, even though in my mind I couldn't wait to get back to work and support him. The future was bright – we sent the news of our baby boy home to both our parents who were quite happy to hear from us. The tribal instinct had subsided on both sides now they were receiving pictures of Junior growing up a chubby healthy baby boy. Our parents wrote us congratulatory letters on the birth of our first son and even sent us names for when we got him christened. My uncles and my respective community families in London visited us too; Uncle Godwin visited the most as he stopped by nearly each morning on his way back from work to see how I was coping with motherhood. Joe and I couldn't get enough time to be with our growing son; our beautiful baby growing on my breast milk. But guess what, it didn't look like he was getting satisfied on that. He would cry after every feed and that left me stressed and confused. I was a nursing mother at home

24/7 while Joe worked at the furniture business near us. He came home for tea and lunch breaks which he spent mostly doting on his son, Junior. He changed his soiled nappies and fed him while I caught up with my TV programme rituals for that hour break. Coronation Street, Emmerdale Farm – you name it I was watching them all.

You could say I was bored stiff as a stay at home mum and running up our phone bill with the number of calls I went through daily. I was calling friends at work during office hours and phoning up quiz games on TV. I never won a penny even though they tended to ask the easiest questions that even I knew the answers to.

My baby was growing and was the only company I had most of the time while his dad was at work or out with his friends. I used to finish my morning routine by midday when Joe might visit for half hour break. He played with our baby throughout before getting back. And we were on our own again. I used to stand on the balcony and watch people go by and couldn't for the life of me imagine what I was thinking on the day I stood there carrying my baby son.

Down on the busy street below the whole area was buzzing with everyday people walking and driving in all directions. I had given Junior a bath that morning after Joe left for work. After creaming and powdering him, I put fresh baby wear on him then took him to the balcony to look out and while away time. He was in my arms as I looked on outside. I must have looked away from admiring my beautiful bundle of joy and recognised the thought in my head saying, 'What if you threw him down? People would gather round his body, ambulance, police and fire brigade would all be in attendance; all the emergency services…'

Fear enveloped me. Slowly, I stepped back and quickly ran into the living room. Holding him tight, I started telling myself off to even have let such horrible thoughts slip into my mind. I was in my bed with him for the next couple of hours or so to protect him. God forbid he should come to any harm.

I kept the incident from Joe for two days. And so, the next evening as he sat eating his dinner I had Junior with me on the end of the settee watching TV.

'Darling,' I began and he looked up at me. 'You're not going to believe it. I was out there and some stupid thinking came into my head.' All the while pointing out the balcony.

'What?'

'I stood there wondering what would happen if I threw Junior down from the balco—'

'You must be gone crazy. I warn you – don't ever step onto that balcony with him again!' He got up and went up the stairs for the bathroom first then to our bedroom.

I came downstairs from putting Junior to bed the next day and followed the cracking sound of some sharp tearing inside the living room. I walked in and Joe was busy. Like a sheep I stood there and watched in silence as he duct-taped the door to the balcony; top to bottom.

'I'm sorry I didn't tell you. I was scared myself. And you don't seriously think I would harm my son, do you?'

'Don't tell me that. You don't go to the balcony ever again, that's all I'm saying to you. A clothes horse is in the bathroom, use it if you want to dry clothes.'

I was now really scared, not just about him being angry with me, but also how to stop the despicable thought creeping into me again. I began to feel it may have to do with some unfinished traditional business – a marriage ritual we had left unaccomplished especially as we were from different tribes. I needed to find out why I was having those weird thoughts about my new baby. I was bored alright. And even though I wasn't working Joe took care of us. I decided to write to my parents for some possible answers.

As time went on I realised I should have talked to my health visitor about it as help was on hand for what I now know was postnatal depression. I'd never informed my GP either so wasn't diagnosed as suffering from it.

And then my house phone developed a fault and Joe asked me to book an appointment with British Telecom for an engineer to come and see to it. The BT engineer arrived just as I had finished breastfeeding Junior and he was still crying. Naturally the engineer was concerned about the crying baby and so I told him my plight and he smiled and asked if I had any Weetabix. He asked me to go get a fresh feeding bottle that I kept in the sterilising unit. And even though I was breastfeeding I had also bought the feeding bottles and all the sterilising gadgets as I would give him cooled boiled water now and then especially when he hiccupped. The guy next asked for scissors and snipped the rubber teet to make it a little wider and I watched as he threw one Weetabix biscuit into the bottle and asked me to mix this with my normal SMA milk measure and give it to him. Without a break to take a breath, Junior took to the mixed food like a fish to water. I put the bottle down, burped him and he dozed off.

He couldn't sleep enough on the first day he had the Weetabix mix. Every few minutes I would look in on him in his room and place my hand on his back as he slept to check he was still breathing, especially when it was close to Joe's return from work. I was making sure his son was alive. There seemed nothing wrong with giving him Weetabix seeing that the baby loved it. That put an end to breast feeding my baby as he grew more interested in the mixture in his bottle. I was feeling relieved and gratified watching my baby blossom. He was into everything and couldn't wait to grow and be up and about. I joined the mothers with babies on reins, walking them everywhere. Life was going according to plan. I had had my baby and was looking forward to getting back into employment.

And then came a Home Office letter requesting that as an overstayer, it was high time I left the country. The letter warned that if they didn't hear from me within fourteen days they would have me arrested and sent back to Nigeria. This was in January of 1983. I wondered how they'd traced me to my present address. Joe had to remind me that I had been profiled from when I received my national insurance number at our previous Albion Grove basement flat. Perhaps, Hackney council had also notified them about my temporary accommodation before permanently rehousing us at our present new abode. All sorts of thoughts were racing through my mind and what possible repercussion lay in waiting for me as a result. How was I to travel home especially now that I had a baby and his father whom I loved? I was so much in despair. Joe insisted we must tie the knot before I travelled. I wrote to the Home Office with the excuse that I would leave the country as soon as I finished the January sales. This bought us time to plan and have our wedding before I left to return to Nigeria. I felt Joe was agreeing to the idea to lay claim on his first child just in case of any eventuality, including if I wasn't able to return to the UK. I never asked him neither did he confirm this.

To make sure I kept my promise, the Home Office wrote back and asked me to send them copies of both my passport and my purchased ticket as evidence, which I did. Meanwhile, Joe and I tied the knot on 26th February 1983 at St. Barnabas Church in Old Street. Our wedding was simple but sweet. Julie Bello was my chief bridesmaid. She and her boyfriend Dominic were living at ours at the time. My uncles and their respective family members attended too and a handful of Okwe and Umuna brethren including Lawrence, Victoria's younger brother. Joe catered for food and drink both at the church reception and the house party that followed. Many of our wedding party guests stayed with us throughout the weekend and into Monday morning before the whole ceremony cooled off. The plan was for me to go back to Nigeria and come back in my married name, Mrs. Adenuga.

I was hopeful it would wipe my overstayer slate clean. I was leaving my six-month-old son behind in the care of his father and our live-in friends, Julie my bridesmaid and her fiancé, Dominic. They were staying with us while they looked for accommodation and both loved Junior to bits.

The day came for my return trip to Nigeria a few weeks after my wedding. The country was far from the land I left in 1980. The nation had increased the number of states prior to my travel. I took a taxi to my mother-in-law's in Festac village where she lived with her family, Joe's stepfather and two younger stepsisters. It would be the first time I'd see her. Joe had prepared me to be duty bound and sensible all the time out there. 'And you won't go wrong. Mummy will love you,' he'd said as he helped me lock my suitcase.

My taxi pulled in front of the one-storey house with a large shop front. Lights were on and I could see there were people sat in the shop's corridor. I walked down after paying the taxi and saw a shadowy figure getting up and walking up towards me.

'My wife, welcome. We've been expecting you,' the middle-aged woman said to me as we met. A number of young teenagers came running towards me too.

'Good evening, ma, please let me carry the bag,' one of them said and took the bag from me.

We walked into the house and continued on to the ground floor living room where a middle-aged man sat watching TV. He was welcoming too.

'Aah aah, our wife, good to see you. Welcome home.

What about baby and his dad?' he asked as the rest of the household all assembled inside the room. I knew the woman that brought me in was my mother-in-law, I could see the resemblance with Joe, and the man we met in the room was Joe's stepfather. Mummie (my mother-in-law) was so very excited as she jumped in to explain to the husband that Joe senior and Junior couldn't come with me.

Mummie had four grandchildren from Joe's middle stepsister: first the twin girls and two younger ones – pretty young things. She turned to one of the twins and said, 'Olutade, let's get your auntie something to eat and show her the room where she will be sleeping.'

It was really nice meeting Joe's extended family members in the flesh – his elder stepsister and her family also visited me in Festac and it was enjoyment galore on the day they came down. They all were so happy to see me and what a rude awakening it was for me to find that they all accepted me regardless of my different tribe. I loved and got on well with every single one of them.

We were getting ready for dinner.

'I must thank you, Mummie, for going to my village.'

'Don't mention! Your people were pleased to see us and they entertained us.'

'Thank you very much, ma. My parents told me you completed the bridal custom, thank you, ma,' I said to her while kneeling before her.

'Ah my wife dearest, your papa is a very God-fearing man. All he asked for was to entertain the villagers and make sure all their traditional rights were catered for and he said he doesn't want a penny for your bride price. A very good man and your mother too.' It was usually not the villagers' business whether or not a father asked and received bride price from their respective in-law as long as the village traditions were met.

With that my stepfather-in-law called us all in the room to prayer. 'Let us pray for Mama junior's safe return journey home. May Almighty God guide and protect Papa junior and Junior the baby, our son, till the mother's safe return to meet them.'

My eyes still closed in prayer, I wondered what my parents would think about my bold move when they saw me in the flesh. At least I'd spent a couple of days with the Yorubas and all I got was love and laughter, even though I was Igbo. Would my people see it like that too?

I shared the presents I'd brought along for everyone the next morning and they all passed my family photos round to look at – of the wedding and Junior. The children were asking me a lot of questions about their cousin in London and I tried as much as possible to answer them.

Mummie couldn't help but ask, 'Mama junior, you're so fluent in Yoruba to think that you are an Igbo girl.'

'I was born in Lagos, ma, and went to primary school before the war.'

'No wonder,' she replied with a smile. 'You ought to have a Yoruba name; I'll give you one. From today I'll call you Abimbola not mama junior, understand?'

'Yes, ma, I do and thank you,' I replied to the jeer of everyone.

We made a few international calls for them to speak with Joe.

'Hello, hello... my Laja, my father-in-law, how are you? How is Junior?'

Laja is Mummie's pet name for Joe meaning 'a mediator'. It was over half an hour by the time the phone was passed round for the nieces to say hello and finally with his stepfather. They even asked to speak with Junior over the phone.

The last time I was in touch with Charlie, my brother, he had just arrived in Lagos. That was about a year or so ago. He was working in the national security (NS) service as an NS Officer (NSO). I was pleased that his education had paid off contrary to our father's premonitions of his academic ability.

Charlie said that he visited my in-laws from time to time.

'Mummie, do you know where Charlie lives so I can go visit?' I asked.

'A few months ago he came and told me he was travelling home and I asked him to greet Mama and Papa for me. I haven't seen or heard from him since then. I know he lives in the Ogunsanya area but I don't know his house, I haven't been.'

I was looking forward to seeing him after all these years to congratulate him. But first I needed to get down to business.

I needed a new passport in my married name but our

passport office was asking for requirements that needed Joe's input. They advised me to renew my existing passport instead and change it at a later date when it would be convenient for Joe and I to complete the process. I was left with no choice than that as much as I feared it might not pass the test at the UK border. I submitted a renewal application and decided to go see my folks in the east and then collect my passport when I got back to Lagos. Mummie gave me provisions for my family when I left for my village two days later.

Seeing Charlie in the village made me so happy, but I wasn't prepared for what he had to tell me. He had just been discharged with redundancy pay from the NSO employment. He had to return home to contemplate what to do next. Many of our villagers didn't believe that I had returned from the white man's land so soon, like I had been to Hausa hill and back and called it London. It remained a rumour I'd heard but wasn't bothered. I had enough on my plate with my brother's job loss and how I could get myself back to my husband and child.

I was chuffed to see my siblings and Mama. She was worried about the rumours and whatever else she might have heard people saying about me.

'I don't want you showing your photos here and there, especially with the elders.' The children and teenagers that giggled excitedly viewing the photos didn't bother her. She needn't explain it 'cause I understood her perfectly.

'And make sure you are not in pair of trousers when they come to welcome you.'

'Haba, Mama, what's the matter?'

'You need to be seen dressing like a married woman; in up and down,' began her lecture. Up and down was a name for an African print blouse with two pieces you wraparound your waist one on top the other. 'You mustn't put on trousers in the village for them to think you'd just returned from prostitution.'

I couldn't believe how far gone I had left all that petty mandatory social understanding behind. I had evolved indeed as I don't think I had one single wrapper at this time. So I had to borrow hers – she lent me her newest ones.

'Here, take these to your room and you can wear them with your English blouse.' She handed me about three pairs of the old classic African prints of horses, broomsticks and opener. And all this was after I had worn trousers all my developing years both in Ezeoke and Queens. Mama ensured we had packets of cabin biscuits in the house to welcome visitors but that was it.

I had to listen to Mama nonetheless to manage all the village politics that could be not just horrible but unfounded, and I still had to do what she said as we kept receiving our village visitors. I was beginning to feel homesick for London. Every evening with my family, I listened to home stories and I answered all the questions about the white man's land they liked to know.

'Did you go to the queen's house?' Rose asked me.

I told her Her Majesty the Queen doesn't live in a house but a palace. 'We go day-outing to central London sometime to see her palace.'

'Mama, why were you so cautious with me with our people? Don't you think some of them may have noticed you didn't want them to see my photos?' I asked.

Standing her ground she said, 'Some of them are evil – people who might afflict you with voodoo and could even get at your husband and child through the photos you're showing them.' It wasn't new or the first time I was hearing such conspiracy theories, but it was doing my brain in as I know my people hold such beliefs.

Mama also had another reason for not wanting me to share my London experiences. 'Listen, don't go discussing your husband or son with anyone. They've come and taken their rights and we don't owe them anything but not everyone is happy about your marriage to a Yoruba man.' Her desire was for my marriage to remain a Pandora's box; as long as it was not talked about, she was fine.

'For how long, Mama?' I asked to no response.

Papa on the other hand was his excited self to have his daughter return from the home of his ex-master, the master that told him his date of birth. I'll never forget the story he told us. He was pleased that I didn't stay too long before returning home like he'd wished. But little did he know.

I sat down with my parents and told them about my circumstances – what brought me home and what I'd done with my passport in order to be able to return to England.

'So wouldn't your husband be annoyed you were unable to change to your married name?'

'I had no choice, Papa,' I replied. 'He will understand and

we can go together and change it at the Nigerian embassy over there.'

We spent hours chatting – he was asking me about the Houses of Parliament, Trafalgar Square, Buckingham Palace and St. Paul's Cathedral.

'I've visited them in the West End, Papa.'

These were places I visited upon arriving to London years ago but I talked about them to Papa like I went weekly to sustain his enthusiasm stemming from his time with the colonial master.

Before I left my village to return to Lagos and travel out, I dreamt of the idea of taking my mother back with me for her to see England and babysit my baby son. I would ask my brother to lend me the money for her flight and pay it back when I got home to London. Mama was an old woman, which should make it easy to take her across the border checkpoint. I would tell them she had come with me to visit her grandson and my nephew by another son or daughter of hers. Charlie agreed to lend me his redundancy money for her journey. Like me, Mama was fearful of heights and no matter how safe I told her the flight was going to be she was not having it. She was quite happy to remain grounded, she said and had no interest risking her life just to fly in an aeroplane. Papa on the other hand was ecstatic about the news that she'd turned my offer down and couldn't wait to be asked to take her place. He relished the idea of visiting the homeland of his colonial master to see all the landmarks he'd been told about, like London Bridge. What an irony. After all our father did to stop my brother's secondary education, Charlie was the one footing the bill to make Papa's dream come true. It took Papa no time to inform his old Lagos brigade that he was travelling to the UK and we were ready a week later to head to Lagos to process his travelling documents.

I did all the talking at the airport now that my English was better and we were both let in. We took the underground and changed at Kings Cross to catch the northern line to Old Street. Papa was all eyes throughout the journey. And when we came out of the station to walk to our street, he couldn't resist taking a swipe at a few people he saw entering the bus.

'God almighty, my in-law, aren't they afraid to sit at the top? I can't imagine the giant of a driver to be wheeling this thing about,' he said to me.

'Papa, the buses are sturdy and the drivers are trained specially to drive them,' I replied as we walked past the post office and turned into Bath Street.

We got into the lift and within a few minutes we walked onto our floor.

'And what floor is this?' Papa asked.

'The seventeenth floor, Papa.' I pressed my doorbell and Joe, who was expecting us, swung into prostrate mode to greet and welcome Papa typical of the Yorubas.

'Na you bi, Joe?' Papa asked as he gazed at Joe lying on the floor before him by the porch and gestured to him to get up.

Joe stood up and nodded. 'Darling I'll be back, make Papa at home. I wanted to see you before going shopping. Julie's got Junior, let me go and I'll be back soon.'

'OK,' I replied and Papa and I continued into the living room. He was still looking around as he walked, taking it all in. As we made ourselves comfortable in the living room, Julie came down with Junior who was now a massive seven-month-old bouncing boy dribbling as he looked steadily at me.

'Wow, looks like my baby has been well fed. Thank you Julie. Oh, Dominic,' I saw him walk in behind Julie, 'I was going to thank you for looking after Junior.'

'You're welcome, Ify. Good to see you. How is naija?'

'So, so, many things have changed indeed.'

I introduced them to Papa. 'Papa, these are our friends who were helping Joe with looking after Junior. Julie was also my bridesmaid.'

'Thank you very much,' Papa said to them.

I was playing with my baby son who I'd missed so much when Dominic said to me, 'You can visit us at our new place any time. Joe knows the place off White Hart Lane, Tottenham.' We said our byes and they left. Joe had been taking Junior to visit them since they moved out after their brief stay with us.

'Let me hold Junior,' Papa said to me when we heard Joe at the front door and he pushed in a Safeway's supermarket trolley full of groceries including a bottle of champagne.

'Welcome, my in-law. You're welcome.'

'Thank you, sir,' Joe kept responding.

I prepared jollof rice, garnished beef and salad for dinner toasted with the champagne.

'May the good Lord guide and protect you over here and

us at home. Give us good health and happiness… Amen,' Papa was saying as he let a couple of drops of the champagne fall onto the floor while baby Junior looked on in his baby walker. Papa enjoyed the evening meal very much as he displayed his 'fork and knife' etiquette to let us know he was still in the know. No sooner did I clear the table than he took Junior to the living room to play with him.

We all watched TV and chatted into the wee hours of the morning including calling to notify my community people in London that Papa was visiting. My two uncles spoke with him promising to visit as soon as. The next day Joe went to Silver Street market during his lunch break and bought Papa winter pullovers and other clothes.

'Thank you, my in-law. It's cold over here.' Papa was announcing another of his observations after seeing the fearless people getting on the top decks of buses never mind the king kong driver.

We threw a welcome party for him at our flat and our people all came to see him. Relatives came by to pick him up to spend time with them at their place. Sometimes Joe and I accompanied him in the evenings, including when he visited Joe's uncle's house in Turnpike Lane. We went everywhere with him for the three weeks he spent with us. We took him to the West End and to the Greenwich time spot. And of course we went to Buckingham Palace and the Houses of Parliament. He made a big album of all his holiday photos, most of which were with and of Junior. He was so proud to be returning with the album to share with folks at home.

Papa got on well with Uncle Henshaw and Joe in particular. He left on a high with his album full of stories, especially of his grandson the first to be born offshore Nigeria.

So began my motherhood experience. I put Junior's name down on a waiting list at St Luke's School, a church school which was in part of our estate on Bath Street. I dressed him up in Pierre Cardin and every designer gear I could afford to take him in his pushchair everywhere. We went to parks, our street market and visited friends who in turn paid us visits especially if we happened to be nursing mums.

My baby was getting bigger and bigger and we celebrated his birthdays like we were having adult parties. Our adult guests would take the celebration into the early hours when the partying children had gone home. Junior embraced music as he hung side by side with his dad whenever he was playing music from his wall to wall record stash. As we watched his music interest grow we bought him musical gadgets like a mini piano and a plastic guitar to play with. He also had a plastic microphone with the stand all of which he used to mime to every other song we played in the house. He was singing to Bob Marley's *One Love* once when he jumped up to do a Bob Marley spin move and was caught under the chin by the plastic guitar. Joe was home on tea break luckily that afternoon. He called his workplace to tell them he was running late back because he had to take his son to hospital where he received five stitches to seal the wound under his chin.

As a stay at home mother, life was becoming a routine of

washing, cleaning and shopping. And I was beginning to knit too. I got on well with other parents on the block and I relied on Mrs. Jump's family and a girl called Kirsty living on the block to look after Junior every now and then for my short trips to the shop or GP appointments. No sooner did I perfect the routine of leaving Junior with carers in my block than I was deciding to get back to work. And so I dropped him with Kirsty and family one day and headed off job hunting. I took the bus to Dalston to my old factory but they were no longer there, so I checked nearby factories where I got lucky with one of them. I got hired alright but as a top presser as opposed to cleaning cotton off finished garments that I did in the past and had experience of. But due to my desperation I had to lie to get the position working with two other men, a Ghanian and a Nigerian. It also meant that I would earn more than I did before. Joe hit the roof when I got back with the news. To say he was not happy with my desire to return to work was an understatement – he just didn't like the idea of anyone else looking after his son.

'That's what mothers do, look after the babies,' he kept reminding me, making it perfectly clear that he was the breadwinner and I should stay home and look after our son. I realised I had worked all through my stay abroad and to have Joe confining me to the house because I'd become a mother wasn't going to work with me. After all, Mama worked nonstop raising us and still did regardless of Papa working full time pre and post-civil war. However, I knew I would have to have Junior well looked after if I was to leave him to return to work. I was optimistic I could do that with the money I was going to earn.

I was there for a couple of years pulling ranks with my male colleagues to make the Greek owner and especially the wife happy. You needed to see me going home after my top-pressing work. Especially during winter after ironing tens of garments for up to eight hours in the warm before stepping onto the chilly street to go home. I had swollen feet like I was suffering from elephantiasis; literally. It didn't seem to bother me. I was earning money and able to afford all I could for my baby son in addition to his doting dad's efforts. I was also bringing garments home for sale to my friends. These were mostly shop soiled or the ones I bought to resell for more profit. And our baby son was inundated with every plaything going from alphabet blocks, singing toys and gadgets to all the musical toy instruments aforementioned as well as a big robotic dragon which he played with on a wooden board in the living room. By the age of two his energy was exhausting especially before and after work, but I dare not complain to his dad who was against my return to work in the first place. I was beginning to shout and yell at Junior to calm down whenever he was stressing me out particularly in public places. I had taken him to Safeway shopping where I refused to let him pick up some kind of chocolate from the counter instead of hurrying along with me to the cashier to check out. My baby threw a tantrum and staggered over a mop and bucket and spilled the dirty water all over the floor. I was furious and so angry as I looked behind me to see him half lying in the dirty water attracting the gaze of many shoppers. I felt at a loss of what to do so calmly picked him up in one hand and continued to the check-out where I apologised to the cashier.

'Don't worry, as long as he's OK,' was her response as she pressed her button for her green flashing light to indicate she wanted to draw the attention of her colleague to the spilled water. As soon as we were outside the supermarket I whacked him on both legs to give him something to cry for. I cried inside as I remembered Mama used to do exactly that to me growing up.

Then I found myself pregnant again. I got Junior into a nursery school on Old Street as soon as he turned three where he attended half days throughout the week, enough to tire him out when I brought him home. My second pregnancy was straightforward as I kind of knew what to expect at every step this time around. For a start I wasn't feeling nauseous like I did with Junior. With one toddler and a baby on the way, boredom set in even more. I had jacked in my top-pressing job as soon as I found out I was pregnant. I would drop Junior at his nursery in the mornings, do housework and watch TV till Joe came home for coffee and lunch breaks as usual. My desire to return to work was now overwhelming even though I was pregnant and knowing how Joe felt about me working as a nursing mum never mind now!

My second pregnancy was a pleasant experience but for my daunting need to be doing something to get out of the routine of waking up, taking Junior to nursery and returning home to wait for the time to pick him up – the daily routine was driving me nuts. My weekends were no better 'cause I cooked and washed and contained my hyperactive toddler while coping with the little blob I was carrying inside of me. Junior's cleverness kept me on my toes still. He had one day joined me in the kitchen as I prepared meat to cook red stew. I craved red meat during this pregnancy, and so I would eat taster meat pieces as I cooked with slices of onion and scotch bonnet. Junior saw me chewing away and cried for some. I held up the scotch bonnet, telling him it was what I was eating and it was very hot and as such I couldn't give it to him. Oblivious to all my explanations he cried even more for me to give it. Stupidly, I handed him the pepper and watched my baby bite into it and scream! Don't ask me why I did it – regrettable now but I was drawing a parallel with how Mama would have handled the situation. I had learned all through Junior's pregnancy that you don't smack or 'bully' kids in England. I immediately thought Mama would have thumped me in the head to get out of the kitchen and not given me anything. I suppose I gave it to him as my way of punishing him for not adhering to my warning. Either way, it was wrong but I'm sure he learned a lesson there whether we realised it then or not – to listen to Mother.

I had dropped Junior at his nursery school one day and decided to go job hunting. I was in and out of job agencies along Old Street and took a bus to Hackney to browse a few job centres. I found no job vacancies, however, I came home with a leaflet advertising a government training scheme to prepare people moving into work. I considered the training to both prepare me to return to work for when I'd given birth but most of all to keep me busy for the next sixteen weeks nearing the time to have my baby. Without discussing it with Joe, I completed the enrolment tear-off slip putting myself down for secretarial studies at RSA3 (Royal Society of Arts) level. All hell broke loose for Joe and I because now he was bothered about any harm coming to me while I dashed around pregnant, studying and looking after a toddler while he was at work all day. I tried to make him see reason that our lives would be better if both of us were earning wages properly now that we were going to have two children.

I was heavily pregnant when I completed the programme on Great Eastern Street; Joe or I would drop Junior at his nursery in the mornings where he now attended full time, and it was easy for me to get back to the nursery and pick him up after school. I was able to complete my training; sometimes it was tough but it was well worth it as I grew in confidence during those sixteen weeks, passing all my secretarial subjects some with distinctions including Teeline shorthand. What's more, I was job ready, skilled and knowledgeable in admin work. But physically, I wasn't ready in the least until my baby was born later in spring of 1985, when I went into labour at Mother's Hospital in Hackney where I had given birth to Junior. A few hours into labour and I was told my baby was in distress and so I would need a C-section. Joe and I had a little cry wondering about all the horrible scenarios that could overtake us including losing my own life.

I woke up in the maternity ward wondering why all the

other mothers had their babies in their cots next to them except me. I began to panic thinking all sorts that may have happened to my baby. A few minutes later doctors and some medical staff came to my bedside and one of them introduced himself as my consultant and told me I had a baby boy whom they had in the ICU (Intensive Care Unit) and that I could go to see him whenever I was ready. They were keeping him there to monitor his progress after his ordeal at birth. His amniotic sac had ruptured in the womb and he'd been inhaling the fluid which was choking him. I couldn't wait to go see my baby son. Joe, who was by my side all along, joined me to pay the baby a visit at the ICU. There, I washed my hands and walked along the row of incubators with babies in them on either side and I saw this baby to my right staring at me. I turned round and asked the nurse whether that was my baby and she was surprised as to how I knew. And so was I! Exactly how I felt as the baby and I stared at each other. I picked him up and on his wrist was Baby Adenuga wristband.

Joe and I deliberated outside the ICU on the name for our baby. Junior's was easy to follow as per the family tradition. Joe had expressed his desire to have all his kids bear the initial J. I looked at him curiously and he told me he would like to build on what his parents started by not just giving their first-born son the name Joseph but to have the rest of his kids share the J initials. I thought about it for a second as it was new to me; never ever heard or seen it before. It did interest me enough, though, to agree with him. We then went through all the biblical names we could think of beginning with J, from

Jeremiah to Josiah till we strayed outside the bible to agree on Jamie; we loved the sound of it. And our second son, Jamie Olanrewaju Ifeanyichukwu Adenuga was born on 4th May 1985. Three months later we invited our friends and family to his christening and partied all night at home in celebration – and our first son nearly choked to death before us on that day in August 1985. He was bouncing about to impress his friends in the house. He unwrapped a sweet and offered it to one of the kids who wouldn't take it from him so he decided to eat it himself. He threw the sweet into his mouth while simultaneously jumping up dancing. He couldn't cough or breathe. My first son was choking, but thanks to Roseline – a neighbour guest that saw him and drew everyone's attention to him – Joe grabbed hold of him and pushed the centre of his back for him to spit it out which he did to everyone's relief. 'Junior is had enough,' Junior announced at the top of his voice after he had recollected himself and the room was filled with laughter.

So there I was with these RSA credits to my name and job ready with two little boys, a home to run and still illegal in the country. I wasted no time formally engaging Mrs. Jump to look after Jamie while Junior was still attending Old Street nursery so that I could go job hunting. I found an office manager's job advert which I pursued and got, managing a small office off Mare Street. I was on £7,000 per annum. It was a private enterprise owned and managed by the proprietor, Mr. Hewitt, a middle-aged Englishman. I liked my job as I perfected my communication skills through answering and using the phone, as well as interacting with the builders and site handymen. When Mr. Hewitt was hit by financial problems, the workers were coming to the office and demanding their wages weeks running. It felt awful for me too, I'd been in the job less than a year and the business was hit by austerity. Although I watched television and listened to the news, I wasn't comfortable with the economic explanations behind the austerity as it was threatening my livelihood.

One of the builders and I talked about my prospect at the office one day in light of the company's predicament. He promised to speak with his sister who was leaving her job in the West End for a better paying one. He rang the sister, Tracy, the next day and we arranged for me to meet with her and to discuss the viability of my application for the job. I met Tracy at a cafe close to her workplace on Little Russell Street where she informed me about the job. She collected copies of my credentials from me and asked me to come for an interview in their office on Friday that week. Come Friday I walked into their office and she introduced me to her bosses at R.J. Lattimore, a group of architects. There were three partners: the principal partner and two other architects one of whom was a woman, and they all shared a medium size office. I got Tracy's phone call later that evening that I'd got the job. I couldn't thank her enough as I was sure she must have put in a word or two on my behalf. I was ecstatic as it meant a couple of grand more than I was earning. We were no longer relying only on Joe's income to care for our growing family. I paid Mrs. Jump the going rate to mind Jamie; her two grown children living with her loved Jamie especially the son who later joined the police service.

I loved the idea of working close to the West End, but less than a year later it was time for me to move on. The business was facing a downturn too and the lead partner informed me about the firm letting me go but promised to keep paying my wages until I secured another job. I looked through the paper daily in search of jobs and saw one for an administrator which I applied to at ASTMS, a trade union (Association of Scientific, Technical and Managerial Staffs). I went for the interview on Camden Road and I got the job to work in a secretarial pool to provide admin support to seven researchers and a national officer. By now my salary increased to £13k per annum – a leap of four more grand a year. I then remembered my parents' motto about education being the route to a better life. I had my RSA qualifications to thank albeit I had completed a year's business administration course prior. I loved my job that also included taking press cuttings; skim reading through the daily newspapers for relevant news topics to inform respective researcher's work with the trade union membership. By now I felt the prime minister was always addressing me personally each time I watched her speak on TV. This was Margaret Thatcher's days of urging people to empower themselves. People were being encouraged to go for home ownership, for example, a move I felt we could make now that we had a combined income.

By late 1986, we packed up our belongings from the 17th floor on Bath Street and moved into our own home at flat 1, 41

Mount Pleasant Road in Tottenham, a two-bed ground floor flat costing £41,000. We were so excited to get on the housing ladder. But our excitement was tempered by the gossip we heard about us within our community that Joe and I had the effrontery to go buying a house with no leg to stand on in the country legally. However, we stuck to our guns and reasoned that if the mortgage process was in order and successful we couldn't care less what anyone was saying about us. We just followed our instinct and braced ourselves for whatever the future was preparing to throw at us.

Chapter 8

We had just moved into our home on Mount Pleasant Road barely a year after the Broadwater Farm riot took place at the bottom of our road. It became clear to us that we had moved into one of the most run down communities in the borough. Nonetheless, we felt it was as good an area as our money could buy. I also had access to more African food shops. We enrolled Junior at Welbourne primary school on Monument Way towards Tottenham Hale and I took Jamie with me to the nursery owned by my employer while I worked next door in Camden Road. Although my employer paid the monthly creche bill, I resumed a cleaning job in some offices in Finsbury Square to boost my earnings with our mortgage in mind. Joe also transitioned from his furniture managerial job to becoming self-employed. He bought our first Amstrad computer which he used to develop his A-Class furniture business, compiling a would-be customers' database and developing his working documents. I helped him whenever I could with typing and producing templates. He also lobbied and secured a few private businesses to provide a furniture recovery service for them as well as for a number of north London councils as time went on.

I felt in need of a car as I thought it would make my run around easier with the children. But I was far from a qualified driver. And Joe had told me during our courtship that he once drove in Nigeria so I quickly worked it out that he could do the driving while I learned to drive. Joe disagreed with my idea of a car regardless of how tough I felt it was working full time with two children.

'You are not serious, darling,' Joe said to me each time I tried bringing up the issue. I had bus routes to move around alright but I was always late by the time I got to work. Not to mention that collecting the children was no less difficult on the way home.

The more I thought about it the more desperate I was becoming to drive to put an end to walking my two boys home, particularly when it was cold or snowy. I browsed local papers for used cars for sale until I found one for £250 by an agent on Enfield Road in Hackney. It was a blue Fiat 126 with sunroof, two doors and a small boot. My hope was to buy a small car which would be easy to manage, relatively affordable and be low key in terms of its visibility so not to attract the law's attention to pull me over and throw the book at me. I hadn't factored the car maintenance and upkeep into my car ownership dream. I was just blinded by the need for me to successfully multitask whenever Joe was working outside London.

Joe and I took the bus to the car dealership and the car I had seen in the paper that morning was still there.

'I've got two hundred pounds for the car.' Joe thought he'd chance the dealer to save us money, but the dealer began to walk away and left us standing there.

'Darling, I don't think he'll agree. Let's pay the asking price, take the car and go home,' I said to Joe as he watched the dealer walking back to us.

'£250 take it or leave it,' the dealer exclaimed.

With the paperwork completed we were ready to drive our car home. I was hoping Joe would drive but was I wrong.

'Here's the key,' I said, passing the car key to Joe.

'You're not serious? It's your idea to get a car; you drive it.'

'You told me you'd driven before back home,' I said to him.

'No. You drive. It's you who will be driving it, remember?' he calmly replied to encourage me to take the wheel. Panic set in me. I hadn't driven a car before in my life, I kept muttering to myself as I climbed behind the wheel. But the car was not going to get to our home if neither of us drove it! I was able to move the car into gear one and then into gear two, which saw my speed increase until we got to Stamford Hill traffic lights.

'You're doing very well, darling,' Joe said. A bus pulled into the bus stop behind us and my heart was pounding. The lights changed and I shifted the gear stick into gear one.

'Gently, darling. You are doing well,' Joe kept saying to me as I released the handbrake and the car started to roll backward. 'Pull the handbrake. Pull the handbrake. You're rolling back!'

'You do it,' I barked back at him in the car, still frightened by the sound of the bus horn that filled the air from behind to alert me of the accident that was about to happen. Joe quickly pulled up the handbrake to bring the car to a halt! I was nearly wetting myself.

I composed myself to concentrate on coordinating my clutch and accelerator then shifted the car into gear one again and was able to drive forward. Off I went into gear two and drove all the way home in the same gear regardless of the noise it was making along the way.

I got the car home, stepped out of it to take another look and was so proud of myself there and then. I couldn't wait to give my boys a spin to drive Junior to school and drop Jamie off at the nursery before heading to work.

Within six months I was having fun driving everywhere. And you are not going to believe this, I found myself pregnant again. I was beginning to draw a parallel with my mother. As I'd decided that this would be my last baby it lit the I'm-desperate-for-a-baby-girl bulb in my head. I had long been admiring mothers with prams and strollers and babies beautifully dressed in pink complete with the hanging pink baby bag. I remember crying at one of my surgery appointments even before Jamie when I confided in my GP following a false pregnancy alarm that I was dying to have a baby girl. He joked that I was looking over my shoulder too much and that I should concentrate on staying healthy. Pregnant this time in late 1987, I was so determined to have a girl that I placed bets with two of my co-workers. And the bet was that I would abandon my baby at the hospital if I gave birth to another boy. You would think I was a hundred per cent sure of having a girl even though uninformed by any medical knowledge. Charity from the admin pool and Tony, one of the researchers, each matched my £10 bet.

Joe shared in my anxiety and we shopped for a baby girl. He had landed himself three councils' furniture recovery contracts and life couldn't be any better. We represented your thriving working class family, except we weren't British. We still hadn't appropriated our legal status in the country. Neither did we discuss this with other Nigerians we knew living illegally out there. You would think it should be our collective worry as important as it was, but it didn't seem to bother us that much. Joe and I concentrated on chasing our dream for our children, the pursuit of the best for them and for our growing family as a unit. Months down the line I had to take my maternity leave.

My office threw me a send-off party at Stranglers club on Camden Road. I cleared my office desk and returned home to await the birth of my baby. As usual my boredom was compounded by the fact that I had given up my morning cleaning job a month into my pregnancy. Following Jamie's caesarean birth, the hospital was encouraging me to look forward to birthing the normal way this time and said it was a possibility. Meanwhile Joe had increased his business to include more private furniture recovery contracts from outside London, taking workmates with him to carry out the work. I looked after the home and the children while on maternity leave. Austerity persisted and we were struggling to keep our heads above water with two little mouths to feed and another on the way. Still in the thick of Margaret Thatcher years, Wall Street crashed in October 1987. Our income was no longer enough to sustain our mortgage repayments as the interest rates soared – let alone look after our home! We hardly had anything left after the mortgage was paid monthly via direct debit. The financial struggle was immense.

Free milk that the children enjoyed in schools was stopped and parents were now contributing towards their children's school dinners. The whole system was changing and it was beginning to feel like I wasn't in the know again. The recession unbearably deepened. It was during these hard times that my Julie Oluwatoyin Chidozie Adenuga came along the following year on 15th July 1988. My princess Julie had also been in distress when at the hospital as they tried in vain to encourage me to give birth to her normally this time around. So much for me trying I thought when we began to panic as we watched the baby's heartbeat on the ECG machine going down the scale rapidly. A lady nurse in the room took a glance at the monitoring equipment and said, 'I think you should ask them for the C-section, after all you've had it before. Don't let these people use you as guinea pig.' Before she could finish, Joe leaped out of the room and rushed for the doctor.

They took a look at the machine's reading and got down to business. I was having the operation under epidural, a spine injection that kept me awake to see my princess delivered. As soon as I was informed I had a bouncing baby girl I looked up at Joe who had tears of joy in his eyes; he slowly nodded as he watched the hospital staff prepare Julie. I got my wish, the baby girl I had wanted and nothing else mattered. I won my £20 bet and was over the moon! We brought Julie home and her brothers were excited to have a baby sister and I looked forward to strapping her down in her chair in the back seat of my Fiat 126!

Joe started his driving lessons before me and I followed suit as soon as I found out. He passed his driving test the first time, a month after we had our princess. It was a huge encouragement for me to give it a go but I failed it the first time. I didn't properly observe a pedestrian who had just stepped onto the zebra crossing as I applied my emergency brake. Joe and the boys couldn't console me enough. A couple of months down the line my instructor got me a cancellation slot to retake my test just around my birthday of that year. I passed it this time and couldn't be happier. And then we hatched the plan to trade in our little Fiat for a bigger car. We walked into a car showroom on Lordship Lane and completed the paperwork for a brand new Fiat Uno 60s on hire purchase.

Meanwhile the austerity persisted and mortgage interest rates continued rising. I had just returned to work after maternity leave and, luckily, my employer was footing the bill for my baby girl's nursery and my workplace creche for Jamie. Julie's nursery was based in Broadwater Farm in Tottenham where I dropped her each morning and drove off to drop Junior at Welbourne before taking Jamie to his nursery to hopefully not be too late for work.

The mortgage payments weren't viable anymore because we had the direct debit date a day after my pay day into our joint account, it was a struggle to even get a penny out for housekeeping before the mortgage had gone out of the account, leaving us little to add to Joe's pay that came at a later date. Whatever that amounted to was what we had to live on till the month end. It was difficult at times to keep the roof over our heads and care for our three little mouths, so I applied for subsidies from social services. It was a means tested assistance to support community members till their next pay day or benefit cheque. I accessed the service quite often during our hard times. Joe and I were stressed and took our frustration out on each other with numerous police call outs involved.

'You think I'm mad at you for asking me for money knowing I have none. I'm mad at myself not being able to provide when you asked for it,' my husband would say to me each time we reconciled.

We tried as much as possible to keep the children out of our arguments whether or not they were present, but it was proving difficult. We mostly argued in Yoruba in any case because the children could neither speak nor understand it, but they must have sensed it all the same to register the difference between an argument and conversation.

Back at work and my employer was in consultation with another trade union for a merger to survive the changing times. And the downside was redundancy looming for the majority of us as ASTMS and TASS unions merged to assume the name MSF (Manufacturing, Science and Finance) Union. It was bad news all round. Joe and I were on the verge of losing our home while I was facing redundancy at work. I was barely able to enjoy my baby girl that I so much prayed for; my life was getting tougher and tougher as the mortgage arrears mounted. We immediately cancelled the direct debit on our joint account for the mortgage repayment as this not only left us skint each month with other bills to pay, but also threatened to starve my whole family especially the kids. Julie's monthly nursery bill was also accumulating as I robbed Peter to pay Paul for survival. My employer paid the nursery allowance of £180 per week into my account which I was supposed to pass on to the nursery but was using for housekeeping. I owed the nursery big time and struggled to keep up with all the excuses to keep my daughter's place so that I could make it to work while battling other debts. I broke down often and hardly slept – I would lie down each night with all the grapevine gossip of us owning a home and no legal status running around my brain.

By late 1988 millions of homeowners were losing their homes; we were on the brink as we walked out of a meeting with our mortgage lender. We made up our minds to give up the flat. The lender had spoken to Joe and I at length to let go of the impossible, particularly as we had taken out a remortgage and cut down on our household expenses to no avail. I cried to the council's housing department on Tottenham High Road for my family to be possibly rehoused into social housing. They promised to write to the mortgage lender to buy us time at our home till they could move us into a temporary accommodation to await permanent housing. A few weeks later the council made good on their promise and moved us into a block of flats on Weir Hall Road in Tottenham, just off White Hart Lane. We were back to living in a block of flats this time on the first floor of a small tower block. There were a lot of children living in the building, and at the back of my mind was the fear for my young sons getting mixed up with the juvenile delinquents said to be characteristic of the area. Suffice to say this was every parent's nightmare, raising their kids in such areas. I drove my children everywhere despite the fact that we were hard up and barely had my vehicle legit on the roads. I couldn't pay multiple parking ticket notices either and as much as I wished the penalty notices away, they all came back to bite my behind in the end as I was made to pay it up all; every single one of them, for however long it took me as ordered by the court in Highgate.

We had lived at Weir Hall Road for a few months when a housing association (HA) project was ready nearby. You can imagine my joy when I received a phone call from the council to go and view the accommodation. It was an offer of one of the terrace houses in an ongoing new building project in Meridian Walk. The houses were in blocks and ours had sixteen, eight on either side. Our house was fourth on the left and had three bedrooms with a toilet and bathroom upstairs, a downstairs toilet, a living room and kitchen with a small front and back garden. Families were moved in as and when the housing phases were completed.

Moving into Meridian meant we had to move the boys to a church school closer home to continue the family tradition, and Julie joined her brothers at the school in the nursery class when she came of school age.

The HA project was completed and more families moved in, from multiple cultural backgrounds, some with little or no English language skills. A few of us tenants, mostly women, toyed with the idea of setting up a tenant association to support ourselves and to maintain orderliness in the estate full of growing children. The Estate's Tenant Association was born and I was first to chair it. We worked in partnership with our landlord the HA, the council and the local borough police team. I provided support for many of the estate's tenants especially our new ethnic minority neighbours, representing them on housing matters to the HA and the council i.e., when in need of repairs in their homes and informing our newcomers on how to get their children into nearby schools. We ran a quarterly newsletter – the Meridian Walk Estate Tenant Association – that kept us abreast on our partnership work with the stakeholders. I was enjoying facilitating others and regardless of the number of bust-ups within and around the estate by the kids, us adults were able to deal with them. We never had any serious issues getting out of hand except when it involved other youths coming to the area. And so here I was, actively involved in community engagement while my boys helped to look after their little sister.

Redundancy loomed still at work. MSF offered voluntary redundancies with a 'good' financial package, they told us. I

had been there going on four years, and the newly formed
MSF was to relocate from Camden to Southwark in south
London. Already a habitual late arriver, it scared me that I
would be at risk of losing my job if I continued to be even
later for work in Southwark. I decided that I would be better
off taking the voluntary redundancy than risk getting sacked
for poor work attendance and I then could look for another
job closer to home.

We decided on a family break for the first time to take
a breather with some of the redundancy money. I'd worry
about unemployment later, I thought. We packed our bags
and off we went to Hastings. We met with another family at
the seaside who had two children, a boy and a girl who were
the same age group as Junior and Jamie.

'Mum, please can we go to their house?' Junior was asking
me. I could see the children were whispering with each other.

'Why do you want to go to their house, Junior?' I pulled
him over to ask.

'They've got Sky and it's WWF night. So we can watch it
with them, please Mummy?'

I left the children to go join the adults and what do you
know, I quickly realised they were as crazy about WWF as we
were.

We enjoyed ourselves with our new family friends both
at the children's swing park and at the beach. We took
photographs and went back to their house to watch WWF's
Royal Rumble that evening. We took the children to a live
wrestling match event the next day and bought them WWF's

souvenirs. The wrestling was one of the reasons we took out a Sky subscription back then for the children's interests – and mine and Joe's, I must add as we watched it religiously as a family. It was and still is one of our best family outings to date. We visited the 1066 Battle of Hastings site, Sea World and the amusement arcade by the pier where the children went on rides, played robot games, the lot.

Back in London and Joe's contracts were drying up, one borough after the other with Haringey the last to go. Luckily Joe had had the foresight to go job hunting ahead of time. He got a job working with Cash Converters on Fore Street, not far from our house. Joe brought gaming gadgets home from work for the children. It was such a relief to know that we were good again, or so I thought. Although my redundancy break was uplifting and enjoyable, it came at a price. Here I was, finished spending my thousands of pounds redundancy pay and no job to return to. No matter what savings we were making from no longer paying the mortgage my jobless-ness wasn't helping in the least. Joe, however, was moonlighting as a cab driver while holding down his Cash Converters job. Although my community work involvement lessened my boredom I had never experienced such a long term unemployment before in the UK. I had tried to find another admin job but to no avail. All the jobs I saw at job agencies and centres were paying nearly £4,000 less than the £13,000 I was earning before redundancy. I talked Joe into a weekend away alone to Hastings, because I was getting really frustrated by my situation. I knew we couldn't afford another family holiday and so we organised for a family friend to keep an eye on the children for us for the short weekend break.

I came back and weeks later I found I was pregnant!

'Seriously?' Joe's face lit up despite his surprised high-pitched voice.

'Can you believe that! So much for not emulating my mother's baby factory mentality.'

'Don't say that about Mummie, darling, you are not God that gives life,' he said, trying so hard to reassure me that all would be well 'in Jesus' name' as he liked to end his wishful thinking. I didn't consider the possibility of falling pregnant when I desperately went off to clear my head. What a weekend break to ease my frustration. Gosh! I went down to our GP and came home with the confirmed news that I was expecting a fourth child.

Still redundant, we were living solely on Joe's pay cheque. It was that time again to think of what I could be doing to earn money especially now that I'd gone and broken the promise I made to myself not to have any more children. And then I heard about a government initiative offering incentives for people to retrain themselves to move into employment through training and education programmes. I have had my parents drill it into me all my life to see education as the key to success, so I started thinking the programme was for me. I would further my education and, what's more, the government's financial support would see me through, so I decided to go for teachers' training by returning to college to study for a degree in teaching studies. I felt I had the skills and experience, considering I was growing in my role as chair of my estate association in a voluntary capacity, a role I continued even while pregnant. It felt natural for me to want to learn to impart knowledge to others especially children, which I guess was reflective of my own childhood. I couldn't be more motivated by the guaranteed financial support for me to do the degree course. But first I had to give birth to my baby.

I was in my mid-thirties with this pregnancy. In an area like the estate buzzing with young people the concern was huge especially for our growing boys. We had always quarrelled over disciplining the kids the traditional way, especially corporal punishment, but we had to keep the kids on the straight and narrow in the area. I knew exactly what Joe was worried about, which were in fact also my worries, but drawing from experience, I made a secret pact with myself not to smack my kids even though I couldn't resist every once in a while. I wasn't going to put my kids through what I experienced growing up. Heaven forbid! Joe was no stranger to corporal punishment by his parents in the name of discipline. The majority of Nigerians who grew up and those still growing up back home would back me on this. What's more, we never questioned or stopped to think about its impact on us, at least I didn't. I just knew I detested corporal punishment and refused to perpetuate it on my kids if I could help it.

And so, raising our children on the estate was quite a challenge not just for us parents but also for them to find the balance in being growing children in the area and doing as they were told by Joe and I. I remember cautioning Junior once.

'Nnadim, I don't like seeing you hanging with X. You know he's trouble and a delinquent. He doesn't even live in our area.'

Nnadim was my pet name for him, it meant my father-in-law. I have one for all my children: Jamie's is my granddad, Nna Nnam, Julie is Nnedim, my mother-in-law and Jason is Nnam, my father. I had been brought up religiously to believe in reincarnation and so their pet names rolled out of my mouth each time I spoke with them.

'But where do you want me to go and play, though? Hackney?' he said with an exacerbated face. I was praying for them not to get involved in anything they couldn't talk to us about.

Fear would grip us when there was news about the rising rate of youth crime especially if they were to name worsening boroughs; ours was making all the table leagues most of the time. It was a worrying time when we heard the number of youth on youth stabbing and shooting incidents across London boroughs. Joe and I had work to do to raise our sons and daughter in the area with a latest addition on the way.

I settled back into my pregnancy routine once more, driving the kids to school and coming back home with nothing else to do. With my baby growing inside me, I was reassuring myself about furthering my education as soon as I gave birth. And following my Julie's C-section, my fourth pregnancy was going to be by elective caesarean.

We got to Middlesex Hospital as arranged and my

consultant refused to grant my wish of delivering my baby under epidural injection. She insisted she wasn't going to do it. It was general anaesthetic or nothing. You might think the reason why I wanted it was probably because I enjoyed the last epidural episode. And you would be right but not entirely. Yes it was painless watching my baby Julie being delivered, but it was crucial for me this time as I wanted to ensure that my baby and I survived the ordeal by remaining awake all throughout the process. That was how much I feared having a baby that late in life. But thanks to my consultant, on Friday 8th May, my baby son was delivered and we named him Jason Olanrewaju Ikechukwu Adenuga. I now had three boys and a girl and that was it for me and I meant it!

Following Jason's christening, I put his name down on the waiting list at St. Paul's where Julie was in the infants while the boys prepared to leave for their secondary school education. We got them into Winchmore Hill secondary school in Enfield. I was now ready, four months after giving birth, to embark on the government training and education programme – my long awaited option on the way forward and the only way I knew. This was it and all hell broke loose again in my house.

'You can't be serious, Ify, planning for higher education with four children.'

'You and I would still look after them as usual.'

'How? When you're at college and I'm at work? Just how do you plan we look after them while you are earning a degree, at your age!' Joe wasn't backing down and whenever he addressed me by name and not 'darling' I knew he was more than serious.

'The sad thing is, it's the children who'll suffer from your irrational decision of going to college,' he kept reminding me.

'We'll have financial support.'

Everything about the government's Back to Work programme rang true for me and I couldn't wait to scout round for a childminder for Jason for when I started college in September.

The financial support included everything. You had allowances for upkeep, childcare needs if you had any, and to cover your study sundries. I was ready to make my move in September. I had been in the country for over a decade, married with four growing children and still had no legal status in the land. I was heading into my forties and hadn't heard from my folks back home since I last visited and came back with Papa. All these shortcomings played on my mind each time I prepped myself to go and enrol for my teaching degree. I went and registered at my local college and later received a letter inviting me to their Foundation Course Open Day. Candidates were first met and addressed in a hall where we were given talks about what our course entailed. To become a primary school teacher you needed to specialise in an aspect of learning, which you taught upon your graduation and I chose special needs in education. You needed English and maths O levels to go straight into the university, which I didn't have. I tried to lean on my RSA English language modules I passed during my secretarial studies but was told it wouldn't suffice for me to train as a primary school teacher. The one-year foundation course was the only other route to attend university and so I settled for that and had to return to attend the induction in September.

I couldn't wait to start at the college on my Induction Day. The teacher addressing us was very encouraging. She informed us about the difference our foundation course would make to our ability to complete our degree at the university and about the difference we would make in the lives of the learners. As schools became more multicultural the education department needed teachers to support learners from all the ethnic backgrounds including those with little or no English language skills.

We were then asked to head to the main hall at the back to process our student ID cards and return to the classroom to finish off our induction. We all trooped down and I got talking with two ladies, Kate and Bridget(RIP), both Nigerians and Igbos, while we waited for the staff members to photograph students and prepare our IDs. Once done, you signed the back of the photo that they put in a lanyard which you wore around your neck in school.

As much as I chatted with my new girlfriends my heart was racing with anxiety as I went to sit down for my photo to be taken. My mind went blank as soon as they said, 'ID please'. I quickly stood up like I'd forgotten something and rushed out of the hall. I knew what he meant and had seen it coming while we waited to get the photos done. But being Nigerian, I wasn't going to discuss my fears with my new found friends just in case they spread the word to anyone else. Remember, legal status in the land has never been a topical issue among our community people.

I went back to the classroom to speak to the teacher. I told her I had no driving licence and that my passport was with the Home Office and so I was unable to complete my ID process.

'Come on.' She beckoned me to follow her back through the long corridor to the photo hall. She told one of the photographers that she was waiting on a few of us to resume her class and would appreciate them prioritising my student ID. She pushed me right in front as she spoke to her colleague who then asked me to sit down on the chair and my photo was taken there and then. Within minutes, I was handed my ID signed and sealed and I headed back to the class. My friends were just settling in as I joined them. Class dismissed and, surprise surprise, the three of us girls were going on the same bus ride home to Tottenham. They both lived in the White Hart Lane area. We chatted about our expectations and calculated the hundreds of pounds' support we would be receiving for signing up to the government empowerment programme.

I was breastfeeding Jason at four months old when we resumed our foundation course. My ever so conscious Joe remained uneasy as I dashed about picking up the children, going to college, shopping and doing the little household chores I could cope with. He was still holding down his job at Cash Converters and spending more time with the children than my busy old self. He constantly rebuked me for going back to school even as I neared the end of my foundation course. Our arguments were unabated nonetheless. We argued one night when he recounted the number of times I had failed to heed his advice. That I was always going against him when he had tried to make me see sense in focusing on raising the family against all the odds in the area. No matter how much I tried to justify my move to further my education, it didn't make sense to him.

I was beginning to make new friends from college and outside our relationship while still keeping with my friends in the community. He said that degree study was costing the family and that I was 'neglecting the children and damning the consequence of the devastating impact of my degree pursuit on them' (paraphrasing him). I felt he was emotionally blackmailing me when I had been there holding the fort when he got busier with work including working outside London for days. I had done my final assignment and put it with my bag in the car ready for the morning and Joe nearly cramped my style on the presentation day when he hid my car. I came out of the house and my car wasn't where I had parked it. I'd worked so hard for this assignment and was chuffed that I was able to finish it on time only to find I wouldn't get the chance to hand it in. So, following the argument the night before, I was hoping that it would all blow over the next day when I was due to present my final essay at college on the 1944 Education Act And The Thinking Behind It. And Joe had hid my car that morning and remained calm as I ran back and forth looking for it. I turned the kitchen upside down in anger when I couldn't make out what had happened. I smashed plates and glasses with cutlery strewn on the kitchen floor while Joe sat in the living room. I stormed out of the house and headed for Pretoria Road junction. I walked up the road and found my car parked by the Irish centre's entrance and I lost my cool. I smashed all the windows with a roadwork light I found lying on the ground. And as I walked home with my bag I ran through what story I was recounting in my head to explain what had happened to my car. I would dial 999 to report my car missing that way if they found it I would say Joe hid the car and smashed the windows. By the time I got home, two police officers, one male and one female, were already in the house.

Joe was the nicest gentleman you could ever meet in the presence of the police officers. He was calmly clearing up the kitchen debris while the male officer was listening to him; the female officer took me into the living room where she spoke with me. And all I could say to her was that Joe had been against my university study from day one and had since been punishing me for it like today when he smashed my car windows just to stop me going to college.

'Other than that he hasn't harmed or hit you?' the officer asked as if what I just said had little or no consequence, and I nodded. She went back to the kitchen entrance and stood behind her colleague and they were both now listening to Joe. I could hear him too from the living room even though the service window in between the living room and kitchen was shut.

The woman officer asked Joe, 'If you say she doesn't cook, or wash or look after the children in the house because of her studies, Mr. Adenuga, where do you come in in all that?'

A lightbulb lit up in my head. Why hadn't I used that punchline the night he was emotionally blackmailing me?

It still didn't explain why he was so against me returning to college. University was the way forward for me to better my job opportunity. The officers whispered between themselves in the corridor for a second and the male officer came to join me in the living room. This time, and first of all, he informed me that nothing was going to happen since no one was hurt but that it would help him a great deal if I could tell him the truth about my smashed car windows. He was looking me straight in the eyes. I did a quick glance at my watch to check the time for my 11.30am college presentation.

Before I could look back at him he said, 'I take it you know what happened to your car, perhaps, you did it out of anger at your husband, Mrs. Adenuga?' I quietly nodded. The officers went ahead to advise us both as well as commending us for studying while raising our children. They said we should try and communicate more with each other to realise the good in my decision to further my education and what that could bring for both of us and the family. We both thanked them individually and managed a little smile all round as I made haste to dash off as soon as the officers walked out of the house. I now had to take the bus to get to college in time for my presentation which I passed with flying colours.

Chapter 9

Igot a B+ for my assignment and passed all my foundation course papers on a high and was ready to go to North London University (now Metropolitan University). Surprise, surprise, as I was getting on with my fresher year at the university in September 1993 Joe was starting his foundation course to a computer science degree at Tottenham college. I took Jason's buggy in the car with me to take him into lecture rooms and the university cafe and library. I would throw my white shawl round me to breastfeed him during lectures and during group work. I had a good friend – a fellow Nigerian student working at the university's library who allowed me time and space to breastfeed or change Jason's nappy while studying at the centre. I was always running late for my lectures and this was impacting my team spirit and relationship with others. A number of them found it difficult to tell me this as much as they loved working with me, but I knew and constantly made them aware of my commitment to not disappoint them at all cost. I suffered the consequences nonetheless as every now and then I was always the last to hear or receive information on group work assignments.

Bridget(RIP), Kate and I were having the time of our lives studying for our degrees – we were not short of money and even had access to hardship grants from the uni bursary when times were hard. My life revolved around my studies and nursing Jason while Joe studied and still retained his Cash Converters position from where he continued to spoil the children with new gadgets. By now my teenage boys were becoming some of the most easily recognised in and around our estate. They played out with their friends, although fights and quarrels did break out every once in a while to the extent that us parents were having a go at each other at times. Youth problems became the focus of estate association meetings. Some tenants raised concerns about unknown youths in the area and accused the estate's youths of inviting them in. We also had to consider the fact that they may be coming in uninvited, so the debate went on. In the end we decided we needed a play area for the estate children. HA and the council installed a playpen, which could be locked, and was only for the use of the estate's children, supervised by the tenants.

Our children were beginning to take charge of themselves since everyone knew the score. Even when it came to a particular luxury like any other kid had, they would ask and if we said no, we always gave them the reason why. They once asked for a go-kart and we told them we couldn't afford it so they went out gathering broken gadgets including broken pallets lying about on street corners and along Commercial

Road. With tools from Joe's toolbox they assembled the go-kart they craved. They would proudly display it in the estate and even gave their friends a go on it. As much as they were mindful of upsetting us they felt free to ask questions and say how they felt in any manner of communication with me. All of these made my study days easier as they busied themselves and that kept them from getting into too much trouble while we were at work and uni.

One of my first-year assignments was on creative writing in which I told about the experience of eating one of our cultural meals, fufu and vegetable soup. My course tutor Elizabeth Burns loved how meticulously I described using the tongue to separate all the soup condiments in my mouth to swallow the fufu lump first before starting to chew and swallow all that was left in my mouth. She was fascinated by my story telling so much that she talked about my essay at the end of year party. She also mentioned the fact that as an adult student and a nursing mother I'd done so well in my first year. I had left Jason with a friend in order to stay behind for the party and was on cloud nine on this particular Friday and had my excellent course modules report to prove it. My life was going right; married with four children. What more could I want? I had a couple of glasses of white wine at the party and was looking forward to getting home and impressing Joe with my end of year report. I checked the time and it was nearly ten past three and I had to be at St. Paul's for Julie and dash to Winchmore Hill to pick up the boys too. Off I went in my car, joined the Seven Sister's Road traffic going down to

Haringey, and the traffic was stretched for nearly half a mile ahead of me to St. Ann's Road junction bridge. I looked at the time again and it was nearly three-thirty. I put my thinking cap on and thought about how to beat the traffic. If only I could risk taking the bus lane and do a left turn a little in front to boycott the long traffic queue and come out by the police station on St. Ann's Road. Running the bus route then attracted a fine of £20. There was no CCTV at the time. They only used the bus driver's image of evidence of motorists driving in the lane, I think, to bring them to court. I soon enough veered into the bus lane, going as fast as I could to turn left into Moreton Road; there was no bus approaching behind to catch me on camera. As I indicated left to turn, a female police officer stepped in front of my car from behind a big conker tree at the beginning of the road, asking me to pull over. I heard myself telling me off as soon as I parked the car. Not only was I breaking the law by taking the bus lane I was likely risking another offence that I hadn't thought about because I was on a high from getting a good end of year result. And then I remembered I had yet to appropriate my legal papers in the country!

'Can I see your licence? Step out of the car please, madam.'

I was regretting taking the bus lane now, but I had no time for regrets as I handed her my driving licence and calmly stepped out of my car. I thought of begging seeing as it was just the two of us and she seemed like a nice woman, maybe she would understand.

'I'm sorry, officer. I only took it 'cause it was a short distance to this road,' I said, pointing to the corner road we were on. 'I'm rushing to pick up my children from school.'

Even though her senior brothers were close by, the school wouldn't allow Junior to pick Julie up unless we gave him a note. And so, I continued pleading with the officer in desperation for her to forgive me and help save my children.

While I rambled on in between confirming my name and address, the officer said to me, 'We've been drinking, have we? How many drinks have you had today and what type of drink?'

I burst into tears and was almost recoiling away from her and dropped all my excuses, still trying to beg my way out of the awful situation I found myself in.

'Please, officer, I only had a drink or two, that's all. I rushed out to go get—'

The officer was having none of my excuses. 'Really? Just one drink or two? What drink did you have?' She was holding her car door open for me to get in.

'What of my car?' I asked as if I didn't know the score.

'Lock your car and let's go. You'll get your phone call and you can call someone to come get it. Come on, come on, let's go.'

I locked the car and, feeling so disappointed with myself, I got into the police car and off we went to Tottenham police station where I was asked to empty my bag on the counter. The custody officer behind the desk introduced himself and drilled me through the process from taking down my details to reading me my rights and informing me on the reason I was there. Hello, I never knew!

'You can make your call now on the phone over there, Ify.'

I called Joe at work but he wasn't there. He'd left when the school called him around half four to say that the children were still in school. I now needed another call to my house which the officer sympathetically agreed to. I called my home.

'Don't worry, I know the junction. I'll go and get the car when the children are settled in bed,' Joe assured me. I began to feel a little resigned to my fate. My children were safe; that's all that mattered.

'You broke the rule, darling, but look on the bright side of finishing your first year at the uni.'

'I love you,' I said to him.

'I love you too,' he responded.

As soon as I put the phone down an officer walked me to my cell and closed the door. All sorts of thoughts were running through my head. I thought about my punishment, a ban surely. How was I going to cope dropping the children to school and getting to uni... I must have dozed off eventually.

I was woken up early morning around six and brought to the custody counter again. I was full of disgust with myself in my sober mood. The sergeant behind the desk asked me to confirm my name and address, again.

'The officers are going to interview you. Last night you said you didn't want a solicitor, is that still the case?' he asked.

'Yes,' I responded.

Two officers took me to the interview room where we sat

down. One officer prepared the cassette tape for the interview recording. My heart was pounding as I watched the officer put the tape into the machine and press play.

'Ready? This interview has been tape recorded. I am... the other officer present is... I'm interviewing,' he turned to me and said, 'please could you state your name and date of birth?

'You were arrested on suspicion of driving under the influence of alcohol...'

Me declining to have a solicitor was also confirmed on the tape, not sure what good a solicitor was going to make; I'd had a drink and drove in the bus lane. Besides, I was more concerned about damage control so not to have my legal status revealed by involving more people in my case.

I was beginning to hate the sound of my name for the amount of times I'd had to confirm who I was and the day I was born! The interview was concluded about ten or so minutes later, and after all that I was handed a court date document and charged with drink-driving and driving in the bus lane. I was free to go after that. I asked for a favour from the custody officer for me to make a call to Joe and he agreed.

I collected my things and walked out to the front desk to wait. Minutes later Joe arrived with baby Jason strapped down on the back seat and we left the station.

I got home and was worried sick about my upcoming court date. I just wanted to curl up and die. How could I have spoilt the wonderful mood I was in when I left uni the day before? I was full of regrets, but Joe was lending me words of endurance. We both had an idea that the outcome of the court case would likely be a year's ban with some penalty points on my licence and a fine. We were almost sure of this seeing as it was my first drink-driving offence. Not even the six weeks summer holiday that I was looking forward to spending with the children could pacify me. Like we thought, I got the year ban and three points on my virgin licence. I can't remember how much fine I had to pay too. It was a great lesson learned. When I thought of embarking on financially supported studies it didn't mean all my worries were over. I had to learn to also be mindful of law and order as I developed myself.

The youths swelled in number in and around the estate during the summer holidays. We got them coming from other pocket areas of Tottenham and some of them went to the same schools as our children. Junior was easily recognised as the leader of the pack in his skinny vivacious self. He and his siblings would let their friends into the house to play and listen to music especially when Joe and I were not around. We tried our best to accommodate the children and their friends. And we got to know some of these friends and their families became close with us too. We were hoping our families' friendship would suffice to keep our children on their best behaviour.

This worked for a while but our house phone rang one night and it was Edmonton police station.

The caller introduced himself as the custody officer and informed us that Junior had been arrested with four or so other youths on suspicion of theft and vandalism.

'Could you come down to the station, Mrs. Adenuga, so that—'

'I'll be there right away, sir.' I put the phone down and didn't dare to look Joe's way where he sat watching TV. I called a cab straight away and arrived at Edmonton police station that late evening.

I didn't know how to handle the fact that my child was grappling with the law like the ones we saw on TV; Black youths in particular being arrested and put through police routines. I hated myself and I was so emotional by the time I stepped into Junior's cell. He had his face covered with both hands as soon as he saw me and shook with fear. And all I could say to him was, 'Nnadim, what happened?'

Junior had gone out with his friends and looted one of the kiosks on Commercial Road. They'd hidden loaves of bread and cans of coke under my dustbin shed in my front garden. I ended up acting as an 'appropriate adult' for Junior and the rest of the boys. The officers coached me on what to do and say during their interviews for my son and the boys.

They all were bailed pending more investigations. I was gripped with the fear of my Junior going off the rails. How was I going to cope if he got worse while I still had the rest of my children to worry about? I kept questioning myself. Joe punished him nonetheless; we grounded him for a time and cautioned him to mind the type of friends he hung with outside the house. Jamie seemed to be managing alright on his own both at home and school and rarely ventured outside the house, preferring to remain in his room and make things, draw or play computer games.

I returned to uni for my second year and with the kids back at school, I could breathe again. Then came the revised immigration rule that said that only children born before 1st January 1983 were deemed British citizens unless one or both their parents are citizens. It hit us like a ton of bricks as we realised only Junior was British out of our family of six. We hired a law firm to rectify the children's statuses first and then hopefully we would be able to appropriate ours. In fact the law firm had advised us to do it this way so that the Home Office would take into consideration the kids' citizenship and not break up the family. A couple of months later we received their citizenship certificates and with a further instruction to the legal firm; our 'leave to remain indefinitely' was stamped into mine and Joe's passports. We were so happy at last after all these years! I felt whole! And all I could think of was HOME. We immediately planned for another family holiday this time to Nigeria with the children to see our parents and folks we'd left behind over fifteen years ago. We went shopping and made sure the children had all their jabs for the trip and the date was set for a two week holiday during the summer vacation of 1995.

The children were looking forward to seeing our folks in the flesh, the majority of whom they had only spoken with over the phone several times. They never ceased to make fun of their telephone conversations with them.

'Hello Junior. How are you?'

'Fine.'

'And your brothers?'

'Fine.'

'And your sister?'

'She's fine too.'

And the conversation would run dry. The children giggled a lot after such conversations with our home folks. We sent money ahead of time for my parents to travel from the east to Lagos to wait for our return. We didn't want to take the kids to the east as well within the short space of time we were going to stay out there, besides my brothers lived and worked in Lagos. Charlie and Henry worked in the commercial transport business. Nelson, who had gone to a technical school after elementary school, was an apprentice at a Lagos furniture firm learning how to build couches and other furniture, while Hope and Rose were married and lived with their respective families in the east. Hope, a stay at home mum, by now had about eight children with her husband in Nkalagu, while Rose, an auxiliary nurse, had had five children and was living with her husband in Okigwe township where she worked at the hospital. Hope definitely followed in our mother's footsteps alright, but hers was down to her husband's religious faith. As catholics, birth control is out of their relationship equation. I looked forward to seeing my parents and seeing my mother-in-law for the second time.

The children were elated when we informed them we were going on a family trip to see their grandparents. We got all the necessary shopping to take with us for the children, canned vegetables and treats.

'Can we buy Grandma and Granddad exercise bikes to keep fit?' Junior asked as we shopped one day and I told him bikes were the last things on their bucket list, so to speak. We got soft play toys and baseball caps for their cousins and shirts for Granddad and uncles and African hollandaise print for Grandma and aunties. It would be the first time the children had flown, apart from Jamie's air force camping experience, during his RAF young cadet membership.

It was a night flight that took us from Heathrow and arrived six in the morning at Lagos Murtala Mohmmed Airport (MMA). With all the expectations the children had flying home, they were very uncomfortable at the airport's humid environment. 'I need a drink, Mummy,' Junior said, the rest of the children looked weary and withdrawn.

'Darling, keep an eye on the children. Let me get some change and drinks.' Joe dashed off to the money exchange stall and ten to fifteen minutes later he came back carrying soft drinks and water for the children. I watched over them while he rushed out of the arrival hall to find an airport taxi that took us to his mother's in Festac village where we stayed throughout the holiday. My folks visited us from Charlie's at Orile Iganmu and we visited them too from Festac village. My brother would have our community people come round whenever we visited his place.

My children were getting to know their cousins and grandparents and having a blast socialising with people around them. However, the sight of many unknown insects and bugs scared the living daylights out of them.

'Don't kill it; chase it away,' one of the children would say to their cousin who was about to stamp on the insect or bug to kill it. Our folks found their empathy for animals fascinating.

'So, what if it's a scorpion coming after you, won't you kill it before it stings you?' Their cousins laughed at them each time they saw the anguish in their faces when they were about to get rid of a bug.

Auntie Morayo's twin daughters and two younger sisters took the children sightseeing. When they came back one evening, Junior said, 'We saw people playing Mario Nintendo. Can we go there and play sometime?'

'OK,' I said.

'Yeah,' came the children's chorus.

Auntie Morayo taught the children how to beat the local drums that they had in the house and the children couldn't get enough of it.

'Here, you can have this and you can have this one too.' Auntie Morayo gave them a mini African drum each to take back to London with them.

'Thank you, Auntie,' Junior and Jamie both said excitedly.

The next day the children went on another sightseeing trip and this time Junior and Jamie, accompanied by their cousins, stopped at the game centre they'd seen the last time. They came back and their cousins told of how Junior and Jamie wowed the people so much. I looked at Jamie's smiling face.

'They didn't know how we could get to that level, Mummy,' Junior said to me and I could see he was very proud of himself.

'The people didn't want us to leave. They said they enjoy watching us play the game,' Jamie said, 'with ease,' he hastened to add, and all the children started laughing.

We moved the fun to Orile Iganmu every now and then and it was so pleasing to see my parents truly happy after all these years I had been in self-exile.

'I know you are a good girl for your mama,' Mama said to my seven-year-old daughter who just grinned at her. She must have been wondering what in the world was her grandma saying. But I could just imagine her trying to find out if she was as good a daughter to me as I was to her, I suppose. But will never know – bless her.

My parents were in turn pleased to see the maturity in me in raising four children. By the time we were ready to return to England, the children had met all their cousins, grandparents and extended relatives in Lagos. They also enjoyed the unusual atmosphere in the different eateries like Suya spots in the bustling rowdy streets of Lagos.

Come the morning my family was returning to the UK, the children said their tear-jerking goodbyes as we left in a chartered taxi for the airport.

By the time we got back, our estate had changed a little. There were stories about youths causing mayhem and these were again discussed at the following estate association meetings. We decided to form a youth wing of the association and Junior was appointed as the chair. With the completion of the final housing phase, new families, mostly bilingual, were moved into the blocks and their children needed to assimilate and mix with the existing estate's youths. I was beginning to get complaints as chair from many parents that some children were not keeping to playing in the designated pen but instead vandalising cars and flower hedges around the estate. This was also becoming a big concern for both the HA and the council. It was decided that we would get CCTVs to improve our neighbourhood watch around the estate for everyone's peace of mind. Most of the young people deemed troublesome were Junior and Jamie's peers, which was a big concern for Joe and I. Junior in particular would have his friends converge at my front porch spending hours chatting at the top of their voices and sometimes I would be with them in my living room as they played and listened to music just to keep them out of public sight. The youths were predominantly Black Africans, Caribbean and Indians as well as some white kids too. By now Junior was turning into a full-blown rap music enthusiastic. By mid-90s he was Tu Pac crazy. He began to wear bandanas on his head like him and sing his lyrics morning, noon and night. He would disappear all evening and when I asked where he'd been upon return, he told me he was DOING MUSIC with friends. That bothered me. Since the Edmonton arrest matter I was concerned about how Joe would react to the excuse that meant we had no idea where he was.

That we were not happy about his new calling was an understatement, especially as we still saw him hanging out with the boys we had cautioned him to stay away from. And the fact that both Joe and I were away all day at work and college wasn't helping matters. Junior carried his vinyl record bag about with him and played music all day long in the house when he wasn't disappearing for the day. Until he started to ask me for lifts, to drop and pick him up from wherever he was doing his music. By now Junior was nearly six feet tall. 'Mum, please could you drive me to the high road? Please, Mum.'

And as much as I was helping him out, I was petrified as to how I'd explain it to Joe should he find out. Tottenham by this time was rife with youth crime in the 90s and into the millennium. Joe and I rushed to Tottenham High Road once, following a stabbing near Northumberland School behind the north London social services (now Spurs' ground).

'People got stabbed on the high road and the police are there. I saw Junior out there too,' a little child came running into my house to tell me. Joe and I jumped into the car and headed for the spot on the high road.

'Junior won't kill me; Nnadim won't kill me o,' I kept voicing aloud, like Mama in those days, as we drove into the high road. We quickly parked a few yards away from the crowd. Joe, who'd been quiet since we left, opened his door, slammed it and began briskly walking to the other side of the road. He wasn't involved in the incident, but he got grounded all the same.

We didn't need a rocket scientist to tell us what the impact of both of us at college was having on the children especially as their interests in music grew. It was one of the toughest times raising them and what a catch-22 it was when we both still loved and played music in the house, bought musical instruments as presents for the children and then turned round to tell them off about playing loud music for fear of upsetting the neighbours. Already many of these neighbours were now almost writing Junior off as the ringleader of the boisterously troublesome kids in the estate. And this was causing arguments at home between Joe and I as I continued to drive Junior to industrial and rundown estates as well as fenced off commercial venues to do his music with his mates.

I had changed courses at the end of my second year at the university and moved from teaching studies to education. I was finding it stressful juggling my life, raising my family, keeping up with my studies and managing my social and private life. Not to mention keeping up appearances within my London community of both Igbos and Nigerians at large. And this was at the height of schools being put under pressure by Ofsted to better children's education and to improve learning opportunities for all the mixed ability groups from different multicultural and ethnic backgrounds. They were coming up with new policies and agendas on how to teach children to increase their potential, particularly those with special needs. As a trainee teacher you self-administered and organised your course work including block practice and coursework diaries. And these got inspected not just by your course tutor but also your school placement teacher who then reported back to your tutor. By the time I'd finished my second-year block practice I ended up in hospital for three weeks with backache.

I consulted my course tutor who agreed with me to change my degree course to reduce the stress I was experiencing with my teaching studies. By this time I had enough modules under my belt, including English language, to finish my remaining year studying education and film production, the latter my way of fulfilling my childhood love for film. I had also kept up with my extra English class at the uni library every Wednesday after lectures for a couple of hours all through my first two years. By now I had been dabbling with scriptwriting in my spare time with no specific aim; just toying with the idea of scripting a blockbuster film to the extent that I had written to head of BBC's film of the year programme. I kept his reply for years, although now I can't remember what he said in response. Neither could I remember why I wrote to him and what it was exactly I wanted. This sounds bonkers now but back then I was seriously dreaming of producing THE script!

Joe meanwhile was also busy with his studies and still working part time at Cash Converters. I was at home with Jason one day when the post came, one brown envelope with tens of stamps on it from Nigeria and addressed to Joe. On the flip side of the envelope were Nelson's details. I was angry at first wondering why my brother should be writing to my husband without my knowledge. I could only think of one reason why and that would be to beg for money behind my back. It wasn't difficult to know why he didn't want me to know. And so I opened the letter. To my horror Nelson was explaining that he had just returned to Lagos from the village where he had gone for the funeral of his big sister, Rose. I read that line again to realise who was dead: none other than the younger of my two sisters. I screamed and felt like jumping out of the window. Pauline from two doors away and another neighbour came by and asked if there was anything they could do for me. Quickly they rang for Joe and and left a message for him at the uni. When I rang home for more information on my deceased sister, I was told that Rose died giving birth to her sixth baby that didn't survive. It took me a while to get over losing one of my sisters, again. I never got to spend time with her in our adult years seeing as I left the country before she went on to gain her auxiliary nurse education, get married and live in Okigwe township with her family.

Chapter 10

With Junior and Jamie attending Winchmore Hill secondary school and Julie doing another couple of years to the end of her primary education at St. Paul's and All Hallows, I visited the school by appointment. Jason was starting school that September 1997. A South African vicar had recently taken over the post and so I was meeting with him for the first time. He got out the register and wasted no time informing me that Jason's place had been withdrawn because his parents hadn't maintained regular Sunday service attendance in the last year. I knew the score but was furious that they hadn't even bothered to find out why I was not seen at the church all that time. I told him their actions were totally unacceptable if the church didn't bother to come looking for me, drop me a note via my daughter or pick up the phone and ring me all this while! To pull my child's place without pre-warning me was discriminatory and against my right both as a parent and a fellowship of the church. I was now faced with finding a school for my baby son in the dying minutes which I feared would be tricky because schools only admitted children in their catchment areas. I could see the guy was playing the 'I'm new here and just following orders' card but I let him have a piece of my mind and promised him I would write a complaint letter to the borough's education board. Not only did I take Jason elsewhere, I also took Julie out of St Paul's. I wrote to the council and copied in both the vicar and the school headmaster, to which I've never received a reply from either of the bodies to date!

And my Julie cried her heart out during the transition to Highfield primary school in Enfield.

'Nnedim, you will like it in Enfield, OK?' I would say to her to get this little girl to trust that I knew what I was doing. I couldn't console her enough.

'Why can't I stay with my friends?'

'You'll make more nice friends in Enfield, you'll see. Besides, I would have to drop you before Junior and Jamie and come back and pick you up afterwards. How do I cope with that and still go to uni?'

'I'll walk,' cried my princess. 'I want to be with my friends.'

Pretty determined, I went to Highfield primary school one day to seek admissions for my two youngest. I already had two children in the secondary school, so I walked in on this day and stood by the corridor and followed a member of staff as she was about to enter the staff room.

'Sorry, can I have a word, ma'am?'

She stepped outside the room and stood next to me.

'I have two boys at the secondary school and was wondering if I could get Jason and Julie admitted here so that

I can collect them together please. That would mean a great deal as I still have to get to uni in Holloway Road and back to pick them up from different places.'

She listened for a second longer than I'd stopped talking and quietly said, 'Wait here. I'll be right back,' and she went into the staff room. I kept willing it in my mind for it to be true that she could help me. A few seconds later, she came back to the door and asked me in. I was taken to see the deputy head where I completed my children's application forms and was handed the necessary documents for them to resume the following Monday. I left there feeling like I'd won the lottery!

So you can imagine me waiting by the corridor one day for Julie and Jason to come out as usual. I saw them coming; Jason ran to hug me before Julie got to me in her moody self since leaving St. Paul's and said, 'Mrs. X says to call you.'

'OK, stay here with your brother, I'm coming. Did she say why?'

'No,' she replied but not looking up at me.

Eager to know, I got to the classroom.

'Hello, Mrs. Adenuga, have a seat. Julie is a very smart girl but she's very moody at times for no reason. She works well with others and can be very helpful but when in that mood swing, she becomes angry and lash—'

'Sorry Mrs. X, she's finding it hard to deal with leaving her friends back at her old school. I'll talk to her.'

'Julie's a very bright child and friends go to her. I'm sure if you talked to her she'll be OK.'

I left there feeling relieved she hadn't done anything

terrible but could understand how she felt. I got back to her and Jason and remained cheerful.

'Let's go,' I said to them as we began to walk out of the building to the car. 'It's nothing, Nnedim. She tells me you have friends that like to work with you.' I was hoping that she'd take the bait, and, she did.

'Yes it's x and...'

It did take her some time to settle in at Highfield but she remained her clever self while looking after her brother Jason. I picked them all up from school, which worked in my favour! At last I had the four of them in the same borough of Enfield.

It didn't bother me that they were no longer attending church schools. The church school education tradition was passed down to me by my parents who inherited it from theirs. But I had come to terms with the fact that I had never understood religion anyways right from childhood and I had grown none the wiser into adulthood. Ever since the Sunday Mama beat the crap out of me in the village for uttering some inappropriate question or comment in the church during service.

I felt wronged by the fact that none of my church brethren thought to come look for me to find out what was stopping me from attending church. I had discovered from my last trip home how much my parents had aged and needed my regular care as the first born even though I was living away from home. Their care demands and news of their wellbeing at risk every now and then because of poor living conditions were enough to stress me out even more as I juxtaposed supporting them in

Nigeria with taking care of my family in the United Kingdom. This made me question what role my faith played in my life if the decision to overturn Jason's place was decided by fallible mortals like myself. The thought of the church being far more concerned about my missing tithes than whether I was sick or stressed was very sad for me. Don't get me wrong – the church needs money for administration, resources and repair costs but church administrators should also have found out what had happened to me. And with that confirmed, I took my leave from religion henceforth and concentrated on my studies and raising my family the best I could. I read widely to support my lifetime decision to quit all belief systems – from Dawkins, Hitchens and many more humanist literature out there. I embraced my divorce from religion but remained in the closet where my community people were concerned. I kept my viewpoints to myself and went with the flow when in their midst. With my departure from religion I began to develop representing the marginalised of our society. I was speaking up at local events and in public against all forms of discrimination, building on my community engagement skills and knowledge as my own way of making a real difference. That sealed it for me. From then on, all the personal profiles I completed got ticked as having NO RELIGION!

I was quite enthusiastic about how far I had come, though my final year at the uni in 1997/98, was another year's stretch 'cause of my change of discipline. Life was still tough but the family was getting on alright at this time; the government introduced a policy that replaced student grants with student loans. You were lent money to complete your degree and would start the repayments as soon as you gained employment and earned over a given salary threshold. Joe and I accessed the loan towards the end of our studies. We continued to do the best we could to keep our children safe and out of trouble in our area yet I knew deep in my heart that it wasn't going to be easy.

I chose to do a research project for my dissertation. I wanted to work with young people, particularly the estate youths. I felt I needed to engage with them in order to gain more understanding of how to effectively communicate with them and find out what they thought about us adults where many of us had so many bad things to say about them. I recruited up to a dozen boys and girls and took them on the journey to explore what the government's New Deal programme had in store for young people versus what they thought about the programme and what they would prefer. They resented the idea of making the programme mandatory which meant they risked a reduction or total stoppage of their benefits if they didn't sign up. The government was determined on delivering New Deal as the golden bullet at the time to tackle youth unemployment while many young people saw it as being geared towards forcing them into any kind of employment or training regardless of what they would really like to do.

My dissertation was a twenty-minute documentary about the government's New Deal programme for young people and what they thought it meant to train and support them into work, apprenticeship or self-employment.

Many young people were chasing their keen interest in music making, so my documentary took my working group to the job centre to learn first-hand about the New Deal options giving them the chance to ask as many questions as they wanted to enhance their decision to embark on the programme. The group also visited a music recording studio by Kings Cross station to understand the elements and skills involved in both making and recording songs as well as how to break into the music industry.

Ansalem, the studio manager, talked them through the musical instruments in the building and out of the blue Junior asked, 'Can we make a song now?' staring at the instruments in front of them.

To Junior's surprise, Ansalem replied, 'Yeah, let's make one.'

Junior looked up at him and everyone's laughter filled the room. And this completed the middle of the documentary.

It ended with the group returning to my house for an overall feedback session. They were fed too: some jollof rice, salad and chicken. The group discussed their experiences in comparing their interests to the two visits. Not a single one of them was in favour of the government's programme, citing the length of time it would take them to earn enough for a pair of 'decent' trainers. But they believed strongly that they could follow their music making calling by 'hustling' on their own until they made it. It sounded easier said than done at the time, but that completed my documentary. Joe worked with me to put it together from the editing right through to post-production at the uni film studio. I handed in my dissertation and passed my degree with Honours (Education & Film Studies) in 1998.

I was now an unemployed graduate with four children. Joe had a year to go while still retaining his part-time work. He was even holding down another part-time job at our uni library one day a week as he studied for his computer science degree. He facilitated students at the library, helping them to use both the computers and the printers to process their coursework. In the end I had to sign on to claim every possible benefit I was entitled to for survival. Meanwhile Simone, the daughter of Pauline the neighbour that came to my rescue upon the news of my younger sister passing, was doing some mobile cleaning work at the time. I swallowed my pride and asked her to introduce me to her contractor, and I secured a contract cleaning private homes. I would drive to three to five homes at different times scheduled on my timesheet to clean these houses from top to bottom each weekday. I dusted, washed dishes, made beds, hoovered the whole house and threw the trash out.

One day, Julie asked, 'Mum, how can you go to university and decide to do cleaning jobs afterwards?' I replied that I would do anything to put food on the table. She just didn't understand I was doing the job because I was bored easily and not making me money. I was willing to do the cleaning job and had my own car for mobility. It was easily earned money where the contractor paid my tax before bagging up my weekly net wages. This brought mine and Pauline's family close together and she and I were spending many evenings together chilling either at mine or hers.

I worked mostly in the Wood Green, Highgate and Hornsey areas. The pay wasn't impressive but I was doing something to earn money and help Joe out. I continued to check the local papers for jobs while I did this until I found one that said my borough council was recruiting for admin positions with the social services. I quickly applied for this and got the job. It was providing admin support to social workers based on Tottenham High Road, a stone's throw from my house. I was one of a pool of admin support team members where I met my beautiful Caribbean friend, Roxanne, a social worker that introduced me to Appropriate Adult (AA) volunteering. I had acted as one before for Junior and his mates in the vandalised kiosk incident on Commercial Road. Roxanne signposted me to Rainer charity organisation to meet with the project manager. The organisation has since changed its name to Catch-22. Their office was also just off Tottenham High Road where we met and discussed my interest in volunteering. I enrolled on the two weeks training and started getting deployed to the police stations to shadow AAs in practice to gain more experience. I was doing this while I worked with the social services.

The experience was both fulfilling and reflective on how I was hoping to raise my own children. I couldn't imagine any of them getting into trouble with the police anymore knowing I was an AA volunteer. It was unspoken and I didn't have to caution them again, they just knew that it would be bad news should they get into trouble and we heard about it. Since becoming a volunteer I told my children that I would be the first to give them up should they mess about with the law. Contrary to the stereotypical saying about African and Caribbean parents strictly ruling for their children not to bring police to their doorsteps and that the police were the enemy.

'You might not believe me, but the police are your friends. You must be on the same side with the law to see them that way,' I told our children.

I couldn't honestly say I knew all that my children got up to outside the house but can tell they knew what I meant when I said, 'Don't get involved in anything outside the house that you can't talk to us about inside.' That would have been incredibly difficult for me to call if I was to stand by my child as an AA volunteer; I had the opportunity and privilege to relate to and counsel the young people I came across whenever I could at police stations and off police premises. By now I had amassed a wealth of experience of working and communicating with the youths. I took time to develop my growing interest to inform, advise and guide them where possible in order that they steered clear of trouble in their journey into adulthood.

My admin position with the social services was renewed at the end of the first year that saw me into the millennium.

And then I read about a Reed's Job Fair event happening locally at the Irish centre near my house. The employment zone was a Reed programme in a number of inner city boroughs including Haringey. I attended the Saturday event where we were informed about Reed's plan to recruit locals from the borough to staff the zones. They would train them up to be personal advisers to move the long term unemployed into sustainable work. And then I saw Bianca was one of the Reed staff addressing us. I couldn't wait to meet her after the event. I hadn't seen her since we graduated from uni a couple of years back. We were good friends and this extended to our families becoming friends. I told her I needed a job and had just finished a contractual one with the council. She invited me to her Hackney office on the Monday where she introduced me to her boss and I was given an interview appointment the next day and asked to email my CV. I talked at length about my AA supportive role during my interview and my social services work experiences. I began to talk about my dissertation on the New Deal programme and Bianca's boss and I couldn't stop talking! I came out feeling I'd given it my all plus the fact that all my skills, knowledge and work experiences were transferable to training as a personal adviser to help people into work. I left to go pick up my children from school that afternoon, we got home and I was fixing the kids' dinner when the phone call came from Bianca offering me the personal adviser job in Hackney.

We helped our unemployed clients to develop their CVs, their interview techniques and held job search workshops specialising in their fields of interest. I had two weeks training to step into this new position where I quickly realised that success in the job depended on more on your ability to work with people than to find a job and shove them into it. I met people of diverse racial and social backgrounds and employment needs. As personal advisers we had up to sixty caseloads at a time and all we did all day was fish for job vacancies to match the CVs, speaking with would-be employers about their job specifications to inform our clients and prep them for possible interviews. We spent up to £5,000 on each client to prepare and move them into work. It was an exciting time in my adult life after my motherhood adventures.

During my second year of working at the zone in 2001, Joe graduated in computer science while still keeping his Cash Converters job. Joe being his DIY old self dreamt big after his graduation. Rather than look for work in the IT industry he thought of starting his own computer centre, and the idea was born seven months later in early 2002. He rented workspace on Great Eastern Street and furnished it ready for training the public. In no time he upped his dream level to doing exactly what Reed was doing. He put the proposal together to the DWP (Dept of Work & Pension), who approved his application and iTech Training Centre was born, preparing unemployed people from Hackney to move into work. I helped with his staff recruitment, interviewing and hiring them while I was still at Reed. I took with me one hell of a wealth of knowledge and skills from Reed's employment when I resigned to join forces and run our family business, the iTech Training Centre's own employment zone.

Joe was the centre's Managing Director and I the

Operations Manager. We employed an administrator and IT facilitator and had between one to ten client referrals daily from all Hackney job centres. Life couldn't be happier, Joe drove to work while I dropped the kids to school before joining him. I would leave work early once a week to shop and was able to get home and prepare dinner most times before Joe came home. iTech business grew so fast that we moved to bigger premises on Mare Street, barely a year after opening up. We were comfortable enough to begin to toy with part owning our Meridian Walk house. You owned your home jointly with the landlord, a scheme at the time that was rolled out to enable more people to get on the housing ladder. We sent our completed application to the HA and received their feedback that our application was receiving attention by the beginning of 2003.

By 2004 my Jamie was in his first year at Greenwich University studying 3D digital design, Julie was at Barnet College studying performing arts while Jason was yet to do his GCSEs at Winchmore Hill. Junior had by now tried a few training places while still not sure what he wanted to do. He was a Corgi registered gas fitter for Purdy Contracts but didn't like the way his co-workers would try to school him which resulted in him being fired. Then he trained and got certificated as a forklift driver, but it wasn't engaging enough. Life couldn't have been happier nonetheless. Joe and I had travelled back to Nigeria a few times and had increased the direct debit amount to our parents from N5k (£20 at the time) each month to £50 for each of our living parents, (both my parents and my mother-in-law). By now Junior, who wasn't relying so much on my rides to do his music anymore, was now heavily involved with pirate radio stations and disappearing to the countryside for days or whole weekends and our worry raised its ugly head again. And then a massive setback nearly finished us. I couldn't imagine what was to befall us next in that beautiful estate that had been home for nearly thirteen years where I'd worked tirelessly to ensure peace and tranquillity for everyone. We had a 'chuck out the chintz' exercise on the Saturday 29th May 2004. The estate threw away our rubbish into skips provided by either the HA or the council, not sure now. Together everyone worked to add their own junk into the skips. What a happy communal time spent together it was that Saturday before the next day that went off like time bomb!

Bridget(RIP) dropped by on Sunday on her way back from church service. I'd had breakfast and was just lying on my living room couch when she came. Joe had left earlier for the office to finish some paperwork in readiness for Monday. Junior, Jamie and Julie were still asleep in their rooms upstairs while Jason was on the computer in the living room. I invited my friend Bridget(RIP) to come with me to my uncle's in south east London. She agreed seeing as she'd planned to spend the rest of that day with me. My car was in for servicing at the garage at the time so I got ready and we both left for Tottenham High Road to catch the bus to Deptford. We got to my uncle's and had a pleasant day; we ate, drank and chatted with him, his wife and two sons all afternoon.

We left them at about 6pm and got on our first bus home.

'Won't you call your baby son to see how he is since we left?' Bridget(RIP) reminded me.

'I know, thanks,' I replied as I got my phone out of my bag and put a call to Jason.

'The police are in our house,' he said.

'What do you mean the police are in our house? Where are you?'

'I'm at Jade's.'

'What happened?'

And then he dropped the bombshell. 'Someone got shot on the estate. Julie and Jamie are at the police station, but we don't know where Junior is.'

I glanced at Bridget(RIP).

'He said somebody was shot on the estate. I'm going to take a cab to Tottenham police station – Jamie and Julie are there.'

We both were running along Kingsland Road. I continued to glance both sides of the road for a cab office. I found one that looked quiet but was glad when the operator pointed me to a car sat outside by the kerb. I left Bridget(RIP) behind for her to catch the next bus home as I left with the cab driver for the police station.

My heart was racing. I tried to make sense of who might have been injured or even shot dead, avoiding the possible thought of where Junior might be. We reached the station and Julie was standing outside with her best friend, Glenda, and her parents.

'Please can you hang on to her for us? I'd like to run home to Jason,' I begged of the mother who didn't hesitate to oblige.

'Don't worry about Julie. We're really sorry about all this,' she said to me and I dashed across the road to a cab office for another cab home.

I never said a word to my sunken daughter leaning her whole body on her friend. What could I say to her when I'd failed her? I hadn't protected her like I'd always promised. But I really didn't know what happened to even begin to console her. And Joe hadn't called me. 'What is going on!' I heard myself think aloud as I stepped out of the cab at the estate.

Joe was there and had Jason with him. I rushed up to him. 'Have you seen Junior?'

There was silence. I got my phone out.

'I rang him; he's OK,' came Joe's reply as he held on to Jason.

I continued to ring Junior in any case and could hear him sobbing.

'Mum, I'm scared to come home. I wasn't there when it all started.'

I believed him as they were all still in their rooms that morning when we left not long before the time of the shooting. But that was the least of my problems at that time.

Jamie had left the station and joined Junior in hiding. Our house had been cordoned off with police incident tape and the house draped with blue tarpaulin. The police forensic team were swarming in and around our house morning, noon and night for a whole week. The news went viral! I felt so lost between keeping up with the investigation while Joe and I faced hopping from one bed and breakfast to another as the council moved us about while they worked on rehousing my family. I was also dealing with police officers who were contacting us wanting to speak with Junior and get a follow-up statement from Jason. The HA decided to evict us, giving us a couple of days to move our belongings out after the investigating team had finished and left the place. This was a tall order for us to move out within forty-eight hours from a house we'd lived in for over a decade. Plus, we had no money to hire a removal van.

'We need to challenge the length of time in court; it's in the West End,' I pondered aloud.

'What about it?' Joe asked.

'We have to get those papers ready and take them first thing.'

We were so exhausted trying to keep our children together and process what was actually happening to us that we were too distressed to even grieve over our crashed business. We were finished. Big time! But it would be weeks later until we had time to digest the wider context. For now we were just dealing with what was in front of us in the moment.

We went to the High Court in the Strand first thing the next morning and got the stay of execution order – an injunction to overturn the landlord's decision to evict us within two days. On 2nd June the council found us temporary accommodation, a privately owned property. So we started to move into Fairway in Palmer's Green, walking distance from

Winchmore Hill school. We had a roof over our heads but our family business wound down abruptly as we never opened up for business from the day of the incident.

A couple of our long term friends lived in the same part of north London and supported us immensely during this nightmarish time. Tina and Emma Okafor came with us to salvage what we could from our belongings from the Meridian Walk property. We could only take a few things 'cause everything else was either damaged or broken entirely; from our framed wedding photos, wardrobes, wall units, mirrors, hanging ornaments and paintings; all strewn everywhere in the house. Worse still was the fact that both the gas and electricity were shut off, and windows and doors boarded up. We used our Nokia 3310 phones as torches. Tina and I laughed as we sheepishly looked through for anything to pick up.

'Ify, bet we'll laugh about this one day. Don't worry. It will come to pass, you'll see.'

And we laughed more. It wasn't funny but I was grateful I had people to rely on at a time like that. Tina and I took everything we could find outside and our husbands loaded them up in their respective cars. It took many trips to our new home that day. Sadly all our kitchen white goods were forfeited: dishwasher, fridge freezer, washing and drying machines, we left them all behind as we couldn't fit them in either of the cars.

The investigating police team had confiscated Junior's DJ equipment, and computers, particularly Jamie's that had all his course work, and I'm told they'd also taken what Jamie, Julie and Jason were wearing that afternoon.

Our two youngest children in particular were left really traumatised, while Joe and I reeled with guilt and engaged in the blame game as we struggled to come to terms with what had happened.

'Who are those hanging outside with Junior?' Joe would ask, frowning as he walked into the house.

'They're friends from the old house,' I would answer lowering my tone.

'What do you mean friends from old house? The reason we're homeless today?'

'Take it easy, Dad. The children aren't stupid to let such things happen here. Besides, what happened had nothing to do with them.'

He would take his car keys and leave. We were so very mindful to keep the negative vibe under wraps especially now that we both were unemployed and seen almost as troublemakers from our old house.

I said no to the officers who came to our temporary accommodation to appeal for Jason to come for another interview this time with a two-way mirror for his protection. Tell it to the birds I thought to myself. Tina was visiting me on this day.

'If you're arresting him I'll hand him over to you but not without a legal representative,' I said. 'My child is traumatised as it is and knows nothing else to tell you other than what he'd already said to you the last time. Sorry, he's not coming.'

And no matter how well the officer meant to say it, I wasn't budging. Tina sat there perplexed at my exchange with the officers – both the one that spoke and his colleague that just stood there looking around my house. I asked them to leave and never return for Jason again.

Junior meanwhile had to be convinced to attend the station 'cause they wanted to speak to him more than they did Jason.

'Junior, we'll go with you. They won't stop until you've gone there and told them what you know,' said Joe.

'Yes Nnadim,' I said to support Dad.

We drove to Tottenham police station. As we got out of the car we noticed TV people in front of the station approaching us. They may have introduced themselves but I was concerned about how Dad would like us to deal with the situation.

'We're only going to film his legs that's all...'

For their evening news broadcast obviously, I thought. Dad and I looked at each other and he told them to go ahead but not before he'd spoken to Junior as he was about to head into the station.

Joe and I went to the cafe a few yards away from the station to wait for Junior. He came out fifteen or so minutes later and showed Dad his bail paper.

'They bailed me to report once a month to the station.'

'Until when?' Dad asked.

He shrugged.

'Until they finish their investigation I suppose,' I added.

The estate shooting incident was a nightmare that I kept a daily record of for fifty-four days from the day of the incident until the day I gained employment working on a Sure Start programme in Barking & Dagenham as an employment training officer. I delivered basic skills training and facilitated learners' empowerment to develop their English language skill and engage with their children's schools to better their learning and their own job opportunities. These were predominantly women from diverse ethnic backgrounds.

At the end of the attempted murder investigation we heard that three young people had been indicted and Junior, who had been reporting monthly at the station, was discharged. He called me at work in the middle of my lesson to tell me.

'Mum, it's finished, Mummy!'

'What do you mean?'

'They said I don't have to report to the station again. They said NFA.'

In my excitement, I dismissed my class an hour early to return home to my family as fast as I could. We were finally rid of the shooting problem. It was a massive weight off my shoulders.

After the shooting and at our new address, I became very protective of my children. Junior embarked on his music making journey moonlighting as DJ. He shared a room with Jamie and between them they equipped it with foam on the walls to absorb the noise as they continued dreaming about music careers. Joe and I were still cautious of history not repeating itself at our new home.

Jamie went back to uni still on his music career journey, Julie was continuing her performing art studies and Jason was back at Winchmore. My position with Barking and Dagenham council had come to an end, so Joe and I were both unemployed. The fact that the children continued their education despite the setback was really gratifying for us. A year went by in our lives with no trouble except for the passing of one of my dearest girlfriends, Bridget(RIP), who had seen me through the shooting and been there for my family and I afterwards. I was very sad when she passed in 2005 of an asthma attack. May she continue to rest easy.

Jamie released his first single and music video in 2005 while still an undergraduate which he filmed on our street. He was this young baby-faced twenty-year-old. It was a good thing that he'd made the video before I knew or I would have stopped it, even though I thought the lyrics posited a good message for young people. I felt it was really nice a song:

'Just cos we come from the gutter and we know about scraping the bottom of the butter, don't mean we have to be sinners, major labels don't want killers. Think! Who's gonna sign a guy with a shank? Or a guy with a nine mill?'

Hearing those lyrics was so pleasing. I felt at least they were talking and expressing themselves; what and how they felt. They were processing their life experiences. This was my own interpretation of their music genre, Grime. But I would still not have allowed him to film the video round our new home in case the council evicted us again. I wasn't taking any chances especially with the rumour that young people being lured to my house often by the children's loud music was what led to our eviction. The song, *Serious*, was released and his stage name Jme was adapted from Jamie. We were now on high alert with the kids and their music again, and my support was no longer like in the early days prior to the shooting incident when I would drive them to their music sessions, wherever that may be.

For me back then, the kids were doing something they loved and they spent every waking day of their lives doing it, both in their room and our living room. I knew it was something they wanted to do and I'm sure other mums out there in my shoes would have supported their children all the same. Without thinking, I just drove them round on a few occasions, giving them the odd bit of money when I could and generally supported their music making interests even though I had no idea how successful they could become. No idea, especially considering Grime had to compete within the mainstream.

But Joe was having kittens at all of this sneaking about, especially late at night! I wasn't just supportive of the children's music antics, I was convinced the more I knew about what they were up to, especially my Junior, the better I could keep an eye on him so to speak to defend and protect them. I was beginning to see how serious they were becoming about producing their brand of music. A few of their friends from the old estate were visiting and hanging around with them and there was nothing we could do about that. In hindsight, their sustained friendship with their mates from the Meridian Estate may have inspired Junior's Man song (*Konnichiwa*) where he professed his trust in having his old mates still with him.

Jamie's single *Serious* generated a whole page write-up in *The Voice*, a newspaper written for and by Afro/Caribbean people based in London, and I couldn't be happier to see how well he was doing both in his higher learning and music interest. The piece was a whole page about how Jamie was a much needed inspiration for teens all over the country. Before you could blink, Junior got off the DJing decks and picked up the mic and started MCing too. His first catchy lyric appears to be the one he's still known for today and that is where he says, 'Go on nen' (then). Both brothers' lyrics are relatable while Junior is much more rooted in the street life but always with a twist and humour too. I admire both styles.

All this while, I was beginning to welcome many of their friends to our home from the music scene. Junior and Jamie went through a period of joining music crews like Meridian crew then there was Roll Deep and Grime was getting talked about in local magazines like *RWD* and the free *Metro* newspaper. Even I signed up to Myspace in order to see what my babies were doing online with their music. I would read their postings and their fans' comments. Having signed up with a false name, I was able to vent my anger in reply to any silly or abusive comments on their posts. Without thinking one day, I began to discuss my reply to a nasty comment on one of Jamie's posts – and I was in for trouble. The boys warned me not to ever do that again. They threatened to block me if I didn't stop replying to comments on their post regardless of my alias. It was like I had a purpose now to guide their interests. The maternal instinct in me to care for my children no matter how old they became had kicked in! I've managed to follow them all through the social media transitions from Myspace to Facebook, Twitter and Instagram. Although Jason blocked me, I'm still following his brothers and sister. I remember signing up to Instagram and wondering how to post. I put my question to the 'Familee' iMessage group and only one reply came back from Julie. 'Click on the settings button and choose "delete account"!' The cheeky sod I thought but immediately sent laughing emojis back to say, 'I got you!' back to her. I now can post as well as watch Junior on Instagram – how savvy is that erh!

Before we knew it, the record label Boy Better Know was born and the likes of Shorty, Jammer, Frisco, Sam and Maximum all became part of our family. Still under the BBK umbrella the individual artists were releasing songs as well as uniting to release BBK's song *Too Many Man*. There came a time when P.Diddy tweeted for music fans to advise him on who out of the British Grime artists he should approach to remix his song; a Grime version of *Hello Good Morning*. Junior got the majority of suggestions which was announced everywhere online. I couldn't stop reading (but no longer commenting on) the posts. I will never forget the day I saw P.Diddy on the computer chatting with Junior over FaceTime. I was awe struck! The Grime remix was made and the video was filmed and P.Diddy was also live to thank the fans that suggested Junior do the remix. I was following everything and watching every YouTube clip reporting all the goings on. I was on cloud nine. My community people were beginning to recognise my boys and calling me up to confirm they saw them here and there in public spaces and in the media. They were by now not just on TV channels like AKA or MTV Base, they were also appearing in print too. Joe and I were embracing the fact that contrary to our generic traditional wish for our children to get a good education to become doctors, lawyers, engineers and so on, our ones are all headed into the music and entertainment industry. What's more, they are good at what they're doing and earning a living from it; who could ask for more?

As far as work went, Joe and I were back to square one again at our temporary home even as I got busy following the kids online. We decided to develop our own projects in partnership with our old borough's strategic board. The aim was to continue to do what we did best – facilitating people's development and empowerment – and my knowledge in helping adults gain skills and work experience provided me with the platform to do this. Armed with my NVQ3 AA certificate I sent in my proposal to the council. My project was shortlisted and then funded on a yearly basis to recruit community members and train them to become AA volunteers. The service was covering up to five police stations in the north London boroughs of Haringey, Enfield and Barnet. I also supported my trainees into employment and further education as they passed out of the AA programme. Joe was delivering a funded programme; a fatherhood community project that engaged and empowered single fathers with kids living in the borough. He took them on excursions and provided them with IT and soft skills training in preparing them for employment. Our projects were both borough-funded until the spending cut exercise in 2011 ending in March 2012.

By mid-September 2010 Papa slept to sleep no more on the 16th. My world came crumbling down again. It was a big blow as I had never imagined life without him in the picture. He was 86, or so he said. I remember him telling the story of how that came about during his service years with his colonial master. His master had asked him his age one day and he was perplexed as to why the question. According to Papa, your age had nothing to do with sequential education. You only started school, in his time, when you could touch your ear with one hand across and over your head onto the other side – with or without hair on your head! In other words clasping your upper arm to the side of your face and your forearm over your head and reaching for your earlobe. Once you could accomplish this, you were said to be ready for school. It didn't matter how old you were. This was the benchmark for school age back then. And so, when he couldn't come up with any reply to his master, he said the Oyibo smiled and said to him, 'You must be born in 1924; you look ten years younger than me.' From that day on Papa believed he was born in 1924 and remained completely unperturbed till the end about the month or date of his birth. 'Who wants to know?' he would jokingly dismiss us! I used to tease him about it and now, he's no more!

For three weeks I had paid through the nose for him and Mama to receive treatment and care in Enugu at the teaching hospital where he used to work. Papa had had a mild stroke and the hospital could not save him. Healthcare is nothing to write home about in Nigeria. It was a horrible experience, but thanks to our sons who were now excelling in their music careers, I was able to give him a befitting burial. I had to return home for the funeral both as the first born and the one out of his children that could fund the funeral project. I had asked that he be put at the nearby mortuary in Umunachi, a stone's throw from Okwelle, near Umuofeke. I had also sent funds for the funeral preparation as I got ready to return from London. I got back and we went shopping for his dress up accessories like gloves and a hat at Anara market. These we took to the mortuary where one of the staff instructed me to put them on him. For the first time in my life, I was face to face with Papa on eye level with his eyes closed. I lifted his head gently with my left hand and placed the hat on his head before gently lowering it back down. All the while I felt calm through that fear of touching my father's head while he slept. I stood up and glanced back at my brother behind me and tears welled up in my eyes.

We'd gone out to get him a special casket draped in the Nigerian flag. A day before the burial day, my Uncle Vin came up to me to ask me to hire a local rainmaker to prevent rain fall on the scheduled burial date. I wasn't sure how to explain to him that I didn't believe that whoever the contractor was could stop rain falling in early November in Nigeria. I just declined point blank to him without any excuse but reminding him the odds were small seeing as we had rainy days in the month. We went ahead on the day to bring him from the mortuary first to the church service where my family was prayed upon for solace at that time in our lives, and then we drove the short distance from the church to our family compound where the grave was covered with a plastic sheet to keep out the rain. It had started raining in the morning so I asked Mama to stay at home and not risk riding in the ambulance bringing her husband to his final resting place. This was tradition but I wasn't going to let Mama out in that rain where the roads were messed up – muddy and slippery especially from Aku stream to the federal road junction. Even as the ambulance came down the Aku bridge on the day, villagers were literally giving the vehicle a push to get it to the church.

Papa was laid in state in the decorated front room and tens of people filed in to pay their last respects – people came from all over the Okwe, Okwelle and Umuna communities as well as Umuduru, Papa's maternal home. We had in-laws and well-wishers from near and far, and the rain trickled to a stop round about midday when the burial ceremony started. Papa's casket was closed and carried to the graveside where the village vicar took us through the procession; I read the eulogy as Charlie couldn't bring himself to read it as the first son. He was reeling in agony about our loss. After the graveyard rituals the party began. My family members wore uniformed material and some close family friends including in-laws joined us too. People ate and drank through to the morning the next day. I returned to London a week later.

The following year which was the Nigerian election year wasn't better either. Following the 2011 spending cuts in the UK that saw the demise of our projects, Joe was determined for both of us to return to Nigeria now that the children were responsible enough to not only manage their own lives but look out for one another and us too. Joe left in 2011 and couple of months later I visited him for an update and, not surprising, we were finding out that things just didn't work in Nigeria the way we were used to here in England. You had far more concerns about sustaining the comfortable lifestyle you had been used to for decades never mind running a business, whatever the business: manufacturing or service industry. We were realising how much of a struggle it was to sustain a living in the nation we'd left some three decades ago and it wasn't fun! First we needed to buy litres of petrol daily to supplement if not replace the electricity supply, and then we had to think about growing our own food including rearing our own chicken and fish, even snails. Again we needed to find people able to do the job and this was a tall order seeing that people mostly wanted better paying jobs than pottering round a compound feeding fishes or chicken. Overall, we were not as relaxed and/or as comfortable as we had envisaged and the idea of getting back home to London got to me, so I began to work on convincing Joe for us to go back as soon as possible.

Meanwhile something happened at the end of 2011 that cheered us up to the max. Junior and Jamie announced to us that they were booked to perform that Christmas in Nigeria and I felt like 'I had arrived,' I must admit. I phoned home to alert both my people and my husband's, particularly those living in Lagos to get ready to come to the show.

The thought of my relatives seeing my boys perform in Nigeria was a massive dream come true for me. It was an atmosphere to behold when Joe and I left our Lagos Eko hotel to join them at Federal Palace hotel the next morning for breakfast before they left for a radio interview, the preamble to their performance that evening. *'Nnadim k'abo ooo'* (welcome) I was gesturing to Junior as he hugged me and joined his already seated entourage in the shuttle to take them to the radio station. It was fab!

We rode in a convoy of exclusive cars to the venue on the night and who did they ask for first? The mother dearest!

'Mummie, could you get your twelve guests including Daddy to go sit over there please? Thank you, ma'am,' the well-dressed young man said to me.

I could see the seating he referred to with what looked like up to three buckets of champagne on the round table and ornaments. Already I knew to bring a dozen guests that included Auntie Morayo and her children, Sunny my brother and his wife Ogechi, Tina (Victoria's younger sister) and her children. We took our place by the front row when for a solid hour and a half, Junior, Jamie, 2Face and Fally Ipupa wowed the crowd at the Ikoyi venue. This was followed by Junior's performance with Nigerian artists like Wizkid and he played a venue with Burna Boy, which Joe and I attended.

And then the boys were flying across Europe and America to perform. Their growth was instant as far as I was concerned because there was never a dull moment where they sat down contemplating the way forward. They just did it and I was pleasantly surprised each time I flicked through my TV to see them. I would even sing along to some of their lyrics. To watch them on YouTube and see fans screaming out for them was crazy. It felt so good discussing them with friends whenever we got together.

Julie on the other hand had now finished with her college education and was enrolled at East London University to study events management, but she was only there for just a year before dropping out. When we asked her why she said she didn't fit in and was struggling to study something she didn't love. Undeterred by it all, Julie started to design and make garments which she shared online. She would even model her own garments and talk about them. This was quickly followed by a series of media work trials like creating a music show on Channel AKA where she hosted up and coming UK artists. Mind you, I was beginning to get worried about my university drop-out princess. What was she trying to do? I even spotted her vocals on Jamie's Lily Allen LDN remix and wondered whether she was heading for a music career after all. The problem was, she was good at all she was trying to do, which gave me no room to advise her on anything. In her early twenties, she seemed to have her head screwed on. Aside from her career, we found little time to talk about girl grooming stuff. This was the period I'd walk into her room and see all the career development plans she had on her wall. She would ask questions like how and what does she need to become a singer, TV presenter, a dancer and for each of these areas she made a list of things. Meanwhile the boys were rising in the ranks of Grime artists in the country as well as selling their merchandise which they kicked off by visiting their old school and giving away Boy Better Know school bags to the children.

Nonetheless, I never stopped worrying about the boys' careers either. I wasn't clued up on how they produced their music i.e., what it cost them to work at studios or the cost of producing their merchandise. I hoped each time that they would succeed especially as Joe and I were beginning to toy with the idea of suggesting they get a second job just in case their music career flopped. But as we worried, their record releases were talked about. I was firmly online to lap it all up.

Come 2013, Mama died. Mother, who had long suffered with a stomach ulcer even before Papa took ill, passed in July of that year. I had been home earlier in the year and spent time with her. I can still remember our last conversation as she sat waiting to leave for church on the Sunday before I returned to Lagos the next day to fly back to London. She asked me for money for offering so I had given her N1k and she was scrambling round to break the money down. I told her I didn't have anything smaller and that they should be able to break it at the church for her. It was important to her to have the money in bits for the number of rounds the offering plate would be passed around. She didn't like the hassle of asking the usher for change thereby letting everyone know how much she had and what she was putting in the offering plate. Neither did she want to spend it all at the same time because she had to make all the offering rounds in church. We couldn't stop laughing as I joked to her that us non-believers don't share in such dilemma! Thanks to Boy Better Know, Mama had a grand old mother farewell too. Again I travelled home for both the burial and funeral ceremony. I was able to find a few old family photos Mama had been keeping in her 'portmanteau', as she called it, a medium sized plastic leather-looking brown box. Me as a baby, a three or so year old and even a family one taken during the war or thereabouts. My parents were now gone to be seen no more. I fought the thought after Mama's passing and each time the feeling about my own mortality overwhelmed me.

And then Joe's mum followed suit in 2015! This coincided with the period when we were about to start the family home project in Ijebu Ode. The children had agreed to Joe's plan to build a home and for it to start in that year. Joe had gone home with the initial work plan and budget when a few days later at the end of March 2015 he'd called us in the UK to report his mother was very ill. Some more days down the line, myself and the children received a FaceTime call from Joe perching on the edge of the bed next to his mother who was lying down and gazing at us all on the phone. I could see she was exacerbated by it all. She looked tired and not her cheerful old self. I immediately informed Joe I was going to ring off in order that his mother got some rest. It was in the afternoon of the next day in early April that Joe cried down the phone to me that she was gone. I couldn't console him enough over the phone. I also reminded him that fate may have intervened for her to hold on until he was in Nigeria before she died – a blessing in disguise, being her only son. Joe managed all the necessary burial and funeral rights that included the extended families both of his senior and junior stepsisters. We miss our parents a great deal. Special dates in our lives that Joe and I tend to observe on our own and for me as a reminder that it will be my turn at some point. No day goes by that I don't contemplate what life would have been like if they were alive to see how our children turned out today.

Joe and I were now flying first class once a year to our family homes both in the east and west of Nigeria. Since then, the rest is history! Both Junior and Jamie have gone on to play SOLD OUT shows at home and abroad. Then along came the Hyundai Mercury award winning album *Konnichiwa* in 2016, followed by Junior's sold out event at Alexandra Palace. To date, he's been managing both his Nike SkAIR shoe and clothing line, MAINS London, which launched in Selfridges. Boy Better Know have headlined festivals all over the country, they played the closing performance at Glastonbury and held a takeover at The O2 across multiple venues, including a performance in the arena. I've lost count of Junior's awards, from the MOBO he won for his music video that cost 'eighty English pounds', to his GRMDaily award, AIM award, his Ivor

Novello and more. And the family has always been there to celebrate with him.

Julie, who had dropped out from higher education, started working at IKEA in Tottenham from where she joined forces with her friend Sian to record a pilot radio show on BBC 1xtra. Then she moved to working in the Apple store on Regent Street. She was there for not too long before joining Rinse FM hosting the Drive with Julie show. We were still rejoicing at how speedily she was moving career wise when she was headhunted to front Apple Music's radio station Beats 1 in London. I have since been a part of some of Julie's projects, first in the documentary she made about her eldest sibling following his Mercury win and the sold out Alexander Palace show. And then I did a four-part radio show with her celebrating Women's History Month. It was nice working with her, like we were both in our living room at home. Jamie is still enjoying his music career and got married to the love of his life in August 2016; they're living not far from our family home where we moved after finally leaving our temporary accommodation of fourteen years. It was fabulous to have that many music artists in attendance at the wedding that saw me rubbing shoulders with the likes of Ed Sheeran, Giggs, Chipmunk, Shorty, Frisco, the lot. They have since had a baby girl; my precious first granddaughter, Miss. Rose Ayomide Nkeiruka Adenuga. Five months later Junior and his girl had a baby girl too, Miss. River Ifenumi Ifeyinwa Adenuga. I've since been smiling like a Cheshire cat as they say.

My Jboy, (Jason), is a producer, graphic designer and

illustrator. He is the genius behind the design of this book. I've come to see all my kids as equally successful as they work separately yet collectively with Jason's artistic designs and music production as a backdrop. Each of their individual success feeds into the other and keeps it in the family, so to speak. Life couldn't get any better than this for me. I've come full circle; a round trip that started at 10 Modile Way when I first had my dream of pursuing a good life influenced by what Papa told me about the white man's lifestyle and what I watched on television at No. 4. Even in my positive exuberant pursuits, never in my wildest dream did I think my children would impact the world like they are doing, coming from my humble beginning both in Lagos and Umuofeke, my tiny village in Imo state of Nigeria. Thanks to the children, both our Ijebu and Umuofeke communities have received grants for their community development. A playing field designated for Odo Aje's youth in Ijebu Ode equipped with apparatus, swings, climbing frames and a football pitch. A football team named Nuga Football Club (NFC) have since been formed, and early in 2017 Odo Aje community conferred a chieftaincy title to Junior bestowing him the title of Chief Amuludun of Odo Aje. The title was the community's expression of who Junior is to them and how he makes them feel! A chief that is a source of the 'feel good factor' in their community. This is contrary to what the British press reported as a 'merry maker' chief. That in my view was understating both the spirit of the title-giver and the recipient. Then again what do they know about my family and my culture!

My first family, Umuofeke community, now have their own village oil mill to process their palm oil and a borehole to access cleaner water as opposed to the Ikwe and Aku streams we used to drink from. I've also advised them to treat the borehole water by pre-boiling it prior to drinking or using it to prepare food. I thank goodness for my children by whom Joe and I were able to improve our respective communities.

I had returned home in 2018 and saw a swell in the number of youths and young adults in my village, many of whom were not in any employment or education. I sat down throughout my three weeks holiday and carried out an initial assessment on fifty-seven of them, who at the time ranged in age from eleven to thirty, and even over forty, begging to be assessed, which I did. My objective was to identify their strengths and work that into their career development action plan to pursue any of their three identified career goal options. Of the total number assessed, twenty wanted to go to university, and the breakdown of the rest varied from business ownership, taxi driving, building material merchant, bakery, tailoring and even a chemist. I returned to the UK and told my family of this and wondered how I could move them forward; many of them came from large families with not enough earning power from both parents combined to send them anywhere after their free secondary school education.

In December 2019 I sent all my discarded clothes, including those that I had been collecting from the children, to Nigeria where they were auctioned as the main attraction at the scholarship launch which currently has one female student studying science laboratory technology at Federal College Nekede in Owerri, the capital of Imo state. I have established this to honour my father, who against all odds championed the education of girls. He'd been named Mokwe 'cause Iye Anyamnele went through many births but only he survived, hence they named him 'by the grace of the immortals' or 'immortals willing, he'd live' and he did indeed. Papa, I couldn't thank you enough for giving me the beginning I needed to pursue my dream and believing it could be possible. On 6th February 2020, a class of thirty-nine attended the Mokwe Adult Education class in Umuofeke attending two days a week under the supervision of two adult trainers. Apparently some adults from our neighbouring villages Alaocha and Umumgbada are today still joining the class.

Not only am I a mother of four, but now a grandmother of two. Oh my goodness! It's like a new leaf, especially now that I have time and feel I have purpose. I have to be careful not to do too much though; I've realised I can be too eager! It took me time to caution myself and not get too carried away with the grandchildren. I have to make sure the mums and dads get time with their babies too! I've now decided to spend one evening a week with each baby unless we have occasions where I had both granddaughters as well as the rest of the family, like birthdays and Junior's housewarming.

It's so gratifying to see my boys so wrapped up with their babies. Both boys look after their daughters daily, giving their mothers time to run errands and get work done. The main pleasure I look forward to weekly is playing with them and watching them develop their personality traits. Junior's first thought is for his daughter and how soon he can return to her from work. Both my sons are mad about their daughters and I'm so pleasantly surprised that the cultural 'son' thing didn't rub off on them. They haven't followed my cultural lure of baby gender preference and that makes me very happy. I like the way they're all family orientated. Julie is the big aunty and loving it. Same as Jason, their uncle. So I promised myself not to take over raising my grandchildren and I plan for them to call me 'GG' (Glamorous Granny) as opposed to Grandma or Nan. They can come over and stay in their own rooms in my house when they are older. They're growing in front of me and it's something to behold. When I was raising my own kids there were things I didn't think about celebrating that are now so clear to me like their first time smiling, their first sound or word and first time crawling and walking, gosh it's bliss.

Any notable regrets? I often asked myself this question having come thus far and my answer has always been categorically no! I may have struggled with my cultural traditions while trying to do things my own way like following my heart to marry someone from a different tribe from me and refusing to follow my African traditional disciplinary code when raising kids. But my accomplishments dwarf the likely impact of my nonconformist style and form of raising my family. Most of all I came to realise that the feeling of freedom and happiness resides in everyone and it's up to individuals to take the necessary steps to pursue those important life goals their own way. Whether you subscribe to a notion that you believe guides you to it, is entirely up to you. I believe in the old Yoruba adage that says, *Bi nwon ba bi eniyan eniyan nturara re bi ni.* Translated it means, once you are born into this world you have to 'reborn' yourself. In other words, you have to forge a way for yourself depending on the time, space and the environment you find yourself on this planet. You have to be able to strive for freedom and happiness in life and to achieve these, you have to re-evaluate all you are born with and to assert who you are. For me, no cultural or traditional specifics were compelling enough to stand in the way of all the contradicting moves I made to get to where I am today. Through it all, one common compelling notion remained constant. I realised I share the same reason Papa left the village to reside in Lagos. The same reason got me to cross Niger Bridge and board the plane for London Bridge to see the queen as they say. I left my birthplace for another part of the world like my father did in search of greener pastures. Little did Papa know that his first born, a girl whom he had desired to train as a nurse would opt for training as a teacher and a seasoned community developer. Wish he could see me now.

Epilogue

One interesting question I was asked as soon as I'd finished writing my life story was to describe myself in one word. I wasted no time to say I am a realist; what you see is what you get, but I'm not oblivious to the consequences of speaking your mind. I have never been afraid to stand alone insofar as my decisions are in my interest and not hurting no one. Yet, I'm lost without friends as a people person that thrives on meeting people. This has allowed me access to broaden my horizons as I've lived my life. Hence, I've been able to reconcile my guiding principles to include and accommodate my experiences beyond my cultural traditions in the interest of my growing and developing family in a foreign environment that we still reside in.

Talk about raising children, I know that everyone is wondering how we did it for all four children to end up in the creative industry rather than mainstream professions. I'll start by saying that we refused to classify ourselves as a dysfunctional family regardless of where or how we lived. Neither did we measure ourselves as being posh.

Engaging with kids on their own terms is extremely vital to the dynamics of your relationship with children. No playing them off one another or between parents. If your children are allowed to be vocal like mine, they will make clear what you are doing to them and tell you where and when to get off in a respectable manner. And that's not a good feeling. They already have the utmost respect for you as a parent – try reciprocating that and don't just see them as children. Let them know that you trust them, because they quite like acting all 'grown up'. When they realise that you are asking questions and not chastising, instructing, advising or even dismissing them, they will engage more. It's confidence boosting and encourages them to reason. We felt it was very important that we created a space where they could feel at ease to relate to us and if that meant 'Hello Mum' in the morning as opposed to 'Good morning Mum or Mother' every once in a while so be it, and it still doesn't scratch the surface of their invaluable affection for us.

We all know the challenges we face in diaspora especially being a black woman whether married or single, with or without children. You have the customs of the nation to contend with, some of which are contradictory to what you know and how you know it to be and others that are new to you that you come across as you go along. If you are lucky you can rely on your relatives, your community and/or closest friends for your support system in order to maintain your position in society while carving out a life for yourself and family as well as in many cases taking care of your folks back home as best as you can. No matter the difficulties, it's never the end of the world as millions like us have gone through it before and those coming after us are looking forward to their turn. You must be willing to be flexible, learning new ways of life that more often than not enhance your understanding of your new environment. That becomes your navigation tool in life not only in the foreign land where you reside but also back home where you come from. Your heart's desire for peace and freedom is universal regardless of what else you commit to in life. Many of us prefer privacy to networking with others, keeping ourselves to ourselves within our community; it's alright and safe but drawing from experience I would claim understanding that what is different to what I know and am used to, has enabled me to understand others in that it's possible for us to co-exist and live side by side in peace.

I'm not saying that having learned the socio-political order of a country you are home and dry because these challenges are different for many of us. Take law and order for example. As a parent, you live permanently with anxiety in most inner city areas where your teenage children are away from you for up to eight hours a day while you work full time to put food on the table and clothes on their backs. Back in the 80s it was common to meet BAME (Black And Minority Ethnics – I hate to use the acronym for non-white people) who told you they'd warned their children to steer clear of trouble by not bringing police to their doorsteps as if that could keep the children out of trouble. If anything it was likely to backfire as such an instruction only translates to the children to dislike the police, resulting in many anti-social young children outside and even within their family environments.

You could say I got lucky because it was understanding the pain that children go through growing up that motivated my major career pursuit. I loved my parents to death; they were and continue to be my God and Goddess, but I resented my childhood that was marred by civil war, poverty and family chores to the extent that I still see it as the reason why I'm not a tall woman at 5ft 3ins today. Both my parents were of average height, but I am the shortest of all my siblings yet the eldest; can you imagine! Had I not carried so many cassava baskets, wood logs, firewood, pails and pails of water, ukwa, palmnuts, you name it, I might have been a tall woman today like my elegant mother. It was how I felt growing up.

After my secretarial studies here in London, I wanted to further my understanding of how a child could and should be raised to achieve the comforts I craved for all those years growing up both in Lagos and my village during that war until after my secondary education when I returned to Lagos. It was this innate quest to know and understand children that prepared me for the whole process of raising my three boys and a girl in the north London inner city areas where they grew up. In the end, I didn't just manage my own children but also provided support to the numerous other children I came across, especially Black Africans in police custody across the north London boroughs I worked in, including youth centres working with at risk young people not in education, employment, or training (NEET). I made a choice to inform myself rather than study a discipline just because I have a number of friends doing it or I could earn more money. I needed to feed my motivation and resolve my personal matter with my parents as well as raise my own children successfully. As a realist, therefore, you could say keeping up with the Jones isn't for me.

It would be unwise to keep quiet if ever you or a member of your family encountered many of the challenges we face. Take for example the worries we get upon hearing the statistics of rising youth crime in the inner cities. You don't keep quiet about it no matter how severe the problem might be; you still need to resolve the matter whether people laugh at you or not. Your utmost goal should be to restore your family's equilibrium. This is when you will be able to relate to friends and family and be HAPPY again. And so, don't be afraid to talk your problems over with anyone you feel comfortable with – even professional shrinks; yes, shrinks. It doesn't mean you are losing it. Having someone listen to you and ask a few questions might help you to a) understand your problems and why they came about, and b) make the most of their support to help you drum up possible solutions and steer clear of any problems in future the best you can. This is why you take time to keep good company – you learn from mistakes to keep bad energy away as much as possible. That's not saying boycott any friend 'cause, believe me, we are bound to need one another some day as long as we remain friends.

You just apply the sense of having a handful of good friends close to you, and still keep company with all your friends as and when your paths cross. As long as you are you – you are unlikely to offend anyone.

I once sought a friend's shoulder to cry on when my eldest child got into police trouble the first time. Roxanne Ali was a colleague; we both worked for social services in my borough and she introduced me to volunteering as an Appropriate Adult for children in trouble with the police, which in turn informed both my career and work development. Also, when we had the shooting incident in our estate, my cry for help got all my friends running to my aid, to feed my family, offer us money, food shopping, and even their company when we felt alone. Thank goodness I had both friends and relatives who travelled from places like south east London and Hertfordshire to visit us with gifts. I am forever indebted to them. They were our saviours at the time – they supported us and we couldn't pay them back enough other than to wish them the good fortune of meeting good Samaritans like themselves in times of need. In our community that's not difficult to do, especially if you have memberships to the different community organisations including religious bodies. I find it fascinating to sustain my friendships in all the respective organisations even without being a member of some of them. I am a pretty determined person and steadfast in my friendships and so far have had hardly any problems in this department because I believe that's what we are on this planet to do: relate to one another.

And to touch a little on those still looking to migrate overseas. Things have changed. I remember preparing to travel back in 1980. The exchange rate was almost a pound to one naira. You were only allowed a thousand naira for travel which at the time fetched me £998. You couldn't dream of that now that it's almost six hundred naira to a pound. And so it's tough just even putting together the funds you need never mind gathering the travel documents. Back then when Alhaji Shehu Shagari was the president, we travelled out and received our visas at the point of border entry. I remember doing this twice, even the last time taking Papa on a visit to his colonial master's homeland that he'd heard so much about. 'Business or pleasure?' Papa was asked at the border and just as I was about to answer, he replied, 'I don come to see what is great in Great Britain.' It was laughs all round.

Such an experience is a thing of the past now; you don't dream of embarking on your migration journey if you haven't first secured your visa from your destination country's embassy in Nigeria, one of the main reasons lives are lost through human trafficking. It isn't worth the hassle if you know you are really not fully prepared to travel out. The risk is more than likely to outweigh what you would have to endure to settle like we did in the 80s. Suffice to mention the hurdle of all the new immigration reforms, rules and other policies almost phased in monthly that you have to abide by as a new arrival while you find your bearing in the foreign land. Try researching all you need to know about your travel and make sure you are dealing with credible agents who will not only tell you the truth about your chances of succeeding, but also advise you on every option available to you to pursue a better life.

Don't be afraid to inform yourself. Education is another tool you can rely on regardless of age or circumstance. Joe and I seized such an opportunity when the UK government rolled out a programme to tackle high unemployment. We went back to school to increase our employment opportunities in the new technological age. I joined the race as a nursing mother. It wasn't easy but I had Joe running the race with me to win.

In all honesty, I wasn't particular about inter-tribal marriage. I was just an Igbo girl who spoke Yoruba very well. I would say it played a huge role in us understanding who we are and what we wanted from each other. My parents also lived much of their adult working life among the Yorubas in Lagos and had no concerns in validating my marriage. They both spoke Yoruba too although not so fluently. Thus, Papa asked one of my uncles to represent him at my wedding including walking me down the aisle. My mother-in-law had wasted no time confirming she had been to complete the bridal ceremony in my village where she spent time with my folks who wrote to inform me about the whole thing especially my age mates. I wouldn't be surprised if my parents had faced a lot of resentment from my community, but they never discussed it with me neither did I ask them. However, the good thing is quite a number of my village sisters are now married to non-Igbo men. Were they following my footsteps?

Should I even be wondering about a feeling that knows no human divide?

My family was no more special or uniquely endowed than anyone else, but we were able to take the plunge and be prepared to learn to swim with every stroke to perfect what we have today. To start off, our children didn't all favour university education like we parents so much believe in, neither did we pressure them to study for mainstream professions like medicine, science and engineering. But all through their developing years we took an interest in what they loved doing and encouraged them in what later became their way of earning their living. The day the boys came to ask Joe if they could load a music production software called Fruity Loops on one of the computers he was building for sale, he allowed them to do it; he didn't tell them to go read their books or to get out and stop disturbing him. When two little speakers were connected to the computer and they could hear the sound their loaded program made, the rest became history. We were more than aware of the influence Joe's career path was likely to have on them as they had free access to all the computer games and electronic gadgets in the house. Some might say we should have planned ahead to channel them into a more mainstream environment, but we didn't because we were far more interested in how they were feeling, and how their enjoyment in what they were doing made us feel accomplished as parents.

We all like to think of ourselves as proud parents but it's no denying the amount of gruesome times we go through worrying about whatever is happening in our lives. We learned a lot from raising children who were bent on being realistic and vivacious like their mother and skilled and creative like their father. They grew up wanting to build and make things themselves as Joe did. The grew up singing and chanting realistically about themselves by themselves and for themselves.

I set and chase realistic goals. For example, I didn't crave for a house if I didn't have land registered in my name. And no matter what big dream I have in my head about these attributes, my dream must undergo a rearrangement for what I accomplish first. Most of all, I don't sit on my equity irrespective of how large or small. For example, I don't own two vehicles if all I need is one unless my work or life engagements dictate as such.

Most important to me today is my family's comfort and wellbeing, and anything after that as an addition I recycle and use to empower and better the life chances of those around me. I once coined the saying that when you protect the interest of the masses; yours is guaranteed. I said it and I live it and couldn't be more gratified in my life as a result. I love to see things done successfully while I'm well aware of when to cut my losses and chase another realistic goal.

Who I am and have become today is the total of all I did, right and wrong, to get to the place I find myself now. In other words, my life has been a composition of my evaluated cultural traditions blended with my love of a democratic lifestyle; live and let live - making my personal culture a fluidity. Many quit at the first, second or third culture clash hurdle but I realistically deal with the situation knowing I will have an understanding of what options are available to iron out such cultural abrasions in the interest of all parties.

Thanks to my children I have a lot of things to keep me busy back home that I return twice a year to supervise. One is my foundation – Mokwe Learning Trust (MLT) which was set up in honour of my late father who ensured that I was educated against all odds back then. The foundation provides scholarships for Umuofeke village youths post-secondary school to attend higher education. We currently have an undergraduate at Federal Polytechnics Owerri studying science laboratory technology, and we also have the MLT's Adult Education programme which is open to all the villagers.

Finally it would be a great joy to hear from my readers who identify with any of what I had to tell of my life, particularly those that were taken back to the east like me and what your life was like; I celebrate you my comrade.

Thank you for stopping by.

Inspiration and
Acknowledgements

Writing my autobiography was an idea that sprang from an epiphany of painful moments in my life, weathering the streets of London as JJC in the early 80s. I was going through these pains and anguish in a foreign land and remembering the times I had found myself under such pressures that were mostly beyond my control right from when I was a kid. I thought: 'Why not write it down?' And so, with the help of the journal I'd always kept, I did a little writing now and then about my life experiences running up to my migration to the United Kingdom. The more I wrote the more I remembered. Most of those times that I was writing about felt like they were yesterday. I would wake up in the middle of the night after some crying session and write. While alone at night in my cold room and writing, it felt as if I was going back in time for real so much so that I began to feel homesick! But I would put on a brave face before friends and relations.

I didn't want to appear vulnerable not when I had gone and married from another tribe and some people never thought the marriage would work out, let alone last. Some would say, 'Give them five years to watch them break up.'

And when that didn't happen, they would set us another milestone as soon as they had been invited to celebrate our most recent wedding anniversary. All these were rumours that we heard through the grapevine. The mendacity was huge, pretending I was OK while suffering. I remember coming home from college on a snowy evening and came down the bus at Camberwell. I walked to the bus stop to continue my journey home and then decided against waiting for another bus in that snow for the couple of stops' ride. I decided to take off my shoes and run home instead, that it would be quicker to take my cold self out of the excruciating weather.

I had to be reminding myself as I landed one foot ahead of the other, like throwing frozen fish on the ground, that I was actually running when I couldn't feel my legs at all. I got home and cried like I did on my first cold sickness experience in this country. My hands were so stiff and painful, I had a passerby with gloves on turn the key in my front door to let me in. I had had something to eat that night then spent couple of hours documenting my pain before I fell asleep.

It has taken me four years to write this book, fairly quick in my view and achievable because I had previously written things down. My choice to substitute the names for some characters in the book, except for my very close friends and family members, has been deliberate because I wanted readers to focus on the characters on the journey with me and understand how they also contributed to shaping me into who I have become. I hope you enjoy reading my book which I couldn't have done without the help of a number of people.

First is Junior who said to me one day, 'Until I see you do that one goal in your life to write your biography will I be truly happy for you, Mummy.' Thank you to Jamie, Julie and Jason for inspiring me to challenge myself with the promise to publish it the family DIY way – BBK and free of charge! Thank you to Jason Morgan and Crystal Mahey-Morgan and the whole OWN IT! team. A big thank you to Hattie Collins who believed I had it in me to write about my life seconded by Grace Ladoja MBE who introduced us. Shout out to all the BBK massive. My dearest brother researcher in Lagos, Olabode Olanipekun who provided me with visuals of some of my childhood memories of life in Lagos. Thank you Elaine Burke whose brainstorming sessions shaped my book introduction. Thank you to my lovely friend, Duchess Nena who researched the scientific names for the native food ingredients mentioned in the book, and how can I forget my bosom girlfriends that stood by me through thick and thin with their families – Chinyere Alaneme, Comfort Momoh MBE, Jenny Chika Okafor, Kate Echeazu, Kehinde Kazeem, Stella Maris-Oji and Tina Okafor; especially during the estate shooting saga. Thanks to Jephta Opara my media production guru and Mummy J Fashion Ltd for fostering my fashion sense.

Thanks to my uncles and families – the Chuks and the

Offomata families who provided me with the reason for my migration, love and shelter in the UK. Thanks to everyone that I have ever chatted with about writing my biography, my social media friends far and wide and neighbours who challenged me to the task. My Fairway neighbour Prisca and her mum thank you. Trust me, many didn't know I was making mental notes of our discussions. I thank you all.

I was in my village late September 2018 when I pledged twenty per cent of my book sales towards Umuofeke Development Programme to provide them with the financial support they need for their development and wellbeing.

Thank you, my reader. Hope you enjoyed it.

Thank you exceptionally Dad Adenuga. Love you till pigs fly with or without your consent xx

ABOUT OWN IT!

OWN IT! is a storytelling lifestyle brand, sharing stories across books, music, art and film. At the heart of everything we do is a desire to share, empower, celebrate and inspire. Whether it's through multi-media digital books, print books, music or film, OWN IT! releases original and authentic stories told in creative new ways.

WWW.OWNIT.LONDON